$ 22.95

D0891298

HENRY
HOLT

Batsford Chess Library

The Leningrad Dutch

Jaan Ehlvest

An Owl Book
Henry Holt and Company
New York

Henry Holt and Company, Inc.
Publishers since 1866
115 West 18th Street
New York, New York 10011

Henry Holt® is a registered trademark
of Henry Holt and Company, Inc.

Library of Congress Catalog Card Number: 93-77841

ISBN 0-8050-2944-3 (An Owl Book: pbk.)

First American Edition—1993

Printed in the United Kingdom
All first editions are printed on acid-free paper. ∞

10   9   8   7   6   5   4   3   2   1

Adviser: R. D. Keene, GM, OBE
Technical Editor: Andrew Kinsman

Contents

Symbols

+	Check
++	Double check
mate	Checkmate
!	Good move
!!	Excellent move
?	Bad move
??	Blunder
!?	Interesting move
?!	Dubious move
±	Small advantage for White
∓	Small advantage for Black
±	Clear advantage for White
∓	Clear advantage for Black
+–	Winning advantage for White
–+	Winning advantage for Black
=	The position is equal
∞	The position is unclear
∞	With counterplay
1–0	White wins
0–1	Black wins
½–½	Draw
ol	Olympiad
izt	Interzonal
zt	Zonal
Ch	Championship
corr	Correspondence

Introduction

The Dutch Leningrad system (1 d4 f5 2 g3 ♘f6 3 ♗g2 g6) was first regularly studied and played in Leningrad during the mid 1930s. For a long time it was quite unpopular, although some top players occasionally used it as a reserve opening. However, the Dutch Defence, and particularly the Leningrad system, appeared more and more often in tournaments in the 1980s. This was due to the fact that, compared to many classical openings, the Dutch Defence in general, and the Leningrad system in particular, are much less heavily analysed. Unlike many other openings, the Leningrad rarely results in symmetrical positions leading to drawish endgames; play instead revolves around strategic situations in which creative solutions are required from both sides.

This book has taken into account the opinion and practice of Mikhail Botvinnik and Mark Taimanov who greatly influeneced the development of the Leningrad system. A great deal of attention has also been paid to the games of grandmasters Mikhail Gurevich and Vladimir Malaniuk - the modern innovators of the Leningrad variation. Naturally all the important games of recent years are included.

How should you read this book? Dear chess-friend, you should not take the analysis presented here as the final word but learning these ideas will help to develop your skills in understanding irregular positions. One should not concentrate on memorising every variation, although their importance should not be under-estimated, but should instead learn the meaning of plans, themes and manoeuvres. After careful study the Leningrad system will be an invaluable addition to your repertoire, leading to dynamic positions with plenty of scope for original ideas.

1 Main Line with 7 ... ♕e8

1	d4	f5
2	g3	♘f6
3	♗g2	g6
4	♘f3	♗g7
5	0-0	0-0
6	c4	d6
7	♘c3	♕e8 (1)

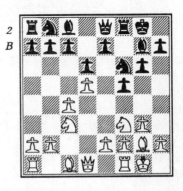

The system characterised by 7 ... ♕e8 began to appear regularly in tournaments at the start of the 1980s and has been used often and successfully by Grandmaster Vladimir Malaniuk. We will explore the following lines for White:

A 8 d5 DONE
B 8 b3
C 8 ♖e1
D 8 ♘d5
E 8 ♕b3
F 8 e4

A

8 d5 (2)

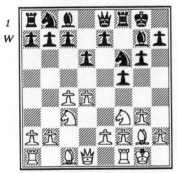

Here Black has:

A1 8 ... ♘a6
A2 8 ... a5

A1

8 ... ♘a6

Now White usually chooses between:

A11 9 ♘d4
A12 9 ♖b1
A13 9 ♗e3 and others

A11

9 ♘d4 (3)
In recent years 9 ♘d4 has

been seen relatively infrequently, as 9 ♖b1 has become the standard choice.

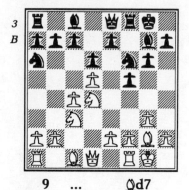

9 ... ♗d7

Instead of this move there has also occurred 9 ... ♘c5 10 b3 (10 b4!?) 10 ... ♗d7 11 ♗b2 a6 12 ♕c2 ♖b8 13 ♖ac1 ♘g4 14 e3 g5 15 b4 ♘a4 16 ♘xa4 ♗xa4 17 ♕e2 ♗d7 18 f4 with a slight advantage for White; Liebert – Okhotnik, Halle 1987.

10 e4

This position has been much played and deeply analysed. Instead of 10 e4, Botvinnik has suggested 10 ♘b3. In practice four more variations have been tried:

a) 10 ♖e1 ♘c5 (If 10 ... c6 11 e4 fxe4 12 ♘xe4 ♘xe4 13 ♗xe4 ♘c7 14 ♖b1 c5 15 ♘e2 with equal chances, Kindermann – Wegner, Hamburg 1991) 11 b3 (11 ♕c2 c6 12 ♘b3? ♘ce4! 13 ♘xe4 fxe4 14 ♗xe4 ♕f7! 15 ♗e3 cxd5 16 cxd5 ♖fc8 17 ♕d3 ♘xe4 18 ♕xe4 ♗f5 19 ♕h4 ♗xb2∓ Prakhov – Bertholdt, Bad Salzungen 1960) 11 ... c6 12 ♗b2 a5 13 ♖b1 g5 14 e3 f4 15 exf4 gxf4 16 ♘ce2

fxg3 17 fxg3 cxd5 18 cxd5 ♗g4 19 ♕d2 and Black has difficulties in defending his pawn weaknesses; Sveshnikov – Gabdarkhmanov, USSR 1984.

b) 10 e3 c6 11 b3 (More active seems 11 ♖b1!? ♖b8 *{11 ... ♘c7 12 b4 cxd5 13 cxd5 ♖c8 14 a4 ♘a8 15 ♕b3± Gavrilov – Gurevich, USSR 1982}* 12 a3 *{12 b4 c5}* 12 ... ♘c5 13 b4 ♘ce4 14 ♘xe4 ♘xe4 15 ♕d3 c5 16 ♘e6 ♗xe6 17 dxe6 cxb4 18 axb4 ♕c8 19 ♗xe4 fxe4 20 ♕xe4 ♖f6 21 ♗b2 ♕xe6 22 ♕d3 ♖ff8 and Black has succeeded in maintaining the balance; Knaak – Espig, East Germany 1984) 11 ... ♘c7 12 ♗b2 c5 13 ♘de2? (Better would be 13 ♘f3 b5 14 ♕c2 with the idea of ♘d2, f4, ♖ae1, e4 – Malaniuk) 13 ... b5 14 ♕c2 ♖b8. Already it is White who has problems and after 15 ♖ac1? bxc4 16 bxc4 ♘g4 Black gained the advantage in Beliavsky – Malaniuk, USSR Ch 1983.

c) 10 b3 c6 (10 ... c5!? 11 ♘c2?! *{11 dxc6 bxc6 12 ♗b2 ♖c8 13 ♖b1 ♘c5 14 b4 ♘ce4 15 ♘b3 ♕f7= Magai – Petelin, USSR 1988}* 11 ... ♘e4 *{11 ... b5!}* 12 ♘xe4 ♗xa1 13 ♘xa1 fxe4 14 ♗xe4 and White has a slight initiative – Tukmakov) 11 ♗b2 ♘c7 12 ♕d2 (12 ♖c1 ♖b8 13 ♕d2 c5 14 ♘f3 a6 *{Dubious is the immediate 14 ... b5 15 cxb5 ♘xb5 16 ♘xb5 ♖xb5 17 ♗xf6 ♗xf6 18 ♕c2 with the idea of ♘d2 – c4 with a slight advantage for White according to Kremenietsky}* 15 ♕c2 b5 16

♘d2 e5!? 17 dxe6 ♗xe6 18 ♘a1 *{18 e4? is not suitable, e.g. 18 ... bxc4 19 bxc4 fxe4 20 ♘cxe4 ♖xb2∓ - Kremenietsky}* 18 ... ♕e7 and a complicated position with equal chances has arisen; F. Lengyel - Kremenietsky, Satu-Mare 1983) 12 ... c5 13 ♘f3 a6 14 ♖ae1 b5 15 ♕d3 ♖b8 16 ♗a1 h6 17 ♘d2 ♘g4 18 e3 (Stefanov - Marasescu, Romania 1983) and White has an opportunity to obtain a dominating position in the centre with the plan h3, f4 and e4.

d) 10 ♖b1!? (Apart from the main line, this is the most logical plan, preparing action on the queenside) 10 ... c6 *(4)* (Not 10 ... c5? 11 ♘e6!±) and now:

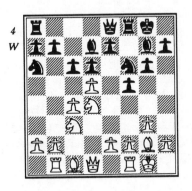

d1) 11 b3 ♘c7 12 b4!? (Serious attention should be paid to 12 dxc6!? bxc6 13 b4 e5 14 ♘b3 ♕e7 15 e4!? with a somewhat better position for White. Dubious, however, is 12 ♗b2?! c5 13 ♘f3 *{13 ♘c2?! b5 14 cxb5 ♘xb5 15 ♘xb5 ♗xb5 16 ♘a3 a5∓ Larsen - Yrjola, Espoo zt 1989 or 13 ♘e6 ♗xe6 14 dxe6 ♖b8= Cvetkovic - Malaniuk, Vrnjacka Banja 1991}* 13 ... ♖b8 14 ♘d2 b5 15 cxb5 ♘xb5 16 ♘c4 g5 17 ♘xb5 ♗xb5 18 ♕c2 f4 19 ♕f5 h6 20 gxf4 ♗d7 and Black has good prospects of counterplay; Ryshkov - Zarubin, Leningrad 1983) 12 ... e5 13 dxe6 (13 dxc6 *{13 ♘b3 cxd5}* 13 ... exd4 14 cxd7 ♕xd7 15 ♘a4 ♘e4 16 ♗b2 b5∓ - Tukmakov) 13 ... ♘xe6 14 ♘b3!? (14 e3) 14 ... ♘g4 15 ♗b2 ♘e5 16 ♘d2 with an unclear position; Tukmakov - Gurevich, USSR 1982.

d2) After 11 b4 Black found the interesting 11 ... ♘xb4 and after 12 ♖xb4 c5 13 ♘cb5 cxb4 14 ♘c7 ♕c8 15 ♘xa8 ♘e4 16 ♗xe4 fxe4 17 ♗g5 ♖f7 18 ♘c2 ♕xa8 19 ♘xb4 ♗h3 achieved a superior position in Karasev - Cherepkov, Leningrad 1984.

Other games with 11 b4 show Black is able to achieve an active position, e.g. 11 ... c5 12 ♘e6 cxb4 13 ♘xf8 ♔xf8 14 ♘b5 ♗xb5 15 cxb5 ♕xb5 16 ♕d2 ♖c8, as in Boguslawsky - Beim, Voskresensk 1992, where Black had very active play for the exchange and went on to win. Or 11 b4 ♖c8 12 ♗a3 ♕f7 13 e3 cxd5 14 ♘xd5 ♖xc4 15 ♘xf6+ Röder - Santo Roman, Lyon Open 1990, with complications.

d3) 11 a3 ♖c8 (11 ... ♘c7 12 e4 e5 - Meulders) 12 b4 c5 13 ♘e6

♗xe6 14 dxe6 cxb4 15 axb4
♖xc4 16 ♗xb7 ♖xc3 17 ♗xa6
with an unclear position; Shvidler - van Mil, Belgium 1987.

Returning to the position after 10 e4 *(5)*.

10 ... fxe4

Of course 10 ... ♘xe4 11 ♘xe4 fxe4 12 ♗xe4 transposes to the main line. An interesting alternative is 10 ... c5 11 dxc6 bxc6 12 exf5 gxf5 and Black had a strong centre in Vukic - Hölzl, Graz 1991.

11 ♘xe4 ♘xe4

This further capture is practically forced: 11 ... c5? 12 ♘e6 ♗xe6 13 dxe6 ♘c7 14 ♘xf6+ ♗xf6 15 ♕e2 ♖b8 16 a4 ♘a6 17 h4! greatly favoured White in Ivkov - Bischoff, Thessaloniki 1984.

12 ♗xe4 *(6)*

This is one of the critical positions of the 7 ... ♕e8 variation.

12 ... ♘c5

Alternatively:

a) 12 ... c6 13 ♗e3 (13 dxc6 bxc6 is considered below under 'b' whilst 13 h4!? ♘c5 14 ♗g2

♖c8 15 ♗e3 a5 16 ♕d2 a4 17 ♖ab1 e5 led to equality in Portisch - Gurevich, Moscow GMA 1990) 13 ... ♘c7 14 ♖b1 (14 ♕d2 c5! 15 ♘e2 b5 16 cxb5 ♗f5 17 ♗g2 ♕xb5 18 ♘c3 ♕d3!∓ Hernandez - Chernin, Cienfuegos 1981 and 14 ♖e1 c5 15 ♘e2 b5 16 cxb5 ♘xb5∞ K. Arkell - King, London {WFW} 1991) 14 ... c5 15 ♘f3 (15 ♘e2!? b5 16 b3 ♖b8 17 ♕d2 was played in Döring - Kindermann, Dortmund 1992) 15 ... ♗g4 16 ♖e1 b5! (16 ... ♕f7 would have given White a plus after 17 ♘g5 ♗xd1 18 ♘xf7 ♖xf7 19 ♖exd1, because of the power of the two bishops in the endgame) 17 h3 ♗xh3 (More modest is 17 ... ♗xf3 18 ♗xf3 bxc4=) 18 ♘g5 ♗f5 19 ♗f4 ♕d7 20 cxb5 ♗xe4 21 ♖xe4 ♕f5? (Correct was 21 ... ♖f5! after which White's centre would have been destroyed) Yrjola - Malaniuk, Tallinn 1987.

b) 12 ... c5?! 13 ♘e6! (Less promising is 13 dxc6 bxc6 14 ♖b1 ♘c5 {*Also possible is 14 ... ♖c8 15 ♗e3 ♕f7 16 ♕e2 e5 17 ♘b3 ♘c7 18 ♗g2 d5 with an*} *obscure position; Schmidt - Grigorov, Prague 1985}* 15 ♘g2 e5 16 ♘e2 ♕e7 17 ♗e3 ♘e6 18 ♕d2 ♖fc8 19 ♖bd1 ♗f8 20 ♘c1 ♘g7 21 ♘d3 ♖c7 22 f4 exf4 23 ♗xf4 with a superior position for White; Vukic - Minic, Yugoslavia 1984, but as Vukic added in his comments, Black had a golden opportunity to play 18 ... c5 19 ♗xa8 ♖xa8 with good compensation) 13 ... ♗xe6 14 dxe6 ♖b8 15 h4! b5 16 h5 gxh5 17 ♔g2 ♘d4; van der Sterren - Malaniuk, Tallinn 1987. Here White could have gained great advantage by 18 ♗h6! (Kijk), for example 18 ... ♖f6 19 ♗g5 ♖f8 20 f4 bxc4 21 ♖b1 with the idea of ♖h1 x h5 with a winning attack.

Returning to the position after 12 ... ♘c5 *(7).*

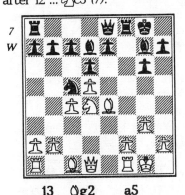

| | 13 | ♗g2 | a5 |
| | 14 | ♗g5 | |

14 ♗e3! with the idea of ♕d2, ♗h6, ♖ae1 - Simic.

	14	...	♕f7
	15	♕d2	♗xd4!?
	16	♕xd4	e5!
	17	♕c3	♕f5
	18	f4	

A position with equal chances has arisen; van der Sterren - Beliavsky, Wijk aan Zee 1984.

A12

| | 9 | ♖b1 *(8)* |

A fashionable and dangerous move.

| | 9 | ... | c5 |

Instead:

a) 9 ... ♗d7 10 b4 (10 ♘d4 transposes to the variation 9 ♘d4 ♗d7 10 ♖b1 whilst 10 b3 c6 11 ♗b2 ♘c7 12 a3 h6 13 ♘d4 ♖b8 14 b4 e5 15 dxe6 ♘xe6 16 ♘b3 ♕e7= Matamoros - Horvath, Gausdal 1986 and 10 ♖e1?! also fails to cause problems for Black: 10 ... c6 11 b3 h6 12 ♗b2 ♕f7 13 ♘d4 ♖ac8= Stone - Chernin, St John 1988) 10 ... c6 (10 ... c5 11 dxc6 is considered below under the move order 9 ... c5 10 dxc6 bxc6 11 b4, but not 10 ... e5? 11 dxe6 ♗xe6 12 ♘d4 ♗xc4 13 ♗xb7 ♖b8 14 ♗c6± Rukavina - Cvitan, Yugoslavia 1986) 11 ♕d3!? (Other variations are not promising for White: 11 ♕b3 ♘c7 12 ♘d4 ♘fxd5 13 cxd5 ♗xd4 14 dxc6 ♗e6 15 ♘d5 bxc6

16 ♘xc7 ♗xb3 17 ♘xe8 ♗xa2 18 ♗b2 ♗xb1 19 ♗xd4 ♗e4 20 f3 with equal chances in Karimov - Ivanchuk, Tashkent 1984; 11 dxc6 bxc6 transposes to the variation 9 ... c5 10 dxc6 bxc6 11 b4; but recently Mikhail Gurevich has experimented with 11 ... ♗xc6 to avoid this variation: 12 b5 ♗xf3 13 ♗xf3 ♘c5 14 ♗e3 ♖c8 15 ♗xc5?! *{15 ♘d5±}* 15 ... ♖xc5 16 ♗xb7 ♖xc4∞ Gelfand - Gurevich, Linares 1991; 11 a3 ♘c7 12 ♘d4 cxd5 13 cxd5 ♕f7 14 ♘b3 and a draw was agreed in Pigusov - Casper, Moscow 1987) 11 ... ♘e4 12 ♘d1 (12 ♘xe4?? fxe4 13 ♕xe4 ♗f5) 12 ... ♘c7 (If 12 ... c5 then 13 b5 retains an edge and not 13 a3?! because after this move Black himself plays 13 ... b5) 13 ♗b2 ♕f7 (13 ... cxd5 is not good: 14 ♗xg7 ♔xg7 15 cxd5 ♕f7 16 ♘g5! ♕xd5?? 17 ♗xe4 fxe4 18 ♕c3+ and White wins - Vogt) 14 ♗xg7 ♔xg7 15 dxc6 bxc6 16 ♘e3 ♕f6 17 ♘d2 ♗xd2 (17 ... ♘c3? 18 ♖b3 ♘xa2 19 ♕c2) 18 ♕xd2 f4 19 ♘c2 ♘e6 20 b5 ♖ac8 21 ♘b4 ♕d4 22 ♖fd1± Vogt - Casper, East Germany 1987.

b) 9 ... c6 10 b4 (10 dxc6 transposes to line 'c' in the next note, but more modest is 10 b3 ♘c7 *{10 ... ♗d7!? 11 ♗b2 ♘c5!? 12 b4 ♘ce4 13 ♘xe4 fxe4 14 ♘g5 cxd5 15 cxd5 ♗f5 16 ♘e6 ♗xe6 17 dxe6 e3 with an unclear position; Skalkotas - Kurtesis, Greece 1988}* 11 ♗b2 h6 12 ♕d2 c5 *{12 ... ♗d7 is more natural}* 13

a4 ♗d7 14 ♖be1 ♕f7 15 e4 fxe4 16 ♘xe4 ♘h7 17 ♖e3 ♗xb2 18 ♕xb2 ♕g7 19 ♕xg7+ ♔xg7± 20 ♘xd6?? exd6 0-1 Timoschenko - Bareev, Irkutsk 1986) 10 ... cxd5 11 ♘xd5 ♘e4 12 ♘g5 ♘c3 13 ♘xc3 ♗xc3 14 ♕b3!? (14 c5!) 14 ... ♗f6 (No better is 14 ... ♗xb4 15 c5+ ♔g7 16 cxd6 ♗xd6 17 ♖fd1 and White has a good position and can exert pressure) 15 c5+ ♔g7 16 cxd6 exd6 and Black's pawn weakness, badly positioned pieces, and open king position ensure a great advantage for White; Yrjola - Gurevich, Tallinn 1987.

c) 9 ... e5 has been the subject of experimentation in the last few years: 10 dxe6 ♗xe6 11 ♘d4 c6 (11 ... ♘c5±) 12 b4! (12 ♘xe6 ♕xe6 13 b3 ♖ad8 14 ♗a3 ♖fe8 15 ♕c2 ♘c7= Jo. Horvath - Santo Roman, Novi Sad ol 1990) 12 ... ♗xc4 13 b5 cxb5 14 ♘dxb5 ♖d8 15 ♗a3 d5 16 ♘d6 with a winning position for White; Salov - Gurevich, Reggio Emilia 1991/92.

Returning to the position after 9 ... c5 *(9)*

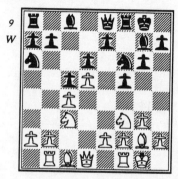

10 b3

Again White has several alternatives:

a) 10 a3 h6 11 b4 g5 12 e3 ♕h5 13 ♖e1 ♘e4 14 ♘b5 ♗d7 15 ♗b2 ♗xb2 16 ♖xb2 ♖fc8 17 ♕e2 ♘c7 18 ♘xc7 ♖xc7= Jelen – Psakhis, Portoroz 1987.

b) 10 ♖e1 ♘c7 11 e4 fxe4 12 ♘g5 ♘g4 13 ♘gxe4 ♕f7 14 ♕e2 h6 15 h3 ♘e5 with an unclear position; Gorin – Dzuraiev, Simferopol 1989.

c) Very fashionable nowadays is 10 dxc6!? bxc6 11 b4 *(10)*

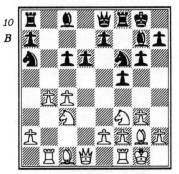

Mikhail Gurevich reached this position twice within a few weeks against Predrag Nikolic in 1990. In the first game he tried 11 ... c5 (11 ... ♖b8 runs into trouble after 12 b5 ♘c5 13 ♘d4 cxb5 14 cxb5 ♕f7 15 ♘c6± Cvetkovic – Legky, Belgrade 1988) 12 bxc5 ♘xc5 13 ♘g5 ♗a6 14 ♗xa8 ♕xa8 with some compensation for the exchange; Nikolic – Gurevich, Moscow GMA 1990. Then he played 11 ... ♗d7 12 a3 ♘c7 13 ♗b2 ♕h8?! 14 c5! dxc5 15 bxc5 ♘g4 16 ♘a4 with advantage to White; Nikolic – Gure-

vich, Manila izt 1990. In this line Black also fails to equalise after 13 ... ♖d8 14 b5 (14 ♘d4 e5 15 ♘b3 ♕e6 with an unclear position – Bareev; 14 ♕d3 f4!, for example 15 ♘e4? is now not possible: 15 ... ♘xe4 16 ♗xg7 ♔xg7 17 ♕xe4 ♘f5 18 ♕d4+ e5) 14 ... ♘e6 15 a4 ♖b8 16 ♗a3! with the idea of ♕d3± (Bareev) and not 16 ♕c2 f4!∞, as in the game Damljanovic – Bareev, Sochi 1988.

After 10 dxc6 bxc6 11 b4 ♗d7 White can also push on with 12 b5 ♘c5 13 ♘d4 ♘fe4 (13 ... cxb5 14 ♗xa8 ♕xa8 15 ♘dxb5 ♖c8 16 ♘d5± Piket – Gurevich, Groningen 1992) 14 ♘xe4 ♘xe4 15 bxc6 ♗xc6 16 ♘e6 ♕c8!∞ Hracek – Malaniuk, Kecskemet 1991.

10 ... ♘c7

Others:

a) 10 ... ♘h5 11 ♗b2 f4 12 ♘e4± – Gufeld.

b) 10 ... h6!? 11 ♗b2 g5 12 ♕d2 (If 12 e3 ♕g6 13 ♕e2 ♖f7 14 ♖be1 ♘e4 15 ♖c1 ♗d7 16 ♘d2 ♘xc3 17 ♗xc3 and White is slightly better; Panzalovic – Cvetkovic Yugoslavia 1991) 12 ... ♕h5 13 e3 ♗d7 14 ♘e1 f4 15 exf4 gxf4 16 ♘e2 fxg3 17 ♘xg3 ♕g6 ½–½ Novikov – Malaniuk, Lvov 1988.

11 a4

An interesting alternative is 11 ♗b2 b5 12 ♘xb5 ♘xb5 13 cxb5 ♕xb5 14 ♘d2 ♘d7 15 ♗xg7 ♔xg7 16 ♖e1 ♕b4 17 e4 with advantage to White; Ivanchuk – Legky, USSR 1987.

11 ... b6

More promising than 11 ... ♘d7 12 ♘b2 b6 13 ♕d2! (13 e4 fxe4 14 ♘g5 e3 – Garzia Martinez; 13 ♘b5 ♕d8! *{13 ... ♘xb5 14 axb5±}* 14 ♘xc7 ♕xc7 15 ♘g5 h6 16 ♘e6 ♗xe6 17 dxe6 and White still has the advantage) 13 ... a6 14 e4 fxe4 15 ♘g5 h6 (15 ... e3 16 ♕xe3 ♘g4 17 ♕e2 with a great advantage to White) 16 ♘gxe4 (± – Vanheste) 16 ... ♘h7? (16 ... b5 was slightly better) 17 ♘e2! and White has a clear advantage; Garcia Martinez – Lin Ta, Dubai 1986.

12 e4!?

On 12 ♘b2 Black plays ... a7 – a6 and ... b7 – b5.

12 ... fxe4
13 ♘g5 e3!

After 13 ... ♗g4 White retains the advantage by 14 ♕c2 e3 15 ♗xe3 ♗f5 16 ♘ge4 – Timoschenko.

14 ♗xe3 ♗f5
15 ♘ge4 ♘xe4
16 ♘xe4 a6 (11)

Black's position is not worse; Timoschenko – Malaniuk, Tashkent 1987.

A13

9 ♗e3 (12)

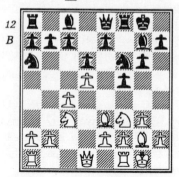

White also hopes to seize the initiative in this position. In comparison with the well-analysed moves 9 ♘d4 and 9 ♖b1, this variation is relatively rare. More rare is 9 ♕c2 which creates no problems for Black, e.g. 9 ... ♘d7 (Or 9 ... c6 10 ♖b1 ♘c7 11 ♖d1 h6 12 b4 cxd5 13 cxd5 ♗d7 14 ♘d4 ♖c8 15 ♕d2 ♕f7 16 ♘b3 ♘e4 17 ♘xe4 fxe4 18 ♕f4 ♕xf4 19 ♗xf4 ♘b5 20 ♖bc1 ♘c3 21 ♖d2 ♖c4 and White's position is critical; Gladysh – Ivanchuk, Tashkent 1984) 10 a3 c6 11 ♘d2 ♖c8 12 b4 ♘c7 13 ♕b3 cxd5 14 cxd5 ♘b5 with advantage to Black; Porth – Gross, Saarlouis 1986.

9 ... h6

The most fashionable move. Others:

a) 9 ... ♘d7 has also been seen: 10 ♕d2 ♘g4 11 ♗f4 ♘c5 12 h3 ♘f6 13 ♘d4 c6 with chances for both sides; Ker – Zsu. Polgar, Wellington 1988.

b) 9 ... c6 10 ♖c1 (An interesting possibility is 10 ♕b3!? c5

{10 ... ♔h8 11 ♖ae1 h6 12 ♘d4 e5 13 dxe6 ♕xe6∞ Naumkin - Tozer, London 1991} 11 ♖ae1 h6 12 ♗c1 ♘c7 13 e4 fxe4 14 ♘d2 ♕f7 15 ♘dxe4 ♖b8 16 ♘xf6+ exf6 17 ♗f4 ♖d8 18 ♘e4 ♗f8 19 ♕c3 ♔g7 20 b4 and Black faces serious difficulties; Naumkin - Dreev, Jaroslavl 1983) 10 ... ♘g4 (10 ... h6?! 11 c5! ½-½ Petrosian - Psakhis, Erevan 1986. Sher and Lysenko considered this position to be better for White, justifying their assessment with the following variation: 11 ... ♘g4 12 ♗d4 ♗xd4 *{12 ... dxc5 13 ♗xg7 ♔xg7 14 dxc6 ♕xc6 15 ♘e5}* 13 ♘xd4 dxc5 14 dxc6 cxd4 15 cxb7) 11 ♗f4 (Also possible are 11 ♗d4? ♗h6! with the idea of ... c5 or 11 ♗d2 ♘c5!? with the idea of ... ♘c5 - e4 - Petrosian) 11 ... h6 12 h3 ♘f6 13 ♗e3 g5 14 ♘d4 ♗d7 (14 ... c5!? 15 ♘e6! - Petrosian) 15 f4! (15 ♕c2 ♘h5 intending ... f4) 15 ... ♘h5 16 ♔h2 e5!? 17 dxe6 ♗xe6 18 ♘xe6 ♕xe6 19 ♗d4 ♕g6 20 ♗xg7 ♔xg7 21 ♕d4+± Petrosian - Kotronias, Lvov 1988.

c) 9 ... c5 10 ♕d2 (Less promising is 10 ♕c1 ♘c7!? 11 ♗h6 b5 12 ♗xg7 ♔xg7 13 cxb5 ♖b8 *{13 ... ♘xb5!?}* 14 a4 ♘cxd5 15 ♘xd5 ♘xd5 16 ♘d4 ♗b4 17 ♘c6 ♘xc6 18 ♗xc6 ♕f7= Djukanovic - Blagojevic, Belgrade 1988) 10 ... ♗d7 (Dubious is 10 ... ♘g4?! *{10 ... ♘c7 11 a4 ♘g4 12 ♗f4 ♗d7 13 e4 ♗xc3 14 ♕xc3 and White has the more active position; Petrosian - Gabdrakhmanov, Pod-*

olsk 1990} 11 ♗f4 h6 12 h3 g5 13 ♗xg5 hxg5 14 hxg4 fxg4 *{14 ... f4 15 ♘xg5 fxg3 16 f4±}* 15 ♘xg5 ♗h6 16 ♘ce4 and the idea of 17 f4 gives the advantage to White - Marin) 11 ♗h6 ♕f7 (11 ... b5!?) 12 ♗xg7 ♕xg7 13 ♘g5± Marin - Timoshenko, Tallinn 1989.

10 ♖c1

Or:

a) 10 ♕c1 ♔h7 11 ♖b1 e5 12 dxe6 ♗xe6 13 ♘d4 c6 14 ♘xe6 ♕xe6 15 b3 ♘c5 16 ♕c2 ♘fe4 17 ♘xe4 ♘xe4 18 ♖bd1 and White has slightly the better game; Larsen - Vasiukov, Graested 1990.

b) 10 ♖b1 ♔h7 11 b4 e5 12 dxe6 ♗xe6 13 c5 ♖d8; Kalantarian - Ryskin USSR Team Ch 1991, where White has good chances of an attack on the queenside.

10 ...   g5

Less committal is 10 ... ♗d7, as in Andersson - Kasparov, Madrid (rapid) 1989, which continued: 11 a3 c5 12 dxc6 bxc6 13 b4 ♘c7 14 c5 ♘g4 15 ♗d2 d5 16 h3 ♘f6 with balanced chances.

11	**♗d4**	**♕h5** *(13)*
12	**♗xf6!**	**♗xf6**
13	**♘d4**	

With the idea of f2 - f4.

13	**...**	**f4**
14	**a3**	**♗xd4**
15	**♕xd4**	**♘c5**
16	**♖ce1**	**♗h3**
17	**f3**	

White has a slight advantage;

Petrosian – Vasiukov, Novi Sad 1988.

A2

8   ...   a5 *(14)*

This an interesting alternative to the standard 8 ... ♘a6. Black anticipates White's activity on the queenside and in some cases is ready to advance his pawn to a4 and a3. White's hopes are associated with activity in the centre.

9   ♘d4

No less than five other moves have been seen here:

a) 9 ♘e1 ♘a6 10 ♘d3 e5 11 e4! (11 dxe6 c6∓) 11 ... c6!? 12 dxc6 bxc6 13 b3 fxe4 14 ♘xe4 ♘xe4 15 ♗xe4 ♗f5 16 ♕e2 ♗xe4 17

♕xe4 ♖d8 18 ♗g5 d5 19 cxd5 cxd5 20 ♕e1 e4 21 ♗xd8 ♕xd8 22 ♘f4 ♗xa1 23 ♕a1 ♕d7; Kremenietsky – Piskov, Moscow 1989. In view of the threat 24 ... ♖xf4, White has no time to deal with the black centre. The position is balanced.

b) 9 ♖e1 ♘a6 10 e4 fxe4 11 ♘xe4 ♘xe4 12 ♖xe4 ♘c5 13 ♖h4 (13 ♖e1 ♕f7 with the idea of ... ♗g4) 13 ... a4! 14 ♘d4 (The only move) 14 ... ♘f6 15 ♖h6 ♕f7 16 ♗e3 ♘d7!∓ Krasnov – Piskov, Moskow 1989.

c) 9 e4 ♘xe4 10 ♘xe4 fxe4 11 ♘g5 a4! (Sometimes threatening ... a4 – a3) 12 ♘xe4 ♗f5! and with ... ♘a6 – c5 following Black is able to transfer his pieces into good positions.

d) 9 ♖b1 ♘a6 10 b3 ♗d7 11 a3 (11 ♘d4 ♘c5 12 a3 c6 13 ♗b2 ♖c8 14 ♗a1 g5 and Black has an active position; Tunik – Gagarin, Smolensk Cup 1991) 11 ... c6 12 b4 axb4 13 axb4 c5 14 bxc5 ♘xc5 15 ♗e3 ♖c8 16 ♘d4 h6 17 ♘d2 g5 18 e3 f4 and Black has seized the initiative; Donchenko – Vyzmanavin, USSR 1986.

e) 9 ♗e3!? ♘a6 (9 ... h6 10 ♘b5 *{Or 10 c5 ♘a6 11 cxd6 exd6 12 ♗d4 b6 [Not 12 ... b5? 13 a4 b4 14 ♘b5 but playable is 12 ... g5 13 ♘d2 f4 14 ♘c4?! b6 15 a4 ♗d7 16 ♘a3 ♕g6 with active play; A. Petrosian – Glek, USSR Team Ch 1991]* 13 ♕c2 ♘c5 14 *♖ad1 ♗d7 15 ♘h4 ♘g4 16 ♗xg7 ♔xg7 17 e3 b5 with a good game for Black; Haritonov –*

Piskov, Moscow GMA 1989} 10 ... ♘a6 11 ♕d2 ♘g4 12 ♘d4 b6 and here, according to Piskov, White has a slight advantage) 10 ♕d2 e5 (Possible is 10 ... ♗d7 *{Worse is 10 ... ♘g4 11 ♗f4 ♘c5 12 h3 ♘f6 13 ♗h6 e5 14 dxe6 ♘fe4 15 ♘xe4 ♘xe4 16 ♕e3 ♗xh6 17 ♕xh6 and Black's king is somewhat exposed; Fominyh - Szabolcsi, Budapest 1992}* 11 ♗h6 *{11 ♖ae1!?}* 11 ... ♘c5 *{11 ... ♕f7?! 12 ♗xg7 ♕xg7 13 ♘d4 ♘c5 14 f4! with advantage to White; Kärner - Raud, Haapsalu 1987}* 12 ♗xg7 ♔xg7 13 ♘d4 e5 14 dxe6 ♗xe6=) 11 dxe6 ♕xe6 12 ♘g5 ♕e7 (12 ... ♕xc4? 13 ♘d5) 13 ♘d5 ♘xd5 14 ♗xd5+ (14 cxd5 b6) 14 ... ♔h8 14 ♕xa5 ♗xb2 and Black maintains the balance, e.g. 16 ♖ab1 ♗f6!

Now we return to the main line with 9 ♘d4. Black's next move follows on naturally from 8 ... a5.

9 ...　　♘a6 *(15)*

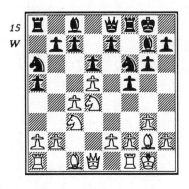

10　e4

More passive is 10 b3 ♘d7 11 ♗b2 and now:

a) 11 ... g5 12 e3 (Probably better are 12 f3 or 12 f4 with advantage to White) 12 ... f4 13 exf4 gxf4 14 ♘e6 ♗xe6 15 dxe6 c6 16 ♘e2 fxg3 and Black has good attacking chances. The game Lukacs - Szabolcsi, Budapest 1991, continued 17 hxg3 ♘g4 18 ♗h3 ♗xb2 19 ♗xg4 ♗xa1 20 ♕xa1 ♕g6 21 ♗h3 ♕h5 0-1.

b) 11 ... ♘c5 12 ♘db5 ♕c8 intending ... e7 - e5 with equal chances.

c) 11 ... c6 12 ♕d2 ♘c7 13 ♖ae1 c5 14 ♘e6! ♗xe6 (14 ... ♘xe6!?) 15 dxe6 ♖b8? (Slightly better was 15 ... ♘xe6 16 ♗xb7 ♖b8±) 16 e4 f4 17 ♗h3 and the weakness of the square e6 gives White a clear advantage; Arulaid - Raud, Haapsalu 1987.

10　...　　fxe4
11　♘xe4　♘xe4
12　♗xe4　♗h3

Not 12 ... ♘c5 13 ♗g2 ♗d7 14 ♗g5 h6 15 ♗e3 a4 16 ♕d2 ♔h7 17 ♖ae1 ♕f7 18 ♘e2! and Black has no compensation for his positional weaknesses.

13　♗g2

A recent game went 13 ♖e1!? ♘c5 14 ♗h1 ♕f7 15 ♗e3 e5 16 dxe6 ♘xe6 17 ♕d2± Otero - L. Valdes, Cuba 1992.

13　...　　♗xg2
14　♔xg2　♘c5 *(16)*

This was the continuation of Cvitan - Piskov, Moscow GMA 1989. According to Piskov, the game should now have gone:

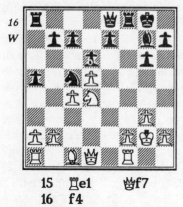

15   ♖e1   ♕f7
16   f4

With a slight advantage for White but Black has also some hope to organise counterplay with 16 ... ♘xd4. Not, however, 15 ♗e3?! ♕f7 (15 ... e6) 16 ♖b1 c6!, when, as in the above-mentioned game, Black has already gained an edge.

B
8   b3

Black again has a wide choice here:

B1   8 ... e5
B2   8 ... ♘a6
B3   8 ... h6
B4   8 ... ♘c6 and others

B1

8   ...   e5 (17)

In this section we shall examine Black's straightforward attempt to solve his problems by advancing ... e7 - e5 immediately. Once it was thought that by this method Black should gain at least equality. But, as we shall see

below, things are not so easy.

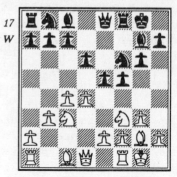

9   dxe5   dxe5
10   e4

Placing the knight in the centre gives White nothing, e.g. 10 ♘d5?! ♘xd5 11 ♕xd5+ ♔h8 12 ♗a3 ♖g8 13 e4 ♘c6 14 exf5 gxf5 15 ♗b2 ♕e7 (Thorsteins - Malaniuk, Warsaw 1989) 16 ♘xe5 (16 ♖fe1!? - Malaniuk) 16 ... ♘xe5 17 ♖ae1 ♗xb2 18 ♖xe7 ♘xe7 19 ♕c5 ♘g6 20 ♕xc7 ♗e5 with an obscure position.

10 ♗a3 also makes little headway, e.g. 10 ... ♖f7 11 ♘g5 (11 e4 ♘c6 transposes to the variation 10 e4 ♘c6 11 ♗a3 ♖f7 considered below) 11 ... ♖d7 12 ♕c1 h6 and the position is equal.

10   ...   ♘c6 (18)

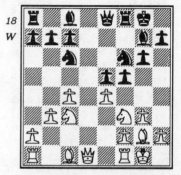

10 ... fxe4 is to be avoided, e.g. 11 ♘xe4 ♘xe4 12 ♕d5+ ♗e6 13 ♕xe4 ♘c6 14 ♘g5± - Vanheste.

11 ♘d5

Alternatively 11 ♗a3 ♖f7 and now:

a) 12 h3 f4 (12 ... h6!?) 13 ♕d3 ♗e6 14 ♖ad1 h6 15 ♖fe1?! (15 g4 ♖d8 16 ♘d5 g5 with the idea of ... ♘h7 - f8 - g6=) 15 ... fxg3! 16 fxg3 ♘h5 17 ♔h2 ♘d4 18 ♖f1 ♖d8∓ Casafus - Lin Ta, Dubai 1986.

b) 12 ♖e1 f4 (A typical continuation of the attack) 13 gxf4?! (Here Beliavsky offers the variation 13 ♘g5! ♖d7 14 ♘d5 h6 15 ♘f3 g5 with equal chances; also possible is 13 ♘d5 ♗g4 14 ♗b2 ♘h5∞ Arbakov - Malaniuk, Budapest 1990) 13 ... ♗g4 (13 ... ♘h5 14 f5 {14 fxe5 ♗g4 15 h3 ♗xf3 16 ♗xf3 ♘f4 17 ♔h2 ♘xe5} 14 ... gxf5 15 ♘g5 ♖d7 16 ♘d5 ♕g6 17 h4 ♘d4 {17 ... ♘f4 18 exf5 ♕xf5 19 ♗e4± - Beliavsky} 18 ♗h3 ♖f7 and Black has succeeded in escaping the worst; Meduna - Beliavsky, Sochi 1986) 14 h3 (14 fxe5 ♘xe5 with the idea of 15 ... ♘h5∓) 14 ... ♗xf3 15 ♗xf3 ♘d4?! (15 ... exf4!? and: 16 e5 ♘xe5 17 ♗xb7 ♖d8 18 ♕c2 c6 19 ♗xc6 ♕xc6 20 ♖xe5 ♘h5 intending 21 ... ♕f3∓; or 16 ♘d5 ♘a5 17 ♗b2 c6∓ - Vanheste) 16 ♘b5 with an unclear position; Balashov - Vyzmanavin, Irkutsk 1986.

c) 12 exf5 ♗xf5 13 ♖e1 ♖d7 14 ♕c1 ♖ad8 15 ♘h4 e4 16 ♘xf5

gxf5 and Black has control of the centre; Temirbaev - Beliavsky, USSR Team Ch 1991.

d) 12 ♘g5 ♖d7 13 ♕b1 h6 14 ♘f3 f4 15 gxf4 ♘h5 with complex play; Tsarev - Malaniuk, Kiev 1989.

11 ... ♕d7 (19)

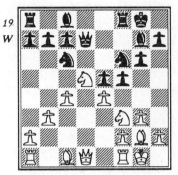

Others:

a) 11 ... fxe4 12 ♘g5 ♘xd5 13 cxd5 ♘d4 14 ♘xe4±.

b) 11 ... ♖f7 12 ♘g5 ♘xe4 (12 ... ♖d7 13 exf5 gxf5 14 ♗b2 h6 {No better is 14 ... ♘g4 15 h3 ♘h6 16 ♕e2 ♕g6 17 f4 ♔h8 18 ♔h2 ♘g8 19 ♖ad1; Lechtynsky - Psakhis, Trnava 1988} 15 ♘xf6+ ♗xf6 16 ♗d5+ ♔g7 17 ♘f3 e4 18 ♗xf6+ ♔xf6 19 ♕c1 exf3 20 ♖e1! - Balashov) 13 ♘xf7 ♕xf7 14 ♗b2 ♗e6 15 ♕e2 and Black lacks sufficent counterplay for the exchange; Balashov - Yrjola, Voronez 1987.

c) 11 ... ♘xd5!? 12 cxd5 (12 exd5 e4; 12 ♕xd5+ ♗e6 13 ♕b5 a6! 14 ♕xb7? ♖a7∓) 12 ... fxe4 (12 ... ♘d4?! 13 ♘xd4 exd4 14 ♗b2 {14 ♗a3! ♖f7 15 e5 f4 16 e6 ♖f5 17 ♖c1 fxg3 18 hxg3 and *White has a winning position;*

Baburin - Ronin, Novosibirsk 1989} 14 ... fxe4 15 ♘xd4 ♗f5 16 ♗xg7 ♔xg7 17 ♕d4+ with the idea of 罝ae1±) 13 ♘g5 (13 dxc6 exf3 14 ♗xf3 e4) 13 ... ♘d4 14 ♘xe4 (14 ♗a3!?) 14 ... ♔h8 15 ♗b2 ♗f5 16 罝c1 (A mistake would be 16 f4?, e.g. 16 ... ♗xe4 17 ♗xe4 exf4 18 罝e1 ♕e5) 16 ... 罝c8 (16 ... ♕f7 17 ♘c5! b6 18 ♘e6± - Blagojevic) 17 罝e1 ♕f7 18 f4 ♕xd5 19 ♘c5 e4 20 ♘xe4 with an obscure position; Gavrikov - Blagojevic, Prague 1988.

12   exf5

Or:

a) 12 ♘xf6+!? ♗xf6 13 ♕xd7 (13 ♗h6 罝e8= 14 罝e1 ♕e7 15 ♕c1 ♘b4 16 c5 ♗e6 17 ♕c3 ♘c6 18 罝ad1 罝ad8 19 罝xd8 罝xd8 20 h4 f4 21 gxf4 exf4 22 e5 ♗xh4 23 ♗xf4 ♗d5 24 b4 ♗xf3 25 ♕xf3 ♗g5 and Black has difficulties in defending his queenside; Hort - Yrjola, Thessaloniki 1988) 13 ... ♗xd7 14 ♗b2 with the idea of 罝fe1 and the square e5 remains weak.

b) 12 ♗a3 and now:

b1) 12 ... 罝e8? (Here attention should be directed at 12 ... ♘xe4!? 13 ♗xf8 ♔xf8 and Black has some compensation) 13 exf5 (13 ♘xf6 ♗xf6 14 ♕d5+ ♕f7 15 ♕xf7+ ♔xf7 16 ♗b2=) 13 ... e4 (13 ... gxf5 14 ♘h4!) 14 ♘g5 (14 ♘h4? g5!∓) 14 ... gxf5 (14 ... ♕xf5 15 f4 exf3 {15 ... ♘xd5 16 cxd5 ♗xa1 17 ♕xa1 ♕xd5 18 罝d1 ♕a5 19 ♕f6!±} 16 ♘xf3 ♘xd5 17 cxd5 ♗xa1 18 ♕xa1 ♕xd5 19 ♕f6 with an attack) 15 ♘xf6+ ♗xf6 16

♕h5! ♗xa1 (Others also fail, e.g. 16 ... ♘d4 17 ♘xh7± - Pinter; or 16 ... 罝d8 17 罝ad1 ♘d4 *(20)*

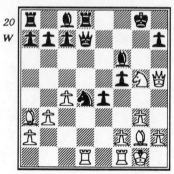

18 罝xd4!! and Black had nothing better than to resign in Magerramov - Malaniuk, Warsaw 1989, because 18 ... ♗xd4 19 罝d1 c5 20 ♗xc5 ♗xc5 21 罝xd7 罝xd7 22 ♘e6 leads to a hopeless position) 17 罝xa1 罝d8 18 ♗b2 ♕e7 19 罝e1 ♘d4 (19 ... ♗d7 20 罝e4!±; 19 ... ♗e6 20 ♕h6!±) 20 ♗xe4!! fxe4 (20 ... ♘f3+ 21 ♕xf3 ♕xg5 22 ♗d5+ ♔f8 23 ♗a3+ ♔g7 24 ♗e7+) 21 罝xe4 ♘f3+ (21 ... ♗e6 22 ♗xd4+; 21 ... ♘e6 22 罝g4) 22 ♔g2!! (22 ♕xf3 ♕xg5∓; 22 ♘xf3 ♕xe4 23 ♕g5+ ♔f7 24 ♘e5+ ♔e6! and no mate) 22 ... ♗h3+ (22 ... ♕xg5 23 罝e8+ 罝xe8 24 ♕xe8 mate) 23 ♔xf3 1-0 Pinter - Karolyi, Budapest 1989, as if 23 ... ♕d7 24 ♕xh3!± or 23 ... ♕f8+! 24 罝f4 ♕d3+ (24 ... ♗f5 25 ♘xh7±) 25 ♔e2 ♗f5 26 ♘e4 ♗xe4 27 罝g4+ with a quick mate - Pinter.

b2) 12 ... 罝d8 13 exf5 e4 14 fxg6? (Better is 14 ♘g5 gxf5 and now not 15 ♘e3?! ♕e8 16 ♕e1 ♘e5 17 罝d1 ♘d3 18 ♕e2

♕g6 19 h4 ♘h6∓ Arkhipov - Videki, Györ 1990, but instead 15 ♘xf6+ ♗xf6 16 ♕h5 ♗xa1 17 ♖xa1∞ as given by Fominyh and Schipkov) 14 ... exf3 15 ♗xf3 hxg6 16 ♖e1 ♕f7 17 ♘xf6+ ♕xf6 18 ♗d5+ ♔h7 with a decisive advantage for Black; Pergericht - Karolyi, London 1989.

12 ... e4

It is not good to capture at once: 12 ... ♗xf5?! 13 ♗b2 e4 14 ♘e5 ♘xe5 15 ♗xe5± - Shabalov.

13 ♘g5 gxf5

Possible is 13 ... ♘xd5 14 cxd5 ♗xa1 15 ♗a3 ♗f6 (15 ... ♖xf5 16 ♕xa1 ♖xg5 17 dxc6 ♕xc6 18 ♖c1 ♕d7 19 ♕c3 with the idea of 20 ♗b2±) 16 dxc6± (Shabalov in *Informator 47*), but after 16 ... ♕xd1 17 ♖xd1 ♗xg5 Black is simply a piece up.

14 ♗e3

If instead 14 ♗f4 h6 15 ♘h3 (15 ♘e6? ♕xe6 16 ♘xc7 ♕f7 17 ♘xa8 ♘h5∓) 15 ... ♘xd5 16 cxd5 ♘d4! (16 ... ♘e7?!= Shabalov - Malaniuk, Moscow GMA 1989) 17 ♖c1 c6 18 d6 (18 dxc6 bxc6 with the idea of ... ♗a6=) 18 ... b6 with a good game for Black - Shabalov.

14 ... ♘xd5

Consideration should also be given to 14 ... h6!? 15 ♘xf6+ ♗xf6 16 ♕xd7 (16 ♘h3 ♗xa1 17 ♕xa1 ♕g7 18 ♕c1 ♔h7 and White has compensation for the sacrificed material) 16 ... ♗xd7 17 ♖ad1± - Piskov.

However, simply bad is 14 ... ♘g4? 15 ♗c5 ♖e8 16 f3± Piskov

- Malaniuk, Moscow GMA 1989.

15	cxd5	♗xa1
16	♕xa1	♕xd5
17	♖d1	♕e5
18	♕c1	*(21)*

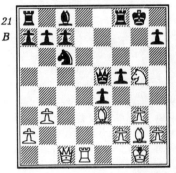

White has good attacking chances for the sacrificed material - Piskov.

B2

8 ... ♘a6 *(22)*

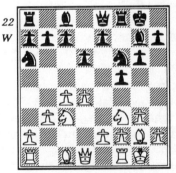

Black started to play in this way in 1988 and 1989, when the forcing variations after 8 ... e5 began to seem dangerous for him (see the previous section). Since then a great amount of practical material on the variation has accumulated. We shall try to find a path through this labyrinth.

9 ♗a3

Alternatively:

a) 9 a4!? has only been seen once: 9 ... h6 (Kramnik recommends 9 ... ♘b4 10 a5 *{10 ♗a3?! a5}* 10 ... e5! 11 ♗a3 c5 12 dxe5 dxe5 13 e4 ♗d7∞) 10 ♗a3 ♘e4 11 ♛c2 ♘xc3 12 ♛xc3 ♘c5 13 ♗xc5 dxc5 14 e3± Mochalov - Kalinichev, USSR 1988.

b) 9 ♗b2 ♗d7 (9 ... h6 10 e4 fxe4 11 ♘d2 ♗g4 12 ♛b1 e3 13 fxe3 c6 14 a3 ♘c7 15 ♛d3 g5 with unclear play; Kaunas - Chernin, Klaipeda 1983) 10 d5 transposes to chapter 5, variation A1111, whilst 10 ♛c2 c6 11 e4? ♘b4! 12 ♛e2 fxe4 13 ♘xe4 ♘xe4 14 ♛xe4 ♗f5 15 ♛e2 ♗d3 was winning for Black in Loginov - Arkhipov, Odessa 1987.

9 ... c6

10 ♛d3

The alternatives are:

a) 10 ♛c2 ♖b8 (10 ... b5 11 ♗b2 ♗d7 12 e4 ♘b4!? 13 ♛d2!? fxe4 14 ♘xe4 ♘xe4 with an obscure position - Piskov) 11 e4 b5 (The exchange in the centre leaves White with a slight advantage: 11 ... fxe4 12 ♘xe4 ♘xe4 13 ♛xe4 ♗f5 14 ♛e3; Schipkov - Gerbakher, Yalta 1988) 12 e5! b4 (12 ... ♘d7 13 cxb5 cxb5 14 ♘d5±) 13 exf6 ♗xf6 14 ♗b2 bxc3 15 ♗xc3 ♛f7 (15 ... e5? 16 dxe5 dxe5 17 ♘xe5! ♗xe5 18 ♖ae1 ♘b4 19 ♗xb4 ♖xb4 20 ♛e2±; 15 ... ♘c7) 16 ♛d2!?± Baburin - Grigorov, Starozagorski Bani 1989.

b) 10 e3 ♖b8 11 ♘e1 (11 ♖c1 b5 12 cxb5 cxb5 13 ♘e2 b4 14 ♗b2 ♘d5 15 ♘f4 ♘ac7 16 ♘xd5 ♘xd5 17 ♖e1 h6 with equal chances; Arbakov - Kramnik, Belgorod 1989) 11 ... b5 12 cxb5 cxb5 13 ♘d5 ♗b7 14 ♘xf6+ ♗xf6 15 ♗xb7 ♖xb7 16 ♘d3 b4 17 ♗b2 ♛b5 ½-½ Huzman - Malaniuk, Baku 1988.

c) An interesting possibility is 10 ♖c1 h6 (Malaniuk suggests here 10 ... ♗d7!? and 10 ... ♖b8 has also been tried: 11 ♗b2 b5 12 cxb5 cxb5 13 d5?! ♘c7 14 b4 a5 15 a3 axb4 16 axb4 ♗b7 17 ♛b3 ♔h8 18 ♖fd1 h6 with an obscure position; Gdanski - Horvath, Leningrad 1989) 11 e3 ♗e6 12 ♛e2 ♛d7 13 ♘d2 ♘c7 14 ♛d3 ♖ab8 15 ♗b2 ♔h8 16 d5 cxd5 17 ♘xd5 ♘cxd5 18 cxd5± Gavrikov - Malaniuk, USSR Ch 1988.

10 ... ♖b8

Other tries:

a) 10 ... ♘c7 (10 ... ♔h8!?) 11 e4 fxe4 12 ♘xe4 ♗f5 13 ♘xf6+ exf6 14 ♛d2 ♛d7= Vegh - Zysk, Budapest 1989.

b) 10 ... ♗d7 11 ♖fe1 ♖d8?! (11 ... d5!? 12 ♘e5±) 12 ♖ad1 ♔h8 13 e4± fxe4 14 ♘xe4 ♗f5 15 ♘xf6 ♗xf6 16 ♛e3 ♛f7 17 h3 ♘c7 18 ♖e2 ♗c8 (18 ... ♖fe8!?) 19 ♘g5 ♛g8 20 ♛d2! ♘e6 21 ♘xe6 ♗xe6 22 ♖de1 ♗d7? (More stubborn resistance could be put up by 22 ... ♗c8!?) *(23)*
23 ♖xe7! ♗xe7 24 ♖xe7 ♖f6 25 d5 ♛f8 26 ♖e3 ♔g8 27 ♗b2 ♖f5 28 ♛d4 ♖e5 29 ♖xe5 dxe5 30 ♛xe5 ♔f7 31 d6! ♗f5 32 c5 h5 33

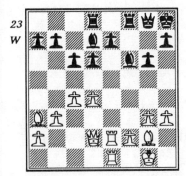

g4! hxg4 34 hxg4 ♘d3 35 ♗d5+! 1-0 Karpov - Malaniuk, USSR 1988 (comments by Karpov and Zaitsev).

c) An interesting move for Black is 10 ... h6!? 11 ♖fe1?! (Malaniuk suggests 11 ♘h4!?. Alternatively, a position with equal chances occurs after 11 e4 fxe4 12 ♘xe4 ♘xe4 13 ♕xe4 ♗f5 14 ♕e3 g5 15 h3 ♕f7 16 ♖ae1; Dzhandzhgava - Basin, Simferopol 1988) 11 ... g5 12 e4 fxe4 13 ♘xe4 ♘xe4 (13 ... ♕g6!?) 14 ♕xe4 ♕h5 and the position is difficult to evaluate; J. Cooper - Kotronias, Thessaloniki ol 1988.

11 ♘d2

White has had varied success with other tries:

a) Nothing is gained by 11 ♖c1?! b5 12 ♗b2 ♘b4 13 ♕b1 bxc4 14 bxc4 h6 15 a3 ♘a6 16 ♕c2 e5 and Black's position is not worse; Wilder - Lund, Preston 1989.

b) In the event of 11 e4 Black must play accurately:

b1) 11 ... b5?! 12 e5 (Less promising is 12 cxb5 cxb5 13 e5

b4 14 exf6 ♗xf6 15 ♗c1 bxc3 16 ♗h6 ♖f7 17 ♘g5 ♗xg5 18 ♗xg5 ♘b4!? and White has no hope of an advantage; Danner - Zysk, Budapest 1989) 12 ... b4 13 exf6 ♗xf6 14 ♗c1 (More modest is 14 ♗b2 bxc3 15 ♗xc3 g5 *{15 ... ♕f7 16 ♖fe1 g5 17 ♕d2 h6 18 d5 c5 19 ♖e2 ♖b7± Lerner - Malaniuk, USSR Ch 1989}* 16 d5 ♘c5 17 ♕c2 cxd5 18 ♗xf6? ♖xf6 19 cxd5 g4 20 ♘d4 ♕h5 and Black has an attack, or 16 ♕d2! ♕h5 17 ♘e1 with the idea of ♘d3± - Dautov) 14 ... bxc3 15 ♗h6! (Dokhoian) 15 ... ♗g7 (15 ... ♖f7 16 ♘g5) 16 ♗xg7 ♔xg7 17 ♕xc3± - Kishnev.

b2) 11 ... fxe4 12 ♘xe4 *(24)*

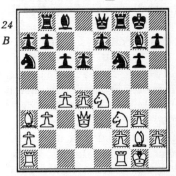

12 ... ♗f5 (12 ... ♘xe4 13 ♕xe4 ♗f5 14 ♕e3 ♕d7 *{14 ... ♕f7 15 ♖fe1 with chances for both sides; Lechtynsky - Salai, Czech Ch 1990. Also interesting is 14 ... ♗f6, preventing ♘h4: 15 ♖ad1 ♘c7 16 ♖fe1 ♕d7 17 ♖d2 ♖be8 18 ♗b2 a6 with equal chances; Basin - Kramnik, Belgorod 1989}* 15 ♘h4 ♗g4 16 f4 with a slight advantage to White - Bareev) 13 ♘xf6+ ♗xf6 (It is

incorrect to take the knight with the pawn: 13 ... exf6? 14 ♕d2 ♖d8 *{14 ... ♕d7 15 ♕f4 ♖bd8 16 ♘h4 ♗h3 17 ♘xh3 ♕xh3 18 ♗xd6 g5 19 ♕f5±}* 15 ♖fe1 ♕f7 16 ♖e2 ♖fe8 17 ♖xe8+ ♕xe8 18 ♖e1 ♕f8 19 ♕a5 *{19 ♘h4 ♗c8 20 ♕a5 f5 21 ♘f3 ♗f6 22 b4±}* 19 ... ♖a8!! 20 b4 ♕d8 21 ♕a4 ♘c7 22 d5 cxd5 23 cxd5 ♕d7 24 ♕d1! *{24 ♕b3 ♖e8 25 ♖c1 ♗e4=}* 24 ... ♗g4 25 ♕d3 ♖e8 26 ♖xe8+ *{26 ♖c1 ♗f5 27 ♕c4 ♘b5 28 ♗b2 ♖c8=}* 26 ... ♕e8 27 ♕c4! and, in spite of the exchanges, Black has not improved his position; Klinger – Bareev, Moscow GMA 1989. Comments by Bareev) 14 ♕e3 (14 ♕d2!? ♘c7 15 ♖ae1 ♕d7 16 h4!?± Ibragimov – Kramnik, Herson 1991) 14 ... b5 15 ♖ac1 (15 ♘g5 bxc4 16 bxc4 ♕d7± – Kramnik) 15 ... ♘c7 (15 ... ♕d7?! 16 cxb5! cxb5 17 ♘g5± Kishnev – Buhman, Budapest 1989) 16 ♖fe1 ♕d7 17 ♖cd1 ♗g4?! (17 ... ♕c8 with the idea of ... ♕a6 – Kramnik) 18 ♖d3!± Miles – Kramnik, Moscow GMA 1989.

c) A further possibility is 11 ♖ad1 b5 12 ♗c1 h6!? (Others are good for White: 12 ... bxc4 13 bxc4 ♘c7 14 ♘d2 ♗a6 15 ♕c2±; 12 ... b4 13 ♘a4 e5 14 dxe5 dxe5 15 ♘d2± – Timoschenko) 13 a3 g5 (This is Alekseev – Timoschenko, USSR 1988. Instead 13 ... b4 14 axb4 ♘xb4 15 ♕b1 e5 16 dxe5 dxe5 17 ♗e3!? results in an unclear position) 14 cxb5 cxb5 15 b4 e6 16 e4 fxe4 17 ♘xe4

♘xe4 18 ♕xe4 ♗b7 19 ♕e2 ♘c7 and Black's position is not worse – Timoschenko.

11 ... ♘c7

Again Black has a choice:

a) 11 ... c5? 12 e3 (12 ♘f3 e5!) 12 ... ♗d7 (12 ... g5 13 ♘b5! ♖a8 14 dxc5 dxc5 15 ♖ad1±) 13 ♖ac1 (13 ♘b5 cxd4 14 exd4 ♕d8!) 13 ... ♕c8? 14 ♖fd1 b6 15 ♘f3 (15 ♘b5 ♘c7 16 ♘xc7 ♕xc7 17 b4±) 15 ... h6? (Dautov – Basin, Minsk 1988) 16 ♘e5!± – Dautov.

b) 11 ... b5!? 12 cxb5 cxb5 13 ♘d5 ♘xd5 14 ♗xd5+ e6?! (Better is 14 ... ♔h8 15 ♖ac1 ♗b7 16 ♗xb7 ♖xb7 17 ♘f3 ♘c7 18 e4 *(25)*

25
B

Dautov considers the diagram position more favourable for White and Piskov thinks that the chances are equal. However, we can agree with neither of them, because after 18 ... ♕f7 there seems to be no good continuation for White: he is threatened with the exchange on e4 and Black gains control over the white squares in the centre. Black's control over square d5 makes his position even more favourable) 15 ♗g2 b4 16 ♗b2 ♘c7 17 ♘c4 ♕d7 (Dautov - Malaniuk, Minsk 1988) 18 ♖ac1 (18 f4?! ♗a6 19 ♕d2 ♘d5 20 ♖ac1 ♖fc8= Savchenko - Malaniuk, Simferopol 1988) 18 ... ♗a6 19 ♕d2 ♘d5 20 ♖c2 ♗b7 21 ♖fc1± (Dautov).

12 ♖ac1 b5

Andrianov suggests 12 ... g5!?. Also possible is 12 ... ♔h8 13 ♖fe1 b5 14 cxb5 cxb5 15 b4 ♕f7 16 ♘b3 ♗e6, as in Kiss - Malaniuk, Budapest 1989.

13 ♗b2

Topalov suggests 13 ♘d1, and if 13 ... ♗d7, then 14 e4 fxe4 15 ♘xe4 with a slight advantage to White.

13 ... g5

Alternatively:

a) 13 ... ♗e6? (13 ... b4!? - Andrianov) 14 cxb5 cxb5 15 d5! ♗f7 16 b4 with a clear advantage in the centre and on the queenside; Dautov - Kramnik, Moscow GMA 1989.

b) 13 ... ♗d7!? 14 e4? (Correct would have been 14 ♘a1! or 14 cxb5! cxb5 15 b4) 14 ... fxe4 15 ♘cxe4 ♘xe4 with the idea of ... bxc4 - Dautov.

c) 13 ... ♗a6!? 14 ♗a1 ♖d8! 15 ♕f3 bxc4 16 ♕xc6 ♕xc6 17 ♗xc6 cxb3 18 ♘xb3± - Kramnik.

14 cxb5

Here three more variations deserve consideration:

a) 14 e4 ♕h5 15 exf5 ♗xf5 16 ♕e2 bxc4 and it is difficult to evaluate the position.

b) 14 ♘d1 ♗d7 15 e4 fxe4 16 ♘xe4 again with an unclear position,

c) 14 cxb5 cxb5 15 b4 ♕h5 16 d5?! f4 17 ♘b3 ♘g4 18 h3 ♘e5 and Black wins a pawn - Topalov.

14 ... cxb5
15 e4 ♕h5
16 f4

Not 16 f3?! fxe4 17 fxe4 b4 18 ♕c4+ ♗e6 19 ♕xc7 ♘g4 and Black gains the opportunity for an attack - Topalov.

16 ... gxf4
17 ♖xf4 fxe4
18 ♘dxe4 *(27)*

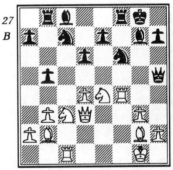

The position promises equal chances; Topalov - Kramnik, Puerto Rico 1989.

B3

8 ... h6 *(28)*

The move examined in this section has all but superceded 8 ... e5 and 8 ... ♘a6. Black does not try to force events, but instead waits to see White's plan in order to choose the right method of counterplay. At the time of writing this modest move with the pawn

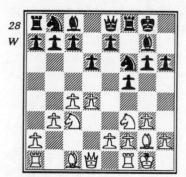

seems the surest way of continuing.

9 ♘d5

This is the most aggressive reaction to Black's move. Let us examine five other variations:

a) 9 ♕c2 ♘c6 10 ♗b2 e5!? (10 ... g5?! 11 d5 ♘b4 12 ♕d2 c5 13 dxc6 bxc6 14 ♘d4 ♗d7 15 e4 and Black finds himself under pressure in the centre; Zakharov – Avshalumov, Lvov 1986) 11 dxe5 dxe5 12 e4 with obscure play – Avshalumov.

b) 9 ♗a3 g5 (9 ... ♖f7!? with the idea of ... e5 – Shabalov or 9 ... ♕f7 10 ♕d3 g5 11 ♖ad1 c6 12 c5 ♖d8 13 cxd6 exd6∞ Blatny – Malaniuk, Alma Ata 1989) 10 ♖c1 (10 e3 c6 {Not so good is 10 ... f4 11 exf4 gxf4 12 ♖e1 – Georgiev} 11 ♕e2 ♘a6 12 ♖fe1 ♖b8 13 ♘d2 b5 14 cxb5 cxb5 15 ♘d5 ♘xd5 16 ♗xd5+ ♔h8 17 ♖ac1 ♕d8! and Black's position is not worse; Kishnev – Shabalov, Debrecen 1989. Georgiev also offers another suggestion: 10 ♕d3!?) 10 ... f4! 11 ♕d3 ♕h5 12 c5! (With the idea of making

use of the c–file after cxd6) 12 ... ♗h3 13 cxd6 cxd6 14 ♘e4 ♘g4 (Georgiev suggests 14 ... ♘bd7!? 15 ♘xf6+ ♖xf6 16 ♖c7 ♖af8 17 ♘d2! with an unclear position, or 14 ... ♘c6!? 15 ♘xf6+ ♗xf6 16 d5 ♘e5 17 ♘xe5 ♗xe5 18 ♖c7 ♖f7 19 ♗xh3 ♕xh3 20 ♕g6+ ♖g7 21 ♕e6+ ♖xe6 22 dxe6±) 15 ♖c7 ♘c6 16 ♗b2 (If 16 ♖xb7, then it is good to play 16 ... d5 17 ♘ed2 ♖f7! with the idea of ... ♖af8, ... ♘xd4) 16 ... ♖f7 17 ♖xb7 ♖af8 18 ♖c1 ♘d8?! (18 ... d5) and in any case White's position remains preferable; Kir. Georgiev – Lukov, Bulgaria 1989.

c) 9 ♗b2 g5 (9 ... ♘a6 10 d5 {Another promising variation for White is 10 ♖e1 g5 11 a3 ♕f7 12 e4 ♘xe4 13 ♘xe4 fxe4 14 ♖xe4 ♘c5 15 ♖e2 ♗g4 16 ♖e3 ♖ae8 17 h3 ♗h5 18 ♕e2 e5 19 g4 e4 20 ♘xg5± Baburin – Shabalov, Leningrad 1989} 10 ... c5 (Better is 10 ... c6, keeping all options open and waiting for White to commit himself in the centre before deciding whether to take on d5 or play ... c5) 11 ♘e1! g5 12 ♘d3 ♕g6 13 e3 f4? 14 exf4 ♗f5 15 ♘e1 gxf4 16 ♘e2!± Espig – Malaniuk, Koszkomot 1989) 10 d5! (Too modest is 10 e3 ♘a6 11 d5 {Preventing 11 ... e5} 11 ... ♗d7 {11 ... c5!?} 12 ♕e2 c6?! {12 ... c5!?; 12 ... ♘c5!?} 13 ♘d4 ♘c7 {13 ... c5 14 ♘e6±} 14 f4± Chekhov – Vyzmanavin, Moscow 1989) 10 ... ♘a6?! 11 ♘d4 f4 12 ♕c2 ♘g4 13 ♘e4 ♕h5

14 h3 ♘e5 15 g4 ♕g6 16 ♘f3!
♘xf3+ 17 ♗xf3 and White has an
undisputed advantage due to
the unfortunate position of
Black's knight; Rozentalis –
Galdunts, Podolsk 1989.

d) 9 ♖e1 is interesting: 9 ... g5
10 ♗b2 (10 e4? ♘xe4 11 ♘xe4
fxe4 12 ♘g5 ♗f5 13 ♖e3 c5! 14
♗b2 ♘c6 intending ... g4∓) 10 ...
♕f7 11 e4 fxe4 12 ♘xe4± Magerramov – Vyzmanavin, Balatonbereny 1989, and Beliavsky –
Bareev, Moscow GMA 1990.

e) Finally, Shirov suggests 9
♕d3!? e5 10 dxe5 dxe5 11 e4 ♘c6
12 ♗b2±.

| 9 | ... | ♘xd5 |
| 10 | cxd5 | (29) |

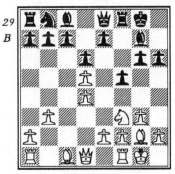

| 10 | ... | ♕f7! |
| 11 | ♗d2 | |

A mistake is 11 ♘e1? ♘d7 12
♘d3 g5 13 ♕c2 ♗xd4 14 ♖b1
♘b6 and White has inadequate
compensation for his pawn, e.g.
15 h4 ♗f6 16 hxg5 hxg5 17 ♘b4
a5 18 ♕xc7 axb4 19 ♕xb6 ♖xa2
20 ♕xb4 ♖xe2∓ Savon – Malaniuk, Moscow GMA 1989.

| 11 | ... | c6 |
| 12 | ♕c1 | g5 |

A sharp position occurs after
12 ... ♔h7, e.g. 13 dxc6 bxc6 (13
... ♘xc6?! 14 d5±) 14 ♖e1 ♗e6 15
e4 fxe4 16 ♖xe4 ♗d5 17 ♖f4
♕e8 18 ♕c2! – Shirov.

| 13 | h4!? | g4 |
| 14 | ♘e1 | ♔h7 |

14 ... h5 15 ♗h6!? cxd5 16
♗xg7 ♔xg7 17 ♘d3 ♔h7 18
♘f4?! (Better was 18 b4! ♘c6 19
e3=) 18 ... e6 19 ♕a3 ♖d8 20
♖ac1 ♘c6 21 ♖fd1?! (21 e3 a5 22
♖c3=) and Black gained the
advantage in Shirov – Malaniuk,
Moscow GMA 1989 (comments
by Shirov).

15 dxc6

15 ♕c4 should also be taken
into consideration: 15 ... b5 16
♕d3 cxd5 17 ♕xb5 e6 18 ♕d3
♗a6 19 ♕e3 ♘c6 20 ♗c3∓.

15	...	♘xc6
16	♗xc6	bxc6
17	♕xc6	♖b8
18	♕c3	♗b7

Black has dangerous threats
– Shirov.

B4

| 8 | ... | ♘c6 | (30) |

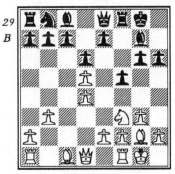

In addition to the other

variations considered, 8 ... c6!? has been seen in recent tournament play:

a) 9 ♘a3 h6 10 ♕c2 (Also possible are 10 ♕d3 g5 11 e4 fxe4 12 ♘xe4 ♕g6= Polugayevsky - Malaniuk, Moscow GMA 1990, and 10 ♖c1 ♘a6 11 ♕d3 g5 12 e4 fxe4 13 ♘xe4 ♕g6 14 ♘xf6+ ♕xf6 15 ♖ce1= Gomez - Sanz, Salamanca 1991) 10 ... g5 (10 ... ♘a6 11 e4 fxe4 12 ♘xe4 g5 13 ♖ae1± Neverov - Piskov, Minsk 1990) 11 e4 fxe4 12 ♘xe4 ♕g6 (12 ... ♘xe4 13 ♕xe4 ♘f5 14 ♕e3 ♕d7! 15 ♖ae1∞ Neurohr - Glek, West Germany 1991) 13 ♘xf6+ ♕xf6 14 ♖ae1 and White has the advantage; Shestoperov - Makarov, Smolensk 1991.

b) 9 ♖e1!? h6 10 e4 fxe4 11 ♘xe4 ♕f7 12 ♗b2 g5 13 ♕d2 ♘a6 14 h4 ♘f5= Pigusov - Malaniuk, Moscow GMA 1990, and Ruban - Malaniuk, Sibenik 1990.

9 ♗b2 transposes to Chapter 5, variation A1111.

Before moving on to the main variation we should mention that 8 ... ♘bd7 leaves Black with difficult problems: 9 ♘b5 ♕d8 10 ♗b2 and, as pointed out by Beliavsky, White has a large advantage.

9   d5!

A natural reaction, but there are three other possibilities:

a) The move 9 ♘b5!? has also been put to test: 9 ... ♕d7?! (Natural and more exact would be 9 ... ♕d8!? as seen three

times recently: 10 ♘a3 ♘e4 11 ♗b2 h6 12 e3 ♔h7 13 ♖c1 ♗d7 14 ♘c3 ♘xc3 15 ♗xc3 e5 16 d5 ♘e7 17 ♘e1 and Black has a solid position; Budnikov - Vyzmanavin, USSR Ch 1991; 10 d5 ♘e5 11 ♗b2 ♘xf3+ 12 ♗xf3 ♗d7 13 ♘d4 ♕e8 14 ♕d3 c6 15 ♖ab1 h5 16 ♗g2= Dzandzgava - Ioseliani, Tbilisi 1991; and finally (10 d5 ♘e5) 11 ♘xe5 dxe5 12 ♗b2 a6 13 ♘a3 e4 14 f3 exf3 15 exf3 f4 16 ♖e1 ♘h5 17 ♗xg7 with an unbalanced position; V. Neverov - Malaniuk, Warsaw 1992) 10 d5 ♘d8 11 ♗b2 e5 12 dxe6 ♘xe6 13 ♘fd4 ♘c5 14 ♘c3 c6 15 ♕c2 ♕e7 16 b4 ♘ce4 17 ♘xe4 fxe4 18 ♖ad1± Vyzmanavin - Makarov, Gorky 1989.

b) 9 ♘a3 ♘e4 10 ♘d5 (Equality results from 10 ♖c1, e.g. 10 ... ♘xc3 11 ♖xc3 f4! 12 ♖d3 ♗g4 13 ♖d2 h6= Kiselev - Makarov, Podolsk 1989) 10 ... ♕d8 11 e3 (More modest is 11 ♖c1 a5 12 e3 e6 13 ♘f4 ♘b4 14 ♕e2 ♕e7 15 ♘e1 c6 16 f3 ♘f6 with a complicated position; Gurevich - Vyzmanavin, Palma de Mallorca 1989) 11 ... ♖e8 12 ♘d2 ♘xd2 13 ♕xd2 e5 14 dxe5 dxe5 15 ♖ad1 ♗e6 16 ♕c1 ♕c8 17 ♕a1 ♗xd5?! 18 ♗xd5+ and White gained the advantage in Anastasian - Makarov, Podolsk 1989.

c) 9 c5 allows Black to carry out his plan with 9 ... e5 10 d5 ♘d8 11 ♖c1, as in Summermatter - Vanka, Prague 1991.

9   ...   ♘e4!

9 ... ♘e5 is better for White:

10 ♘xe5 dxe5 11 a4!?± or 10 ♘d4!?± - Baburin.

10   ♘b5

The only move.

10   ...   ♗xa1

Not:

a) 10 ... ♕d8? 11 dxc6 ♗xa1 12 ♕d5+ e6 13 cxb7 ♖b8 14 bxc8(♕) ♕xc8 15 ♕d3 ♘f6+- Baburin - Belousov, Voronez 1989.

b) Also bad is 10 ... ♖b8?! 11 ♗e3 ♗xa1 12 ♕xa1 a6 (The only move) 13 ♘xc7 ♕d8 (13 ... ♕d7 14 ♘e6±) 14 ♗b6! ♖f7 15 dxc6 bxc6 16 c5! ♘xc5 17 ♘g5 ♖xb6 18 ♕h8+!+- Baburin.

11   ♘xc7

Less accurate is 11 ♗h6 ♘f6 12 ♘xc7 ♕d8 13 ♘xa8 ♖e8 14 dxc6 bxc6 15 ♕c2 ♗b7 16 ♘d2 ♘xd2 17 ♗xd2 ♕xa8 ½-½ Hasin - Makarov, Gorky 1989.

	11	...	**♕d8**
	12	♘xa8	♘e5
	13	♗h6	♗c3
	14	♗xf8	♔xf8
	15	♘d4	♗d7
	16	♗xe4	fxe4
	17	♘e6+	♗xe6
	18	dxe6	♕xa8
	19	♕c2 (31)	

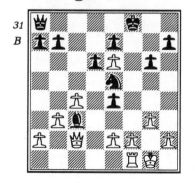

The chaotic position of the black pieces gives White the advantage.

C

8   ♖e1 (32)

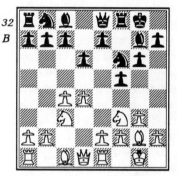

This move, preparing to advance the e-pawn, was for some time considered the route to obtaining the advantage for White. After 8 ... e5 (not 8 ... ♘e4? 9 ♘xe4 fxe4 10 ♘g5 winning) White indeed had a noticeable advantage, but soon an effective reply, 8 ... ♕f7, was found for Black and as a result the system has disappeared from practice. Nevertheless, some questions concerning this variation remain unresolved.

8   ...   ♕f7

Other moves:

a) 8 ... e5 (White's eighth move was designed to prevent this logical reply) 9 dxe5 dxe5 10 e4 fxe4 (Somewhat better is 10 ... ♘c6 11 ♘d5! fxe4 {*Black cannot avoid a disadvantage by 11 ... ♖f7, e.g. 12 exf5 gxf5 13 ♕a4?! ♘e4 14 ♘g5 ♘xg5 15*

♗xg5 ♗e6 16 ♘e3± *Abramov -
Petelin, Dimitrograd 1988, or 13
♘xe5 ♘xe5 14 ♘xf6+ ♗xf6 15
f4± }* 12 ♘g5 ♕d8 *{12 ... ♘xd5 13
cxd5 ♘d4 14 ♗e3! ♘f3+ 15 ♘xf3
exf3 16 ♗xf3! e4? 17 ♗c5! with a
winning position}* 13 ♘xf6+
♕xf6 14 ♘xe4 ♕f7 15 ♗e3!
though White's position is still
favourable) 11 ♘g5 (And not 11
♘xe4? 12 ♖xe4 ♘c6 when Black
gets out of his difficulties) 11 ...
♘c6 (11 ... ♗g4 is of no use: 12
♕b3 ♘c6 13 ♗e3! ♘d4 14 ♗xd4
exd4 15 ♘cxe4 - Lukacs, and 11
... c6 does not work either: 12
♘cxe4 ♘xe4 13 ♘xe4 ♘a6 14
b3 ♘b4 15 ♗e3 ♘a6 16 ♘d6 ♕e7
17 ♘xc8 and positionally Black's
set-up has no prospects; Mich-
aelsen - Lauterbach, Munich
1988) 12 ♗e3! h6 13 ♘gxe4 ♔h7
14 ♘xf6+! ♖xf6 15 ♘d5 ♖f7 16
h4! *(33)*

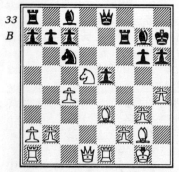

White has a great advantage;
Lukacs - Vaiser, Sochi 1984.

b) 8 ... c6 9 e4 ♘xe4 10 ♘xe4
fxe4 11 ♖xe4 ♗f5 12 ♖e3 ♘d7 13
b3 ♗g4 14 ♗b2 ♘h6 15 ♖e4 ♗xf3
16 ♗xf3 ♕f7 17 ♔g2 e5! 18 dxe5
♘xe5 19 ♗xe5 dxe5 20 ♕e2 and

White retains a slight advantage; Gheorghiu - Grigorov,
Prague 1985.

c) Of all the options here 8
... ♘c6!? is the most worthy of
consideration: 9 d5 (The variation 9 e4 ♘xe4 10 ♘xe4 fxe4 11
♖xe4 ♗f5 is not the best plan
for White) 9 ... ♘a5 (Weaker is
9 ... ♘e5 10 ♘xe5 dxe5 11 c5
♔h8?! 12 b4 ♗d7?! 13 ♗b2 g5 14
b5 e4 15 c6 bxc6 16 bxc6±
Ricardi - Remon, Havana 1986)
10 b3 c5 11 ♗d2 a6 12 e4 fxe4 13
♘g5 ♗g4 14 ♕c1 b5 15 ♘cxe4
♘xe4 16 ♖xe4 ♗f5 17 ♘e6 ♗xe6
18 ♖xe6 ♗xa1 19 ♕xa1 ♘b7 and
White has good compensation
for the sacrificed material;
Petran - Grigorov, Tbilisi 1986,
e.g. 20 h4 ♘d8 21 ♗h3 ♖f7 22
♗h6 with advantage to White.

Now we return to the position after 8 ... ♕f7 *(34)*.

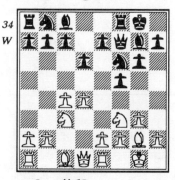

9 ♕d3

Others:

a) 9 b3?! gives Black an
opportunity for a useful knight
deployment: 9 ... ♘e4 (9 ... h6 10
♗b2 g5 11 e4 fxe4 12 ♘xe4 ♗f5
{12 ... c6 is playable: 13 ♕d2 ♘a6

14 h4 ♗f5 15 ♘xf6+ exf6 16 ♖e3 ♖fe8= Pigusov - Malaniuk, *Moscow GMA 1990)* 13 ♘xf6+ ♕xf6 14 ♖e3 ♘a6 15 ♗c3 ♖f7 16 ♕e2 ♖af8 17 ♖e1 with advantage to White; Beliavsky - Bareev, Moscow GMA 1990) 10 ♗b2 ♘c6 (Or 10 ... c5!? 11 ♕d3 ♘c6 12 ♘xe4 fxe4 13 ♕xe4 cxd4 14 ♔h1 ♗f5 15 ♕d5 ♕xd5 16 cxd5 ♘b4 with an unbalanced position in Chabanon - Hoffmann, Lippstadter 1991, but not 10 ... ♘a6?! 11 ♕c2 ♘xc3 12 ♗xc3 h6 13 e4!± Lukacs - Schroll, Kecskemet 1991) 11 ♖c1 (Two other alternatives have been played here: 11 e3 e5 12 ♖c1 ♘xc3 13 ♗xc3 e4 14 ♘d2 a5 with an active position for Black in Hulak - Bareev, Marseille 1990; and 11 ♕d3 ♘xc3 12 ♗xc3 e5 13 dxe5 dxe5 14 ♘g5 ♕e7 15 ♗d5+ ♔h8 16 ♗xc6 bxc6 when Black has the bishop pair as compensation for his weak pawns; Shneider - Bareev, USSR Ch 1990, and Hulak - Malaniuk, Moscow GMA 1990) 11 ... h6 (Vanheste analyses the variation 11 ... e5 12 d5 ♘e7 13 ♖f1 ♘xc3 14 ♗xc3 h6 with a good game for Black) 12 ♖f1 (An alternative would be 12 d5!? ♘b4 13 ♗d4 *{The only move: 13 a3 ♗xc3 14 ♗xc3 ♘a2; 13 ♘xe4 ♗xb2}* 13 ... ♘xc3 14 ♖xc3 ♘xa2 15 ♖e3! with an unclear position - Vanheste) 12 ... ♘xc3 13 ♗xc3 e5 and Black has equalised; Gavrikov - Malaniuk, USSR Ch 1986.

b) At the cost of a pawn,

White hopes by 9 ♘g5!? to exploit the insecure position of the black queen: 9 ... ♕xc4 10 ♘f1 and now:

b1) 10 ... ♕b4 meets more of White's needs than Black's: 11 a3 ♕a5 (11 ... ♕b6!? - Tukmakov) 12 b4 ♕b6 13 ♕b3+ d5 14 e4! (If 14 ♘xd5, then 14 ... ♘xd5 15 ♕xd5+ e6 with the following 16 ... ♗xd4 and White's initiative is neutralised - Tukmakov) 14 ... fxe4 15 ♘xd5 ♘xd5 16 ♕xd5+ e6 17 ♕xe4 ♕xd4 18 ♖a2 *(35)*

Here White has a promising position; Huzman - Vyzmanavin, Novosibirsk 1986;.

b2) The modest 10 ... ♔h8 should also be taken into consideration: 11 d5 (11 e4!? ♕g8 12 e5) 11 ... ♕c5 12 ♗e3 ♕a5 13 a3 c6 14 b4 ♕d8 15 dxc6 ♘xc6 16 ♕b3 ♘g4! with advantage to Black; Huzman - Malaniuk, Novosibirsk 1986.

b3) 10 ... ♕c6 11 e4 (Neverov suggests here 11 ♕b3+!? d5 12 ♘f4) 11 ... fxe4 12 ♗b5 ♕b6 13 ♗c4+ ♔h8 14 ♘f7+ ♖xf7 15 ♗xf7 ♗f5 (15 ... ♗g4 16 ♕a4 *{16 ♕b3 ♘c6! [16 ... ♗f3 17 ♘d5]* 17 ♕xb6

[Not 17 ♘xe4? ♗xd4 18 ♕xb6 axb6] and in the closed position White has difficulties in making use of his rooks} 16 ... ♘c6 17 ♗e3 with advantage to White, for example: 17 ... ♕xb2 18 ♘b5 ♕b4 19 ♕xb4 ♘xb4 20 ♘xc7 ♖c8 *{20 ... ♖f8 21 ♘b3}* 21 ♘e6 ♘c2 22 ♖ac1) 16 ♗e3 c6 (After 16 ... ♘bd7 17 d5 ♕a6 18 ♗e6 ♘f8 *{18 ... ♗xe6 19 dxe6 ♘f8 20 ♘d5}* 19 ♗xf5 gxf5 20 ♗d4 and White stands better) 17 d5 ♕a6 18 ♗d4 ♘bd7 19 ♗e6 ♖f8! and Black has overcome his most serious difficulties; Neverov – Gurevich, Baku 1986.

9 ... h6

Risky is 9 ... ♘c6 10 ♘g5 ♘b4 (10 ... ♕e8 11 ♘d5 ♘xd5 12 cxd5 ♘d8 *{12 ... ♗xd4 13 e3 ♘b5 14 a4 and Black has to give up his knight; or 12 ... ♘b4 13 ♕c4± Lukacs – Espig, Leipzig 1986}* 13 ♕c4 h6 14 ♘f3 b5!? 15 ♕xc7 ♗b7 16 ♘d2 ♗xd4 17 ♘b3 ♗g7 18 ♕c2 e6 19 ♗e3 ♕f7 20 ♕d2 g5 and here, in the game between Lukacs and Pyhala, Espoo 1987, White could have attempted to gain an advantage by 21 f4! – Lukacs) 11 ♘xf7 ♘xd3 12 ♘h6+ ♗xh6 13 exd3 ♗xc1 14 ♖axc1 e6 (The only move) 15 f4! (There is no advantage in 15 c5!? d5 16 c6 b6! Neverov – Legky, USSR 1987) 15 ... ♖e8 (15 ... ♗d7 16 ♘b5 ♘e8 17 d5 exd5 18 ♗xd5+ ♔h8 19 ♖e7± – Legky) 16 ♘b5 (16 d5?! a6 17 dxe6 c6!) 16 ... ♖e7 17 d5 *(36)*

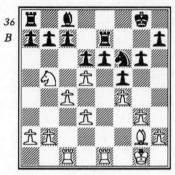

Legky and Moskalenko consider the endgame slightly favourable for White.

10 b3

10 d5 is not suitable: 10 ... e5 11 dxe6 ♗xe6 12 c5 ♘c6 13 cxd6 ♖ad8 14 ♕c2 ♖xd6 and Black has a slight advantage; Kotronias – Casper, Moscow 1987.

10 ... ♘c6

Possible is 10 ... ♘a6 11 ♗a3 c6 12 ♖ad1 g5 13 e3 ♘c7 14 ♘d2 ♗d7; Maiorov – Bareev, Minsk 1986. Another idea is 10 ... c5!?.

11 ♗a3

Less well analysed is 11 ♗b2 e5 12 dxe5 dxe5 13 e4! ♗e6 14 ♖ad1 ♖ad8 15 ♕e2 ♘d4 16 ♘xd4 exd4 17 exf5 ♗xf5 18 ♘d5± Hamann – Yrjola, Copenhagen 1987.

11 ... ♘e4

Others:

a) 11 ... ♖e8 12 d5!.

b) 11 ... g5 12 d5!.

c) 11 ... a5 12 ♘b5 ♘e8 13 ♖ad1 ♘b4 14 ♕b1 c6 15 ♘c3 e5 16 dxe5 dxe5 17 ♗b2 e4 18 ♘d4 with chances for both sides; Neverov – Vasiukov, Voskresensk 1990.

d) 11 ... e5 12 dxe5 dxe5 13 ♗xf8 e4 14 ♕d2 ♗xf8 (14 ... exf3 15 ♗xg7) 15 ♘d4 ♗d7 (15 ... ♗c5 16 ♘xc6 bxc6 17 e3) 16 ♘xc6 ♗xc6 17 e3 and Black has insufficent compensation for his material losses – Lukacs.

12 ♖ad1

Or:

a) 12 ♘b5 e6 13 ♖ad1 ♖e8 (Less dangerous is 13 ... a6 14 ♘c3 ♘xc3) 14 d5! and Black came under slight pressure in Farago – Yrjola, Judenburgh 1987.

b) 12 ♘xe4 fxe4 13 ♕xe4 ♘xd4 14 ♘xd4 ♕xf2+ 15 ♔h1 ♕xd4 16 ♕xe7 ♗f5 (16 ... ♕b6 17 ♗d5+ ♔h8 18 ♗b2! with a winning position; 16 ... ♖f7 17 ♕e8+ {17 ♕d8+ ♔h7!} 17 ... ♖f8 18 ♕xg6 ♗f5 19 ♕h5 ♖ae8 20 ♖ad1±) 17 ♕xc7 ♗e4 with a powerful attack, but not 17 ... ♕xa1 18 ♗d5+ ♔h8 19 ♖xa1 ♗xa1 20 ♗xd6 with better chances for White.

Returning to the position after 12 ♖ad1 (37).

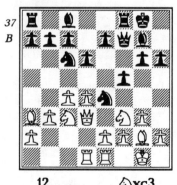

```
12   ...      ♘xc3
13   ♕xc3     f4
```

Also worth mentioning are:

a) 13 ... e5 14 dxe5 ♘xe5 15 ♘d4±.

b) 13 ... ♖e8 14 e4!? (14 ♕c2 e5 15 d5 ♘e7!? 16 c5!±) 14 ... e5! (14 ... fxe4?! 15 ♖xe4) 15 dxe5 dxe5 16 exf5 gxf5 (16 ... e4? 17 fxg6 ♕xg6 18 ♕e3!) 17 ♕e3 with an unclear position – Lukacs.

c) 13 ... g5 14 e3 f4?! 15 exf4 g4 leads to an unclear position, Lukacs – van Mil, Copenhagen 1987.

14 ♕d2

Instead 14 e3 fxg3 15 fxg3 e5 16 d5 (16 ♖f1 ♕e8) 16 ... e4 17 ♘d4 ♘xd4 18 exd4 ♗g4 gives nothing to White.

14 ... ♗g4

14 ... g5!? deserves consideration.

```
15   d5       ♘e5
16   ♕xf4     ♕xf4
17   gxf4     ♗xf3
18   fxe5     ♗xg2
19   ♔xg2     ♗xe5
```

The game is equal; Dokhoian – Malaniuk, Moscow 1989.

D

8 ♘d5 (38)

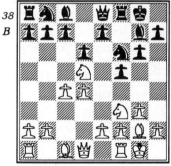

White attempts to strength-en his central position with the exchange of knights.

8   ...   ♘xd5

It is risky to leave the knight in the centre: 8 ... ♘a6?! 9 ♗g5 (9 ♘xf6+ ♗xf6 10 ♗h6 ♗g7 11 ♕d2 c6 12 b4 ♗c7 13 ♗xg7 ♔xg7 14 d5! with the idea of continu-ing with ♖fe1 and e4 and White gained the advantage in the game Uhlmann - Banas, Stary Smokovec 1985) 9 ... c6 10 ♘xf6+ ♗xf6 11 ♗h6 ♗g7 12 ♗xg7 ♔xg7 13 ♕d2 ♕f7 14 ♖ac1 and, thanks to the badly placed knight, White stands better, Knezevic - Remon, Havana 1986.

9   cxd5   c6

Formerly Black successfully played 9 ... ♕b5 but the advan-tages of the white knight re-treat, 10 ♘e1, became apparent:

a) Simply bad is 10 ♕b3 ♕xb3 11 axb3 c6 12 ♗g5 ♖e8 13 ♖fc1 e6 14 dxe6 ♗xe6 15 ♖c3 ♘d7 16 ♗f4 ♘f6! and Black has an indisputable superiority in the endgame; Zukhovitsky - Mi. Tseitlin, Kalinin 1986.

b) An interesting try is 10 a4!? ♕xd5 11 ♘g5 ♕c4 (11 ... ♕xd4? 12 ♕b3+ ♔h8 13 ♗xb7) 12 ♗e3 c6 and now Perelstein - Glek, Budapest 1991, continued 13 ♖c1 ♕b4 14 b3 d5 15 h4 a5 16 ♘h3 ♘d7 17 ♘f4 ♘f6 and Black went on to win.

c) Recently 10 ♘g5 has come into vogue. Black has:

c1) 10 ... c6 11 e4!? fxe4 12 ♘xe4 ♕c4 13 ♗e3± Linen Bueno

- T. Georgadze, Malaga 1991.

c2) 10 ... ♕b6 11 ♘e3 ♖b8 (11 ... ♘a6 12 ♕d2±) 12 h4! a5 13 ♕d2 with good attacking chances for White.

c3) 10 ... ♘a6 11 h4 (11 a4 ♕b6 12 e3 h6 13 ♘h3 g5∞) 11 ... c5 12 dxc6! (12 dxc5 ♘xc5 13 ♖b1 ♗d7∞ Pinter - Norri, Debrecen 1992) 12 ... bxc6 13 a4 ♕b6 14 d5 c5 15 h5± Malaniuk.

c4) 10 ... h6!? 11 a4 ♕b6 12 ♘f3 a5! 13 ♗e3 ♘a6 14 ♕d2 ♔h7 15 ♘e1 ♘b4 L. B. Hansen - Malaniuk, Copenhagen 1992.

d) 10 ♘e1 *(39)* and now Black has some interesting alter-natives:

39
B

d1) 10 ... a5!? 11 e3 (Worse is 11 ♗e3 ♘a6 12 ♕d2 ♗d7 13 ♘c2 c5 14 dxc5 ♘xc5∓ Dumitrache - Malaniuk, Baku 1988) 11 ... a4 12 ♘c2 c6 13 ♘a3 ♕b6 14 b3 cxd5 15 ♗xd5+ e6 16 ♗f3 axb3 17 axb3 ♕d8 18 ♗b2 d5 with equal-ity; Lputian - Malaniuk, Sim-feropol 1988.

d2) 10 ... c6!? 11 a4 ♕a6 12 e3 (12 ♘c2 e6 13 dxe6 ♗xe6 14 d5 ♗f7 15 ♘b4 ♕b6 16 dxc6 ♘xc6 17 ♘d5± Isaev - Galdunts,

Podolsk 1990) 12 ... ♕b6 13 a5 ♕b5 14 ♕d3 ♗d7 15 dxc6 ♗xc6 16 ♗d2 e5 17 ♗xc6 bxc6 and Black seized the initiative in Groszpeter – Gurevich, Palma de Mallorca 1989.

d3) 10 ... ♕b6 11 e3 (11 ♗e3!? ♕xb2 {11 ... c6 12 dxc6 bxc6 13 ♖b1 a5 14 ♕c2 ♗d7 15 ♘d3 ♘a6 16 a3 ♖fc8 17 b4±} 12 ♘d3 {12 a4!?} 12 ... ♕a3 13 ♕c2 c6 and White has compensation for the sacrificed pawn) 11 ... c6 12 ♘d3 cxd5 (12 ... ♗d7 13 ♗d2 ♘a6 14 ♕b3 and according to Chekhov and Dautov, the position favours White) 13 ♗xd5+ e6 14 ♗b3 *(40)*.

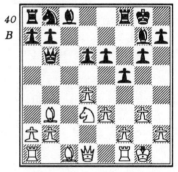

40
B

The diagram position appeared in the game between Dautov and Ragozin, USSR 1986, and is slightly better for White.

d4) 10 ... ♘a6 11 a4 (11 e3 ♗d7 12 ♘d3 {12 ♕b3?? ♕xb3 13 axb3 ♗b5} 12 ... c5 {12 ... c6? 13 a4 or 13 ♕b3} 13 dxc6 ♗xc6 14 ♗xc6 bxc6 15 ♕b3+ ♖f7! {If 15 ... ♕xb3 16 axb3 and White has better chances in the endgame} 16 ♕xb5 {16 ♗d2 ♖b8 17 ♕xb5 ♖xb5 18 ♖fc1 c5=} 16 ... cxb5 17

♗d2 e5 and Black has overcome his opening difficulties; Balashov – Malaniuk, USSR Ch 1986) 11 ... ♕b6 12 ♗e3 ♘b4 (Dangerous is 12 ... ♕xb2, e.g. 13 ♘d3 ♕c3 14 ♖c1 ♕a3 15 ♕c2 ♘b4 16 ♘xb4 ♕xb4 17 ♖b1! ♕a5 18 ♗d2 ♕a6 19 e3 and Black is not able to defend his queenside) 13 ♘d3 ♘xd3 (Bad is 13 ... a5 14 ♘xb4 axb4 15 ♕b3) 14 ♕xd3 a5?! (14 ♗d7 b4!) 15 ♖fc1 ♗d7, as in Dautov – Legky, Tashkent 1987, and now White could have played 16 ♖c3! ♖fc8 17 h4!? (Nothing is achieved by 17 ♖b3 ♕a6 18 ♕xa6 bxa6 19 ♖c3 ♖ab8 20 b3 e5 and Black maintains the balance) 17 ... ♕a6 18 ♕d2 b5 (Even worse is 18 ... c5 19 dxc5! ♗xc3 20 ♕xc3 dxc5 21 ♗g5) 19 ♗h6± – Dautov.

Returning to the position after 9 ... c6 *(41)*.

41
W

10 ♕b3

Also possible is 10 dxc6 bxc6 11 ♖e1 (11 ♕c2 {11 d5!?} 11 ... ♔h8 12 ♗e3?! {12 ♗d2!?} 12 ... ♘a6 with ... ♘b4 or ... ♘c7 to follow, putting pressure on the d5-square but not 12 ... ♗d7 13

♕c4+, as was played in the game between Semkov and Grigorov in Sofia in 1984) 11 ... ♘d7 12 e4 fxe4 13 ♘g5 ♘f6 14 ♘xe4 ♘xe4 15 ♗xe4 ♗d7 16 ♗g5 ♖b8 17 ♗xe7!? ♖xb2∞ Ortega – Remon, Havana 1986.

10   ...   cxd5

Not 10 ... ♚h8?! 11 ♘g5 ♘a6 12 dxc6 bxc6 13 ♕a4 and White enjoyed clear superiority in Uhlmann – S. Grünberg, Kecskemet 1984.

11   ♕xd5+

11 e4!? has been suggested.

11   ...   ♚h8
12   ♗d2   ♘c6
13   ♗c3   ♘d8

If 13 ... ♗d7?! (13 ... f4!?) 14 ♕b3 e5 (14 ... ♘d8? 15 d5) 15 dxe5 dxe5 16 ♕xb7 ♖b8 17 ♕c7 e4 (Hjartarson – Beliavsky, Szirak izt 1987) and now 18 ♖fd1 retains the pawn – Hjartarson.

14   ♕b3

In the case of 14 ♖ac1, then 14 ... ♗e6 15 ♕a5 b6 with the idea of ... ♗d5∓ – Hjartarson.

14   ...   e5
15   dxe5   dxe5
16   e3 *(42)*

This position is considered as equal by Hjartarson.

E

8   ♕b3 *(43)*

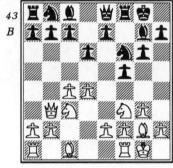

The queen move, introduced by Grandmaster Lerner and taken up by Anatoly Karpov, indirectly prepares the advance e2 – e4, accompanied by a dynamic development of pieces. Recently this idea has been abandoned, because Malaniuk has found excellent possibilities of organising counterplay for Black with 8 ... ♘a6.

8   ...   ♘a6

According to Lerner, two other lines do not enable Black to maintain the balance: 8 ... ♚h8 9 ♘d5! and 8 ... ♘e4 9 ♘xe4 fxe4 10 ♘g5 ♗xd4 11 ♘xe4.

More recently 8 ... c6 has been tried: 9 d5 ♘a6 10 ♗e3 ♘g4 11 ♗f4 (an attempted improvement on 11 ♗d4 e5 12 dxe6 ♘e5! 13 ♖ad1 ♕xe6∞ Karpov – Gurevich, Reggio Emilia 1989/90) 11 ... ♘c5 12 ♕c2 h6 13 h3 e5 and Black comes

out of the complications slightly better; Karpov - Gurevich,
Amsterdam 1991.

9 ♗g5   ♔h8!?

In addition to this extravagant move, Black has other
continuations to consider:

a) 9 ... ♘h5 10 ♘d5 ♖f7 11 c5
e6 12 ♘f4 (It is not clear who
will stand better after 12 ♘b4
♘xb4 13 ♕xb4 a5 14 ♕a3 ♖a6)
12 ... ♘f6! 13 ♗xf6 ♗xf6 14 cxd6
cxd6 15 h4 ♗g7 16 ♖ac1 h6 17
♖fe1 e5 18 dxe5 dxe5 19 ♘d5
e4= Vyzmanavin - Malaniuk,
Novosibirsk 1986.

b) 9 ... c5 10 ♗xf6 (10 d5!? -
Lerner) 10 ... ♗xf6 11 ♖ad1 (11
♖fd1 ♗g7 12 e3 ♔h8 13 ♖ac1 h6
14 dxc5 ♘xc5 15 ♕c2 ♘d7 16
♘d4 ♖b8 17 ♕e2 a6 18 b3 g5 19
♘d5 e5 20 ♘c2 b5 and Black
has a better position; Vainer-
man - Malaniuk, USSR 1986) 11
... ♔h8 *(11 ... ♗g7 {11 ... e5?! 12
dxe5 dxe5 13 e4 f4 14 gxf4 exf4
15 e5 ♗g7 16 ♖fe1 and White's
superiority in the centre is
decisive - Lerner} 12 ♘d5 {12 e3
[12 ♖fe1 intending e2 - e4 is
worth consideration according
to Lerner] 12 ... h6 [An unclear
position arises after 12 ... ♔h8
13 ♖d2 h6 14 ♖e1 ♕f7 15 ♘b5 g5;
Ubilava - Malaniuk, Tbilisi
1986] 13 dxc5 [13 h4!? - Lerner]
13 ... ♘xc5 14 ♕c2 ♗e6 15 b3 ♖c8
16 ♘d4 ♗f7 17 e4?! [17 f4] 17 ...
f4! 18 ♘ce2 a6! when Black
plans to play ... g6 - g5 and ...
e7 - e5 with a complicated
position; Lerner - Malaniuk,*

USSR Ch 1986} 12 ... e5? *{Cor-
rect was 12 ... ♔h8!?}* 13 dxe5
dxe5 14 e4! f4 15 gxf4 exf4 16 e5
♖b8 17 ♖fe1 ♕e6! *{17 ... ♘e6? 18
♘f6+}* 18 ♖e4 *{Malaniuk claims
that White could have gained
advantage by 18 ♕d3, when 18 ...
g5? runs into 19 ♘xg5 ♕h6 20
♘f6+ ♗xf6 21 ♕d5+ with a
decisive superiority}* 18 ... g5! 19
♘xg5 ♕h6 with compenstion
for the sacrificed material;
Lputian - Malaniuk, Novosibirsk
1986)* 12 ♕c2 (Tukmakov offers
the line 12 e4 cxd4 13 ♘xd4 f4
14 gxf4 ♘c5 15 ♕c2 ♗xd4 16
♖xd4 ♘e6∓) 12 ... ♖b8 13 e4 (13
♕d2!? - Tukmakov) 13 ... fxe4
(Bad is 13 ... cxd4 14 ♘xd4 f4 15
gxf4 ♗xd4 16 ♖xd4 ♖xf4 17
♘d5 with advantage for White
- Malanuik) 14 ♕xe4 (According
to Malaniuk, on 14 ♘xe4 an
equal game would be achieved
by 14 ... ♗g7; Tukmakov suggests 14 ... ♗f5 15 ♕e2 ♗xe4 16
♕xe4 and Black has several
promising replies: 16 ... ♕f7, 16
... cxd4!? and 16 ... b5!?) 14 ...
♗d7 (Weaker is 14 ... ♗f5 15 ♕e3
- Tukmakov) 15 ♘d5 ♗c6 and
chances are equal; Tukmakov -
Malaniuk, Novosibirsk 1986.

Returning to the position
after 9 ... ♔h8 *(44)*.

10 ♘d5

If White now exchanges on
f6, Black has sufficient possibilities: 10 ♗xf6 ♗xf6 11 e4 e5 12
♖fe1 (White could have tried 12
dxe5 dxe5 13 ♖fe1, whilst 13
exf5 gxf5 14 ♖fe1 ♘c5 leads to

an unclear position) 12 ... exd4
13 exf5 ♕d8 14 ♘b5 ♘c5 15 ♕a3
♗xf5 (Weaker is 15 ... d3?! 16
fxg6 hxg6 17 ♖ad1) 16 ♘bxd4
♗g4 17 ♖ad1 ♕d7 18 h3 ♗xf3
(The text move leads to a
drawn endgame, but 18 ... ♗xh3
would have been too risky: 19
♗xh3 ♕xh3 20 b4 ♘d7 21 ♘e6
♖fc8 22 ♘fg5 ♗xg5 23 ♘xg5
with a dangerous attack) 19
♘xf3 ♕a4! 20 ♕xa4 ♘xa4 21 b3
and the game soon ended in a
draw; Lputian - Vyzmanavin,
Irkutsk 1986.

| | **10** | **...** | **♘g8** |

Strangely enough, this retreat gives Black good chances.

11	**♗d2**	**e5**
12	**dxe5**	**dxe5**
13	**e4**	**c6**
14	**♘c3**	**f4**
15	**gxf4?**	

A critical moment! Better
seems to be 15 ♘a4!? *(45)*
15 ... ♕e7?! (15 ... h6!?) 16 gxf4
exf4 17 ♗c3 g5 18 ♘d4 g4 19
♖fe1 ♘h6 20 ♖ad1 ♕f7 21 e5 f3
22 e6 ♕h5 23 ♗f1 and Black's
attack on the kingside has
failed; Kravtshenko - Malaniuk,

Tallinn 1987.

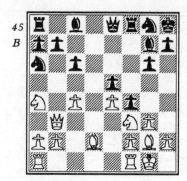

| **15** | **...** | **exf4** |
| **16** | **e5** | **g5!** |

The pawn cannot be taken
because of 17 ... ♕g6.

17	**♖fe1**	**♘c5**
18	**♕a3**	**♘d3**
19	**♘e4**	

White lacks sufficent counterplay for the exchange; Lerner
- Malaniuk, Tallinn 1987. No
better would have been 19 ♖e2
g4, nor 19 ♖e4 ♗f5, nor 19 ♖d1
♘xe5. In each case White loses
material.

F

| **8** | **e4** *(46)* |

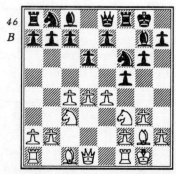

In this last section we shall
examine variations that have

not been endorsed in master practice.

The text move seems to be the most direct way to undermine Black's strategy. Nevertheless, White cannot achieve his goal by such unprepared pawn advances.

Even if e4 is prepared by 8 ♕c2 Black has no problems: 8 ... e5 9 dxe5 dxe5 10 e4?! ♘c6 11 ♗e3 f4! 12 gxf4 ♘h5, as in Reilein – Zysk, Munich 1987.

Also to be considered is 8 ♗e3 e5 (The continuations 8 ... a5 9 d5 and 8 ... c6 9 d5 lead to the variations examined above, but 8 ... ♘g4!? deserves examination) 9 dxe5 dxe5 10 ♗c5 ♖f7 11 ♘g5 ♖d7 12 ♕b3 and White has a minimal advantage.

8	...	fxe4
9	♘g5	♘c6
10	♗e3	♗g4

Black can also attempt to solve his problems in the centre: 10 ... e5!? 11 d5 ♗g4 12 ♕d2 ♘d4?! 13 ♗xd4 exd4 14 ♕xd4 ♘d7 15 ♕e3 ♘e5 16 ♕xe4 ♗f5 17

♕h4 h6 18 ♘e6 g5 19 ♘xg7 gxh4 20 ♘xe8 ♖axe8 21 b3 h3 22 ♗h1 ♗g4 23 f4 ♘d3 24 ♗e4 ♘c5 25 ♖ae1 and the advantage of White's extra pawn is clear; Dziuban – Legky, USSR 1985.

11 ♕b3

Black also has good play after 11 ♕d2 ♕d7 12 ♘gxe4 ♘xe4 13 ♗xe4 ♗f3 14 ♗xf3 ♖xf3, as in Afifi – Yusupov, Tunis 1985.

11	...	♕d7
12	♘gxe4	♘xe4
13	♗xe4	♗f3
14	♗xf3	♖xf3
15	♖ad1	*(47)*

Black has a good game.

2 Main Line with 7 ... c6

1	d4	f5
2	g3	♘f6
3	♗g2	g6
4	♘f3	♗g7
5	0-0	0-0
6	c4	d6
7	♘c3	c6 *(48)*

This move has a long history. If we compare it with the move 7 ... ♘c6, play is less forcing here, but unlike 7 ... ♕e8, where Black retains a choice of several plans, the move 7 ... c6 is usually connected with the advance ... e7 - e5. The main reply for White is 8 d5, which we shall examine first, though White has several possibilities:

A 8 d5
B 8 ♕c2
C 8 ♖e1
D 8 b3
E 8 ♗g5 and others

A

        8   d5

Normally Black reacts to this with the immediate 8 ... e5 but other lines are sometimes tried:

A1 8 ... e5
A2 8 ... ♕c7
A3 8 ... ♗d7 and others

A1

        8   ...   e5 *(49)*

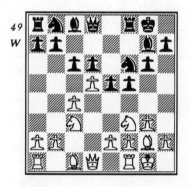

And now:

A11 9 dxe6
A12 9 dxc6 and others

A11

9 dxe6

The most natural move.

9 ... ♗xe6

Again White has a choice here:

A111 10 ♕d3
A112 10 b3 and others

A111

10 ♕d3 *(50)*

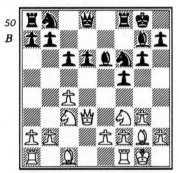

White's intention is to exploit Black's potential weakness - the d6-pawn. A drawback of the plan is that the white queen may be vulnerable to attack by the black pieces. The basic theory of the variation was worked out many years ago, but recent tournament practice has made several important additions.

10 ... ♘a6

Black has tried several other moves here:

a) 10 ... ♔h8 11 ♗f4 ♘e8 (Neither will equality be achieved by 11 ... ♘h5, e.g. 12 ♗xd6 ♗xc4 13 ♕xc4 ♕xd6 14 ♘g5 ♕c7 15 ♘e6 ♕f7 16 ♕b3 ♖e8 17

♘xg7 with advantage to White; Davis - Gallego, Lisbon 1986, nor by 11 ... d5 12 ♘g5 ♗g8 13 cxd5 cxd5 and Black has a potential weakness on d5, Shvedchikov - Alieva, Moscow 1991) 12 ♘g5 ♗g8 13 e4 ♘a6 14 ♖ad1 ♘c5 15 ♕e2 ♕e7 16 ♖fe1 with an unclear position; Hübner - Akvist, Oslo 1974.

b) 10 ... ♘g4 11 b3 (11 ♘g5 ♕e7 12 ♘d5 ♗xd5 13 cxd5 c5 14 ♘e6 and White has a stronghold on e6; Ostenstad - Gretarsson, Gausdal 1992) 11 ... ♘a6 12 ♗b2 (12 ♗f4!? ♘c5 13 ♕d2 ♕a5 14 ♖ac1± Aseev - Kalinichev, Berlin 1991) 12 ... ♘c5 13 ♕d2 ♕e7 14 ♘g5 ♗c8 15 ♖ad1, and the position is more favourable for White; Scanavina - Pelikan, Argentina 1961.

c) 10 ... ♘e4 11 ♘d4 (Accepting the pawn sacrifice leads to equality: 11 ♘xe4 fxe4 12 ♕xe4 ♗f5 13 ♕h4 *(13 ♕e3 ♕b6 [13 ... ♖e8 14 ♕b3 ♘a6 15 ♕xb7 ♘c5 16 ♕b4 ♖xe2 with good counterplay for the sacrificed pawn] 14 a4 ♘a6 15 ♕xb6 axb6 and Black has sufficent compensation; Margolit - Leonidov, USSR 1960}* 13 ... ♕xh4 14 ♘xh4 ♗e6=) 11 ... ♗f7 12 ♗xe4 (12 ♘xe4 fxe4 13 ♗xe4 ♘d7 with counterplay for the pawn) 12 ... fxe4 13 ♘xe4 (13 ♕xe4 ♖e8 14 ♕g4 ♘d7 15 ♗g5 ♘e5 16 ♕h4 ♕b6 and Black regains his pawn in a good position) 13 ... ♘d7 14 ♘g5 (14 ♘xd6?! ♘c5 15 ♘xf7 ♖xf7 16 ♕a3 ♕xd4 17 ♗e3 ♕xb2 18 ♕xc5

♕xe2, and the position favours Black; 14 ♘f3 d5 15 cxd5 ♕xd5 16 ♗g5 ♕b6 with counterplay) 14 ... ♘e5 15 ♘xf7 ♖xf7 16 ♕c2 ♕d7 17 ♗f4 and Black is behind in material - Leonidov.

d) 10 ... ♘bd7 11 ♗f4 ♘b6 12 b3 ♘e4 13 ♘d4 ♘xc3 14 ♘xe6 ♕e7 15 ♗d2 ♕xe6 16 ♗xc3 ♖ae8 17 ♗xg7 ♔xg7 18 e3± Uhlmann - Zwaig, Halle 1967; Botvinnik suggests that Black should play 16 ... ♗xc3 17 ♕xc3 d5!?.

11 ♗f4

White can also try to gain an advantage by 11 ♘g5 *(51)*:

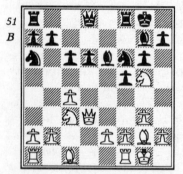

51
B

a) 11 ... ♗c8 (This bishop retreat is unpleasant for Black) 12 ♖d1 (12 ♗f4 ♘h5 *{12 ... ♘e8 13 ♖fd1 h6 14 ♘f3 ♗e6 15 ♕e3! ♗xc4 16 ♗xh6± Keene - Wirthenson, Hannover 1977}* 13 ♕xd6 *{No more than equality is gained by 13 ♖ad1?! ♘xf4 14 gxf4 h6 15 ♘f3 ♖f6 16 ♖d2 ♗e6= Csom - Sax, Budapest 1973}* 13 ... ♘xf4 14 ♕xf4 h6 15 ♘f3 g5 16 ♕c1 ♗e6 17 ♖d1 ♕f6 18 ♘d4 with better chances for White, because 18 ... ♗xc4 19 ♘e4 fxe4 20 ♕xc4+ ♔h8 21

♘e6! gives White a dangerous initiative; Simagin - Hasin, Moscow 1956) 12 ... h6 13 ♘f3 ♗e6? (13 ... ♘e8 or 13 ... ♘e4! 14 ♘xe4 fxe4 15 ♕xe4 ♗f5 16 ♕h4 g5 17 ♕h5 ♕f6 with good compensation - Bellin) 14 ♕xd6 ♕xd6 15 ♖xd6 ♗xc4 16 ♘e5 ♗f7 17 ♗xh6 with an extra pawn for White; Ivkov - Sahovic, Zemun 1982.

b) 11 ... ♖e8 12 ♗f4 ♕b6 13 b3 with a more favourable position for White; Smejkal - Lutikov, Leipzig 1977.

c) 11 ... ♘c5 12 ♘xe6 ♘xe6 13 ♖d1 ♕e8 14 b3 with a better position for White - Taimanov.

d) 11 ... ♕e7 12 ♗f4 ♖ad8 (12 ... ♘e8? 13 ♘d5 ♕xd5 14 cxd5 c5 15 ♘e6 and the white knight vigorously limits Black's chances) 13 ♖ad1 ♘h5 (13 ... ♘g4 14 ♘xe6 *{14 ♘d5!? ♕e8 15 ♕a3 ♘e5 with complications - Knezevic}* 14 ... ♕xe6 15 e4 *{15 b3 ♘c5 16 ♕c2 ♕f6 [16 ... ♖fe8!?] and the game is equal; Ubilava - Knezevic, Trencianske Teplice 1985}* 15 ... ♘c5 16 exf5 gxf5 17 ♕c2 ♘e5 18 b3± Fridstein - Lutikov, Moscow 1958) 14 ♘d5 (Too spectacular) 14 ... ♕d7 15 ♗e3 ♔h8 16 ♘f4 ♗xf4 17 gxf4 (17 ♗xf4!? - Suetin) 17 ... ♗g8 18 ♕c2 ♕c7 19 a3 ♘c5 20 b4 ♘d7 21 ♗d4 ♘b6 with an excellent game for Black; Kremenietsky - Berkovich, Moscow 1983.

Timid is 11 ♖d1 ♘c5 12 ♕xd6 ♕xd6 13 ♖xd6 ♗xc4 with no problems for Black; Radev -

Kaiszauri, USSR 1977.

11 ... ♘e4

This move considerably sharpens the struggle. Others are indifferent or just plain bad:

a) 11 ... ♖e8!? 12 ♘g5?! ♘g4 13 ♘xe6 ♖xe6 14 ♖ad1 ♘e5 15 ♕c2 ♕a5 16 e4?! ♘xc4 and White gained no counterplay for his pawn; Bany – Kuczynsky, Polanica Zdroj 1987.

b) 11 ... ♕a5 12 ♘g5 (Also good is 12 ♗xd6 ♖fd8 13 ♖ad1 ♗f7? 14 ♘g5 ♘e8 15 ♘xf7 ♔xf7 16 c5 ♘xc5 17 ♗d5+ and the black king remained exposed in Shneider – Palatnik, Herson 1989) 12 ... ♖fe8 (If 12 ... ♘c5?! 13 ♕b1! and 13 ... ♗xc4 loses to 14 b4 ♕a3 15 bxc5 ♕xc3 16 ♖c1 ♕d4 17 ♗e3+-) 13 ♗xd6 ♖ad8 14 ♘xe6 ♖xe6 15 b4 ♕a3 16 c5± – Taimanov.

c) 11 ... d5?! 12 ♘g5 ♘c5 13 ♕c2 d4 14 ♘a4 ♘fd7 15 ♖ad1 ♕e7 16 ♘xc5 ♘xc5 17 b4 ♘d7 18 e3 dxe3 19 ♖fe1 with advantage to White; Andersson – Marovic, Banja Luka 1979.

d) 11 ... ♘e8 12 ♘g5 (Passive is 12 b3 ♕f6 13 ♖ac1 d5 14 cxd5 ♘b4 15 ♕d2 ♘xd5 16 ♗e5 ♕e7 17 ♗xg7 ♘xg7 18 ♘d4 ♘xc3 19 ♖xc3 ♗f7= Neverov – Malaniuk, Herson 1989) 12 ... ♕d7 (Consideration should be given to 12 ... ♘c5 13 ♘xe6 ♘xe6 – Taimanov) 13 b3 h6 14 ♘xe6 ♕xe6 15 ♗e3 ♘f6 with a slightly more comfortable position for White; Romanishin – Vaganian, USSR 1976.

Returning to the position after 11 ... ♘e4 (52).

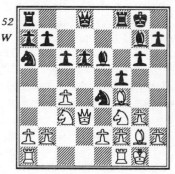

12 ♘xe4

The attempt to play 12 ♘d4 does not give anything more than equality: 12 ... ♗f7 13 ♘xe4 fxe4 14 ♕xe4 ♘c5 15 ♕e3 ♗xc4.

12 ... fxe4
13 ♕xe4 ♘c5

13 ... ♗f5 14 ♕e3 ♗xb2 (Possible is 14 ... ♕b6 15 ♕xb6 axb6 16 ♗xd6 ♖fe8 17 ♘h4 ♗xb2 18 ♘xf5 ♗xa1 19 ♘e7+ ♔f7 20 ♖xa1 ♖ad8 21 ♘a3 ♖d2 22 ♗h3 ♘c5 23 ♗xc5 bxc5 24 ♘c8 ♖exe2 and the active black rooks maintain the balance; Berg – Fleck, West Germany 1987) 15 ♖ad1 ♖e8 16 ♕d2 ♕f6 17 e3! ♗a3 18 ♘d4 ♗b4 19 ♕e2 ♗d7 20 h4 with good attacking chances; Vukic – Kaiszauri, Skara 1980.

14 ♕e3

Not 14 ♕c2? ♗f5 15 ♕d2 ♘e4 16 ♕e3 ♖e8 17 ♕a3 ♕b6 18 ♗c1 d5 with a strong initiative for the pawn; Nordström – Niklasson, Sweden 1974.

14	...	♗xc4
15	♖ad1	♖e8
16	♕c1	♗xe2

17	♖xd6	♕a5
18	♗d2	♕b5
19	♘d4	♘d3

Weaker is 19 ... ♕d3?! 20 ♗e3 ♘e4?! 21 ♖d7 c5 and now White should have played 22 ♖e1! cxd4 23 ♖xg7+ ♔xg7 24 ♗h6+ ♔f7 25 ♕f4+ ♘f6 26 ♗d5+ winning; Yusupov - Barbero, Mendoza 1985.

20	♘xb5	♘xc1
21	♘c7	♗xf1
22	♗xf1	♖ed8
23	♖xd8+	♖xd8
24	♗xc1	♖d1
25	♗e3	♔f7 (53)

Black's chances are by no means worse in the endgame; Shneider - Berkovich, Nikolaev 1987.

A112

10 b3 *(54)*

White tries to gain a positional advantage with quiet moves, not risking complicated tactical variations. Other tenth moves are not promising for White:

a) 10 ♘g5?! (The pawn sacrifice is incorrect) 10 ... ♗xc4 11

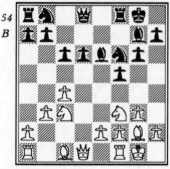

b3 ♗f7 12 ♗a3 ♘e8 13 ♘xf7 ♖xf7 14 ♖c1 ♘a6 15 h4 ♘ac7 16 e4 f4∓ Ribli - Sax, Hungary 1971.

b) 10 ♘d2 (Artificial) 10 ... ♘bd7 11 ♕c2 ♘b6 12 ♘a4 ♘xa4 13 ♕xa4 ♕e7 and White had wasted time on the queenside in Etruk - Holmov, Moscow 1965; Botvinnik suggests 12 b3 d5 with equality.

c) Nothing more than equality is gained by 10 ♗f4 ♗xc4 11 ♗xd6 ♖e8 12 ♕d4 (12 ♘e5 ♗e6 13 ♕d3 ♘bd7 14 ♘xd7 ♘xd7 15 ♖fd1 ♕f6= Aronson - Hasin, Moscow 1956) 12 ... ♗d5 13 ♗xb8 ♗xf3 14 ♕xd8 ♖xd8 15 ♗xf3 ♖axb8= Larsen - Palatnik, Palma de Mallorca 1989.

10 ...   ♘a6

Other moves have also been tried (Botvinnik recommends 10 ... a5!?):

a) 10 ... h6 11 ♘d4 ♗f7 12 ♗b2 ♘a6 13 ♖c1 ♖e8 (13 ... d5!? – Botvinnik) 14 ♖c2 d5 15 cxd5 ♘xd5 16 ♘xd5 ♗xd5 17 ♖d2 with advantage to White; Spiridonov - Stanciu, Bucharest 1973.

b) 10 ... ♔h8 11 ♘a3 (More passive is 11 ♗b2 ♘a6 12 e3 d5 13 cxd5 ♘xd5= Najdorf – Panno, Mar del Plata 1968) 11 ... ♘e8 12 ♕c2 ♘a6 13 ♖ad1 ♕a5 (13 ... ♕e7!? – Botvinnik) 14 ♗b2 ♖d8 15 e3 ♕c7 16 ♘e2 ♘c5 17 ♘f4 ♗g8 18 ♘g5 ♕e7 19 h4± Chaplinsky – Dmitriev, USSR 1973.

c) 10 ... ♘e4?! (Unjustified active play) 11 ♘xe4 ♗xa1 (11 ... fxe4 12 ♘d4 ♗f7 13 ♗xe4 ♕e7 14 ♗g2 c5 15 ♘c2 ♗xa1 16 ♘xa1 ♘c6 17 ♘c2 with more than sufficient compensation; Kärner – Etruk, Parnu 1967) 12 ♕xd6 (Alternatively: 12 ♘xd6 ♗g7 {12 ... ♕e7 13 e4 with an *unclear position – Botvinnik*} 13 ♘xb7 ♕xd1 14 ♖xd1± Krogius – Elizarov, USSR 1967; or 12 ♘h6 ♗g7 13 ♗xg7 ♔xg7 14 ♕d4+ ♔g8 15 ♘xd6 ♕e7 16 e4 fxe4 17 ♘xe4 ♘d7 18 ♖e1∞ Bukhman – Blekhtsin, Leningrad 1968; or 12 ♗g5!? {12 ♘eg5!?} 12 ... ♕c7 13 ♕xd6 – Botvinnik) 12 ... ♕xd6 (Others are bad: 12 ... ♗f7 13 ♗g5 ♕d7 14 ♗h6± – Leonidov; or 12 ... ♖e8 13 ♕xd8 ♖xd8 14 ♘c5±; or 12 ... ♕e8 13 ♘c5 ♗c8 14 ♗h6 ♗g7 15 ♗xg7 ♔xg7 16 ♘g5 with an attack – Malich) 13 ♘xd6 ♗c8 (13 ... b6 14 ♗g5 ♗f6 {14 ... ♗c3 15 ♗e7 ♘a6 16 ♘g5 ♗d7 17 ♗xf8 ♖xf8 and Black has no real compensation for the pawn; Ibragimov – Beshukov, Smolensk 1991} 15 ♗xf6 ♖xf6 16 ♘e8 ♖f7 17 ♘g5 ♖e7 18 ♘xe6 with a decisive advantage for White – Malich) 14 ♗g5 ♗f6

15 ♗xf6 ♖xf6 16 ♘xc8 ♘a6 17 ♘e7+ ♔f8 18 ♘xc6 bxc6 19 ♘e5 with a White advantage; Syre – Paehtz, East Germany 1975.

Returning to the position after 10 ... ♘a6 (55).

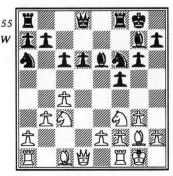

11 ♗b2

Also possible are:

a) 11 ♗e3 ♕e7 12 ♖c1 ♘c5 13 ♗d4 ♗d7 (13 ... a5!?) 14 ♕d2 ♘e6 with possibilities for both sides; Vaganian – Knezevic, Leningrad 1977.

b) 11 ♘g5!? ♕e7 (The retreat 11 ... ♗c8!? deserves consideration: 12 ♖b1 {12 ♗b2 ♘c5 13 ♕c2 ♕e7 14 ♖ad1 ♗d7 15 ♕d2 ♘e8 16 ♖fe1 ♖d8 17 f4 and White is on top; Gulko – Dolmatov, Moscow GMA 1990} 12 ... ♕e7 13 ♕c2 ♗d7 {13 ... h6?! 14 ♘f3 ♘c5 15 ♗a3? [15 ♘h4!? – Taimanov] 15 ... ♗e6 16 ♖bd1 ♖ad8 17 e3 ♗f7 with an excellent game for Black; Petrosian – Knezevic, Banja Luka 1979} 14 e3 ♖ad8 15 ♖d1 ♗c8 16 ♘f3 ♖fe8 with an equal game; Paehtz – Kuczynsky, Dresden 1988) 12 ♘xe6 (12 ♗b2 is considered under the move order 11 ♗b2 ♕e7 12 ♘g5)

12 ... ♕xe6 13 ♘a3 ♖ad8 14 ♖c1 with an unclear position – Taimanov.

c) After the forcing 11 ♘a3?! ♕a5 12 ♕xd6? ♖fe8 13 ♗b2 ♘e4 14 ♘xe4 ♕xb2 15 ♘eg5 ♖ad8 White loses the exchange.

d) 11 ♗f4!? ♘h5 12 ♗d2 (White gains nothing more than equality after 12 ♗g5 ♕a5 13 ♘d4 ♕xc3 14 ♘xe6 ♕xa1 15 ♕xa1 ♗xa1 16 ♘xf8 ♗h8 17 ♘e6 ♖e8 18 ♘f4 ♘xf4 19 ♗xf4 ♖xe2 20 ♗xd6 ♖xa2) 12 ... ♘c5 13 ♕c2 a5 14 ♖ad1 f4 15 ♗c1 ♕e7 (Tukmakov recommends 15 ... ♗f5!? 16 ♕d2 fxg3 17 hxg3 ♕b6 18 ♘d4 ♗d7∞) 16 ♘d4 ♗d7 17 a3 with an unbalanced position; Uhlmann – Vaiser, Szirak 1985.

11 ... ♕e7

Very serious consideration should be given to 11 ... ♘c5!? 12 ♘g5 ♕e7 13 ♕d2 ♖ad8 14 ♘xe6 ♕xe6 15 ♖ad1 ♖fe8 16 ♕c2 *(56)*

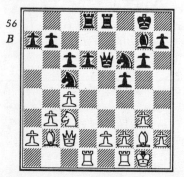

This position arose in the game Bukic – Rakic, Ljubljana 1981. The situation should be considered equal, as Black's pieces control the central squares, but White has a useful bishop pair.

12 ♘g5

12 ♘d4 leads to equality after 12 ... ♘f7 13 ♘a3 ♘c5 14 ♖c1 ♖ad8 15 e3 ♖fe8 16 ♘ce2 ♕c7 17 ♕c2 a6 18 ♘f4 ♘ce4 ½–½ Pinter – Dolmatov, Beersheva 1991.

A more complicated alternative is 12 ♕c2 d5 13 cxd5 and now:

a) 13 ... ♘xd5 14 ♘a4 (14 ♘xd5 ♗xd5 15 ♗xg7 ♕xg7 *{Kimmelfeld – Leonidov, USSR 1969}* 16 ♖ad1 when the following ♘g5 gives White a slightly preferable position according to Kir. Georgiev) 14 ... ♘f6 (14 ... ♘ab4= – Kir. Georgiev) 15 ♖ad1 ♖ad8 16 ♘c3 ♘d5 17 ♘xd5 ♗xd5 18 ♗xg7 ♔xg7 (18 ... ♕xg7 19 ♘xg5±) 19 ♕c3+ ♕f6 20 ♕e3 b6 21 ♘e5 ♘b4 22 f4 with slightly better chances for White; Kir. Georgiev – Ivkov, Sarajevo 1986.

b) 13 ... ♘b4! 14 ♕c1 ♘fxd5 15 ♘a4 ♖ad8 16 ♗xg7 ♕xg7 17 a3 ♘a6 18 e3 ♗c8= Scheeren – Kovacevic, Thessaloniki 1984.

12 ... ♘c5

Also playable are:

a) 12 ... ♖ad8!? 13 ♘xe6 ♕xe6 14 ♕c2± Farago – Borngässer, Dortmund 1978.

b) 12 ... ♗d7 13 ♕c2 (or 13 ♕d2 ♖ad8 14 ♖ad1 ♗c8 15 ♖fe1 h6 16 ♘f3± Dorfman – Dolmatov, Moscow GMA 1990) 13 ... ♖ad8 14 ♖ad1 h6 15 ♘f3 ♗e6 16 ♖fe1 ♘c5 17 ♘d4 gives White a slightly better game; Farago – Renner, Bad Worishofen 1991.

13	♕c2	♗d7?!	
14	♖ad1	♖ad8	
15	b4	♘e6	
16	♘f3		

The exchange on e6 gives Black a good game: 16 ♘xe6 ♗xe6 17 b5 ♗xc4 18 bxc6 bxc6 19 ♗xc6 ♕e6 20 ♘b5 ♖c8 21 ♗xc4 ♕xc4= O'Kelly - Botvinnik, Palma de Mallorca 1967.

16	...	♗c8
17	e3	

White has a slight spatial advantage; Uhlmann - Lutikov, Leipzig 1977.

A12

9	dxc6 (57)

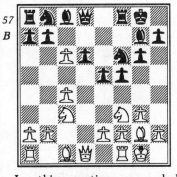

In this section we shall examine the possibilities where White avoids the usual 9 dxe6 and chooses more off-beat continuations. Black normally achieves an equal game without too many difficulties.

No problems for Black arise after 9 e4 cxd5 (9 ... c5?! 10 exf5 gxf5 11 ♘h4 *{11 ♘g5!? - Botvinnik}* 11 ... ♘a6 12 f4 e4 13 ♗h3 ♘e8 14 a3 ♘ac7 15 ♗e3 intending ♕h5; with a slight advan-

tage for White; Bertok - Knezevic, Yugoslavia 1967) 10 cxd5 ♘a6 11 exf5 (11 ♗g5?! h6 12 ♗xf6 ♕xf6 13 exf5 gxf5 and Black's chances are better; Cvetkov - Kotkov, Bulgaria - USSR 1957) 11 ... gxf5 (After 11 ... ♗xf5 12 ♘g5 ♕e7 13 h3 h6 14 ♘ge4 White has a powerful central knight; Magerramov - Vaiser, Nimes 1991) 12 ♘h4 (12 ♘g5!?) with possibilities for both sides - Botvinnik.

9	...	bxc6

Also interesting is 9 ... ♘xc6 10 ♘b5?! (10 ♗g5!?) 10 ... e4 11 ♘fd4 d5 12 c5 ♘e8 13 ♖b1 a6 14 ♘xc6 bxc6 15 ♘d4 ♕f6 16 e3 a5∓ Glek - Palatnik, Tallinn 1986.

10	b3

There is no danger in 10 ♕d2 e4 11 ♘d4 ♕e7 12 ♘c2 ♗e6 13 b3 ♘a6 14 ♗a3 ♘c5 15 ♖ad1 ♖fd8 16 f3 ♗f7 17 ♕e3 with an obscure position; Chikovani - Holmov, Vani 1985.

10	...	e4! (58)

After 10 ... e4 Black gains space for manoeuvre. Other moves are weaker:

a) 10 ... ♖e8 11 ♘a3 d5 12 cxd5 cxd5?! 13 ♖c1 ♗b7 14 ♘b5 ♗c6 15 ♘d6 ♖e6 16 ♘c4 ♘e4 17 ♗b2 and Black finds himself in a critical situation; Vogt - Casper, East Germany 1979.

b) 10 ... ♕e7 11 ♘a3 ♖d8 12 e4 ♘a6 13 ♖e1 ♘xe4 14 ♘xe4 fxe4 15 ♘d2 ♘c5 16 ♘xe4 ♘xe4 17 ♗xe4 ♗b7 (Dvoretsky - Kaiszauri, Vilnius 1978) 18 ♕f3 with a more active position for White.

11	♘d4	♕e7
12	♗a3	♗b7
13	♕d2	♘a6
14	♖ad1	♖ad8
15	♘a4	♖fe8

Black maintains equality; Eingorn - Dolmatov, USSR Ch 1989.

A2

| | 8 | ... | ♕c7 *(59)* |

Black avoids forcing the course of the game by ... e7 - e5. His positional plan is analogous to the variation 7 ... ♕e8, but in this case, if White plays accurately, Black runs into difficulties and thus this variation is not often seen nowadays.

| | 9 | ♘d4 |

It is too early yet to play 9 e4 cxd5 10 cxd5 fxe4 11 ♘g5 ♘a6 (The deployment of the black bishop with 11 ... ♗g4 12 ♕e1 ♘a6 13 ♘cxe4 ♘xe4 14 ♕xe4 ♗f5 15 ♕h4 h6 *{S. Sokolov - Antoshin, USSR 1963}* 16 ♘e6 gives White a slight initiative) 12 ♘cxe4 ♘xe4 13 ♘xe4 ♗f5 and, according to Antoshin, the game is equal.

| | 9 | ... | c5 |

Black remains under attack following 9 ... ♖e8?! 10 e4 fxe4 11 ♘xe4 c5 12 ♘e6 ♗xe6 13 dxe6 ♘xe4 14 ♗xe4 ♘c6 15 h4; Chaplinsky - Yablanovsky, Moscow 1968. Even worse is 9 ... e5? 10 dxe6 ♘a6 11 ♗f4 ♘h5?! 12 ♘db5! with a winning position for White; Gaprindashvili - Gurieli, USSR 1980.

| | 10 | ♘c2 |

An inappropriate attacking move is 10 ♘e6?! ♗xe6 11 dxe6 ♘c6 12 e4 (After 12 ♖b1 ♖ab8 13 b3 ♕c8 14 ♗b2 ♔h8 15 ♗d5 ♘d4 White lost a pawn in Barcza - Antoshin, USSR 1964) 12 ... fxe4 13 ♘xe4 ♘xe4 14 ♗xe4 ♔h8 15 h4 ♗d4 16 ♔g2 ♕c8 17 ♗d5 ♘b4 and Black is fine; Bertok - Antoshin, Zagreb 1965.

| | 10 | ... | ♘bd7 |
| | 11 | ♖b1 |

The immediate 11 f4 is not sufficient for an advantage: 11 ... a6 12 a4 ♖e8 13 ♕d3 ♘f8= Szabo - Antoshin, Budapest

1973.

11 ... a6
12 b3 ♘e5
13 ♗b2 ♖b8

Also better for White is 13 ...
♗d7 14 f4 ♘eg4 15 e4 ♖ae8 16
h3 ♘h6 17 exf5 gxf5 18 ♘e3, as
in Vyzmanavin - Antoshin,
Moscow 1983.

14 f4 ♘f7
15 a4

15 ♕d3?! (This allows Black
to relieve the pressure) 15 ... b5
16 ♘e3 ♗d7= Toran - Tal,
Skopje 1972.

15 ... ♗d7
16 ♕d3 *(60)*

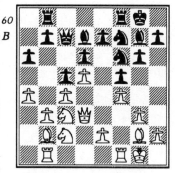

Botvinnik considers this
position slightly preferable for
White.

A3

8 ... ♗d7 *(61)*

In this section we shall look
at continuations for Black that
lost their popularity long ago
and are important only from
the point of view of the development of Leningrad theory.

Here are the remaining
branches on the eighth move:

a) 8 ... cxd5 9 cxd5 ♘a6 (9 ...
a5 10 ♗e3 ♘bd7 11 ♗d4 ♘c5 12
a4 ♗d7 13 ♗xc5 dxc5 14 ♕b3
♔h8 15 ♖ad1 ♘e8 16 e4 with a
marked advantage to White;
Vaganian - Borngässer, Mex-
ico 1977) 10 ♗e3 (10 ♘d4 ♘c5 11
h3 *{11 b3 ♗d7 12 ♗b2 ♕b6 13 ♖c1
a5 with an equal game in
Schmidt - Pytel, Poland 1974; or
11 ♘b3 ♘ce4 12 ♗e3 ♘xc3 13
bxc3 ♗d7 14 ♖c1 ♕e8 15 c4 b6=
Kavalek - Ciocaltea, Harrachov
1966}* 11 ... a5 *{11 ... ♗d7 12 ♔h2
♖c8= Pytel - Eisling, Wijk aan
Zee 1974}* 12 ♗e3 ♗d7 13 ♔h2
♘h5 14 f4 a4 15 ♖c1 ♕a5 and
Black has no problems; Dun-
kelblum - Ciocaltea, Netanya
1965) 10 ... ♗d7 11 ♗d4 h6 12 ♘d2
g5 13 e4 fxe4 14 ♘dxe4 ♗f5 15
♕d2 ♘xe4 16 ♘xe4 ♗xd4 17
♕xd4 ♕b6= Langeweg - Pytel,
Dortmund 1975; 15 ♖e1 ♘c7 16
♕d2 ♕d7 17 ♖ac1± - Botvinnik.

b) 8 ... c5?! (A clear loss of
time) 9 ♕c2± - Botvinnik.

c) 8 ... ♕b6?! 9 ♖b1 ♗d7 10
♗e3 ♕b4 11 ♕d3 ♘a6 12 a3 ♕a5
13 b4 ♕d8 14 ♘d4 and White
is better; Ruehrig - Buecker,

West Germany 1987.

d) 8 ... ♕a5 *(62)* and now:

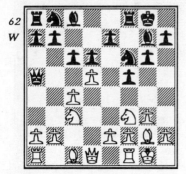

d1) Black gains a slight advantage after 9 ♕b3?! cxd5 10 cxd5 ♘a6 11 ♗e3 ♗d7 12 ♖fc1 ♖fc8 13 ♕d1 ♘c5 14 ♘d4 ♘a4 with an active game; O'Kelly - Liebert, Varna 1962.

d2) Also ineffective is 9 a3 ♕a6 10 ♘d2 cxd5 (10 ... e5 11 b4 e4! 12 dxc6 bxc6 with the initiative; Dolezal - Liebert, Dresden 1957) 11 cxd5 ♘bd7 12 a4 ♘e5 13 ♘b5 ♕b6 14 ♘f3 ♘xf3+ 15 ♗xf3 ♗d7 16 ♗e3 ♕a5= Gheorghiu - Lombardy, Buenos Aires 1979.

d3) Interesting is 9 ♘d2!? ♕a6 10 ♖b1 cxd5 11 cxd5 ♘bd7 12 ♖e1 b5 13 a3 ♕b6 14 ♘f3 ♘c5?! 15 ♗e3 and Black's position is very constricted; Andersson - Panno, Buenos Aires 1979.

d4) Another idea is 9 ♗d2!? ♕b6 (9 ... ♕a6 10 b3 cxd5 11 cxd5 ♘bd7 with equal chances; Wirthensohn - Jansa, Caorle 1972) 10 ♖b1 ♔h8 11 ♗e3 ♕a6 12 b3 cxd5 13 cxd5 ♘bd7 14 a4 and the threat of 15 ♘b5 gives White the advantage; Ivkov -

Lombardy.

d5) 9 ♘d4 ♕c5 and now:

d51) 10 ♗e3 ♘g4!? 11 ♘xf? ♘xe3 12 ♘xe3 ♔h8 13 a3 a5 14 ♖c1 ♕a7 15 ♕d2 a4 with some compensation for the sacrificed pawn in Gauglitz - Lukov, Halle 1987; whilst after 10 ... ♕xc4 White seizes a decisive initiative: 11 ♖c1 ♕a6 12 dxc6 ♘xc6 (12 ... bxc6 13 ♘cb5) 13 ♕b3+ ♔h8 14 ♘cb5 ♘xd4 15 ♗xd4 ♕a5 16 ♘c7 ♖b8 17 ♘e6 ♗xe6 18 ♕xe6 ♖fe8 19 ♖c2 ♘h5 20 ♗xg7+ ♘xg7 21 ♕f7 ♕d8 22 ♖fc1 ♖f8 23 ♕d5.

d52) 10 ♗g5 (Jansa) 10 ... h6 11 ♗xf6 ♗xf6 12 dxc6 bxc6 13 ♘xc6 ♘xc6 14 ♕d5+ ♕xd5 15 ♗xd5+ ♔g7 16 ♗xc6 ♖b8 with counterplay for the pawn - Taimanov.

d53) 10 ♕d3?! ♘g4 11 ♘f3 (Ogaard - Akvist, Oslo 1974) 11 ... ♘d7 with a favourable position for Black - Botvinnik.

d54) 10 dxc6 bxc6 11 ♘db5 ♕b6 with possibilities for both sides in Langeweg - Jansa, Amsterdam 1974, e.g. 12 c5 dxc5 13 ♕b3+ ♔h8 14 ♗f4 ♘a6 with an unclear position.

9 ♖b1

Other moves are:

a) 9 ♘d4 ♕b6 10 e3 (10 ♘b3 ♘a6 11 ♗e3 c5 12 ♖b1 ♘c7 13 ♘d2 ♕a6 14 ♕c2 and Black has no problems; Kestler - Buecker, Bundesliga 1990/91) 10 ... ♘a6 11 ♖b1 (11 b3 ♘c5 12 ♗b2 a5= Spiridonov - Akesson, Polanica Zdroj 1981) 11 ... ♘c5 (11 ...

♘c7 12 dxc6 bxc6 13 b4 e5∞ Harding) 12 b4 ♘ce4 13 ♘a4 ♕a6?! (13 ... ♕c7 14 f3 ♘g5 15 e4± Palatnik - Gulko, Kiev 1973; 15 ... e5!?) 14 f3 ♘g5 15 b5 cxb5 16 cxb5 ♕a5 17 ♗d2 ♕d8 18 ♕b3 with a good game for White; Ivkov - Buecker, Dortmund 1989.

b) 9 ♗e3 ♘a6 10 ♕d2 ♘g4 11 ♗f4 ♘c5 12 h3 ♘f6 13 ♗h6 ♘ce4 14 ♘xe4 fxe4 15 ♘h4?! ♖f7∓ Kaerner - Gavrikov, Tallinn 1987.

c) Also ineffective is 9 ♕c2 ♘a6 10 a3 cxd5 11 cxd5 ♖c8 12 ♘d4 ♘c5∓ - Harding.

| 9 | ... | ♘a6 |
| 10 | b3 | |

If 10 b4 ♘c7 11 ♘d4 e5 12 dxe6 ♘xe6 13 e3 f4 14 ♘ce2 fxg3 15 hxg3 ♘g5 and Black has good counterplay; Schoen - Buecker, Bundesliga 1990/91.

10	...	♘c5
11	♗b2	a5
12	♕d2	♕b6
13	♘d4	(63)

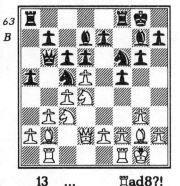

13 ... ♖ad8?!

Probably 13 ... cxd5!? is worth trying.

14 ♖fd1

White's chances are slightly preferable; Ribli - Mestel, London 1986.

B

| 8 | ♕c2 | (64) |

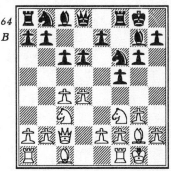

In the present section we discuss 8 ♕c2 which prepares the advance e2 - e4. In comparison with the usual 8 d5, this presents less difficulties for Black who usually intends to play ... e7 - e5; the surest way to equality. In practice this variation has not been particularly successful for White. Black has several alternative eighth moves:

B1 8 ... ♕c7
B2 8 ... ♘a6
B3 8 ... ♔h8 and others

B1

| 8 | ... | ♕c7 |
| 9 | e4 | |

Others fail to impress:

a) 9 d5 does not give the advantage: 9 ... cxd5 10 cxd5 ♘e4 11 ♗d2 ♗d7 12 ♖ac1 ♖c8

with equality; Soloviev - Alekseev, Moscow 1972.

b) 9 ♗g5 e5 10 dxe5 dxe5 11
e4 ♘a6 12 exf5 ♗xf5 13 ♕e2
♖ae8 14 ♘d2 ♘c5 and the black
pieces are well developed;
Fuderer - Dimic, Yugoslavia
1953.

c) 9 b3 e5 10 dxe5 dxe5 11 ♗a3
♖d8 (11 ... ♖e8 12 ♖ad1 ♗f8 13
♗xf8 ♖xf8 14 e4 f4 with an
unclear position in Scherbakov
- Volovic, USSR 1966) 12 e4
fxe4 13 ♘g5 ♗f5 14 ♘gxe4
♘xe4 15 ♘xe4 ♘d7= Keller -
Nilsson, Munich 1958.

d) 9 ♖e1 ♘a6 10 e4 fxe4 11
♘xe4 ♗f5 12 ♘h4? (Equality is
achieved after 12 ♘xf6+ exf6 13
♕c3 - Botvinnik) 12 ... ♘g4 with
a black initiative in Urbanec -
Vesely, Prague 1957.

e) 9 ♖d1 also results in
equality: 9 ... a5 10 b3 ♘a6 11 a3
e5; Lokvenc - Hort, Marianske Lazne 1962.

9 ... fxe4

The immediate 9 ... e5!? is
possible: 10 dxe5 dxe5 11 exf5
♗xf5 (Problems arise after 11 ...
gxf5 12 ♖e1 ♘e8 13 ♕e2 ♘d7 14
♗g5 e4 15 ♗f4± Koblencs -
Ostrauskas, USSR 1961) 12 ♕e2
♘bd7 13 ♗e3 ♖ae8 14 h3 ♘e4 15
♘xe4 ♗xe4= Filip - Nei, Beverwijk 1966.

10 ♘xe4 ♘xe4

Not bad is 10 ... ♗f5 11 ♘h4
♘xe4 12 ♗xe4 e6 13 ♗e3 ♘d7 14
♘xf5 exf5 15 ♗g2 ♘f6= Starck
- Liebert, East Germany 1962.

11 ♕xe4 ♗f5

12	♕h4	e5
13	dxe5	dxe5
14	♗h6	♘a6
15	♖ad1	♖ae8
16	♕g5	♗xh6
17	♕xh6	♗g4
18	♗h3	♗xh3
19	♕xh3	

The game is equal; Gofstein
- Bikhovsky, USSR 1977.

B2

8 ... ♘a6 (65)

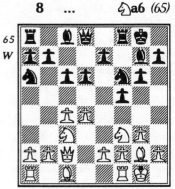

65
W

Black's last move leads to a
slow position in which White
has no reason to hope for the
advantage.

9 ♖d1

Four other possibilities have
been tried without success:

a) 9 d5?! e5 (9 ... cxd5 10 cxd5
♗d7 with a good game for
Black) 10 dxe6 ♗xe6 11 b3 ♘b4?!
(11 ... ♕e7 {11 ... ♘c5} 12 ♗a3!?
and if 12 ... ♘e4, then 13 ♘xe4
fxe4 14 ♕xe4 ♗xa1 15 ♖xa1 and
White has adequate compensation) 12 ♕d2 ♕e7 13 ♗a3 a5 14
♘g5 ♖ad8 15 ♘xe6 ♕xe6 16
♖ad1± Maliutin - Oratovsky,
Jurmala 1989.

b) 9 ♘d2?! ♘h5 10 d5 e5 11 dxe6 ♗xe6 12 b3 f4 13 ♖ad1 ♗f5 14 ♕c1 g5 15 ♗e1 ♕e7 with a black initiative; Lisitsin – Lutikov, USSR 1955.

c) 9 a3?! ♕e8 (Black has several satisfactory alternatives here: 9 ... ♘c7 10 ♖d1 ♔h8 11 d5 ♗d7 12 dxc6 bxc6 13 h3 ♘e6 14 b4 a5= Averbakh – Hasin, USSR 1956; 9 ... ♘h5 10 e4?! *{10 ♖d1 ♕e8 11 d5= – Botvinnik}* 10 ... f4 11 ♘e2 e5 12 dxe5 dxe5 13 c5 ♘c7 and Black has good prospects of becoming active on the kingside; Hernandez – Knezevic, Varna 1976; or 9 ... ♔h8 10 ♗g5 ♗e6 11 b3 ♖c8 12 ♕d3 ♗g8 13 ♖ad1 ♕a5 and after ... e7 – e5 Black's position may be considered preferable; Zamikovsky – Borisenko, USSR 1956) 10 d5 e5 11 dxe6 ♗xe6 12 b3 d5 13 cxd5 ♘xd5 14 ♗b2 f4 and Black seized the initiative in Beninson – Pelikan, Argentina 1959.

d) 9 b3 ♕e8 10 ♗a3 ♖b8 11 b4 ♘c7 12 ♖ad1 ♔h8 13 d5 cxd5 14 cxd5 ♗d7 15 ♘d4 ♖c8 with an equal game; Doda – Bertholdt, Leningrad 1960.

9 ...   ♕e8 *(66)*

10 b3

Also possible is 10 d5 h6?! (10 ... cxd5 11 cxd5 ♗d7 12 ♘d4 ♖c8=; 10 ... e5!? – Botvinnik) 11 ♘d4 e5 12 dxe6 ♗xe6 13 e4 ♗xc4 14 exf5 with advantage to White; Eliskases – Pelikan, Argentina 1960.

10 ...   h6

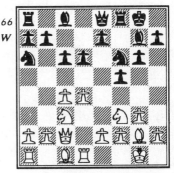

66
W

11 ♗b2   g5

11 ... e5 should also be taken into account here: 12 dxe5 dxe5 13 e3?! (13 ♗a3 ♖f7 14 ♗d6∞ – Botvinnik) 13 ... e4 14 ♘e1 ♘g4 15 ♘e2 ♘e5 and Black is better; Goldenberg – Pelikan, Argentina 1960.

12 d5   c5
13 ♘e1   ♕h5
14 e3   f4
15 exf4   gxf4
16 ♕e2

A state of dynamic equilibrum exists on the board; Goldenberg – Pelikan, Mar del Plata 1961.

B3

8 ...   ♔h8 *(67)*

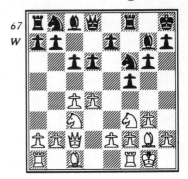

67
W

Here we conclude our survey of the variations with 8 ♕c2. First, we consider some examples where Black chooses rarely-seen possibilities on his eighth move.

a) 8 ... h6? 9 ♘h4 (9 ♖d1 ♕e8 10 d5 cxd5 11 cxd5 ♘a6 12 ♘d4 ♗d7 13 b3 ♕f7 with equal chances; Polugayevsky - Liebert, Reykjavik 1957) 9 ... ♕e8 10 f4 with e4 to follow (±) - Liebert.

b) 8 ... ♘h5 9 b3 (9 d5± - Botvinnik) 9 ... e5 10 dxe5 dxe5 11 ♗a3 ♖e8 12 ♖ad1 ♕f6 13 ♖d6 ♗e6 (Ilievsky - Knezevic, Skopje 1967) 14 ♘d5!±.

8 ... ♔h8 is a useful but rarely seen alternative to the popular 8 ... ♕c7 and 8 ... ♘a6.

9 ♗g5

More solid is 9 b3 ♗e6 10 ♗b2 (10 ♘g5!? ♗g8 11 e4 fxe4 12 ♘cxe4 ♘bd7 13 ♗b2 worked out well for White in Neverov - Savchenko, Herson 1989) 10 ... ♘bd7 (10 ... ♗g8 11 ♖ad1 ♘bd7 12 e3 ♖c8 13 ♘e1 b5 14 cxb5 cxb5 15 ♕e2 a6= Bolbochan - Apschneek, Buenos Aires 1939) 11 e4 fxe4 12 ♘xe4 ♗f5 13 ♘h4 ♗xe4 14 ♗xe4 ♘xe4 15 ♕xe4 e5 16 ♖ad1 (16 dxe5 dxe5 17 ♖ad1±; 16 ... ♘xe5=) 16 ... ♘f6 17 ♕g2 e4∓ Arbakov - Palatnik, Uzgorod 1988.

9 ... ♗e6
10 b3

Better than 10 d5 cxd5 11 ♘d4 ♗g8 12 cxd5 ♘a6 13 ♖fd1 ♖c8 14 ♕d2 (14 ♘db5 ♘b4 15 ♕b3 a5 with equal chances -

Botvinnik) 14 ... ♘c5 15 ♘b3 (15 ♗xf6 ♗xf6 16 e3= - Botvinnik) 15 ... ♘ce4 16 ♘xe4 ♘xe4 17 ♗xe4 fxe4 18 ♗e3 ♖f5 with advantage to Black; Mecking - Botvinnik, Hastings 1966/67.

10 ... ♘bd7
11 ♖ad1 d5!

With equal chances; Beliavsky - Yusupov, Reykjavik 1988.

C

8 ♖e1 (68)

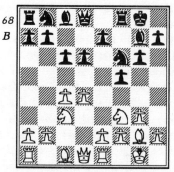

In this short section we shall take a glance at the unfashionable rook move which, as with 8 ♕c2, creates no serious problems for Black, as White is not easily able to achieve e2 - e4.

8 ... ♘e4

Black takes advantage of the lack of protection of the e4-square. Since e2 - e4 is not threatened immediately, other moves are possible:

a) 8 ... ♘a6 9 b3 (9 a3 ♕c7 {9 ... ♗e6} 10 b4 ♗d7 11 ♕b3 ♖ae8 12 c5+ with a better game for White - Schwarz) 9 ... ♕a5 (9 ... ♘e4!? - Botvinnik) 10 ♗d2 ♕c7 11 e4 ♘xe4 12 ♘xe4 fxe4 13

♖xe4 ♘f5 14 ♖e3 c5 (14 ... e5!? – Botvinnik) 15 ♗c3 ♗g4 16 h3 cxd4 17 ♗xd4 with a slight advantage to White; Popov – Eisling, Wijk aan Zee 1974.

b) 8 ... ♕c7 (Black in his turn prepares to play ... e7 – e5, relieving the pressure) 9 e4 fxe4 10 ♘xe4 ♘xe4 11 ♖xe4 e5 12 dxe5 dxe5 13 ♗g5 h6 14 ♗d2 ♗f5 15 ♖e1 ♘d7 with the intention of ... ♖ae8= Bondarevsky – Liebert, Rostov 1961,

c) 8 ... ♘h5 (With the idea of answering e2 – e4 with ... f5 – f4) 9 h3 (9 d5 f4 10 ♘d4 ♕b6 11 e3 fxg3 12 hxg3 c5 13 ♘e6∞ K. Arkell – Pein, British Ch 1989) 9 ... e5 10 dxe5 (10 e4 exd4 11 ♘xd4 f4 12 g4 ♘f6 13 ♘ce2 ♕b6 and Black's position is not worse; Gheorghiu – Sax, Teesside 1972) 10 ... dxe5 11 ♕xd8 ♖xd8 12 e4 ♖e8 and Black maintains the balance – Taimanov.

9 ♕d3

Alternatively, 9 ♕c2 ♘xc3 (9 ... d5!? 10 e3 and according to Taimanov, the manoeuvre ♘c3 – e2 – f4 – d3 gives a slight advantage to White. But this takes a great deal of time and evidently Black's chances of equality after ... ♗e6 and ... ♘d7 are good; or 10 ♘e5 e6 11 f3 ♘d6 12 b3 ♘d7 13 ♘xd7 ♕xd7 14 ♗e3 b6 15 cxd5 exd5 and Black has no real weaknesses; Burmakin – Vasiukov, Leningrad 1991) 10 bxc3 e5 and the chances are equal according to Taim-

anov.

9 ... ♘xc3

Not 9 ... ♘a6 10 ♘xe4 ♘b4 11 ♘f6+ ♗xf6 12 ♕b3 ♘a6 13 ♗h6 ♖e8 14 c5+ and White maintains a slight initiative; Renman – Kristiansen, Copenhagen 1991.

10 bxc3

Or 10 ♕xc3 e5 11 dxe5 dxe5 12 e4 f4 13 c5 ♕e7 14 b4 a5 15 a3 axb4 16 axb4 ♖xa1 17 ♕xa1 ♘a6 18 ♕a3 ♗g4 and Black seized the initiative in Hillarp Persson – Kaiszauri, Stockholm 1988.

10 ... e5
11 e4 ♕a5

Botvinnik recommends two other possibilities: 11 ... fxe4!? and 11 ... d5!?.

12 ♗g5 d5

Not 12 ... ♖e8? 13 ♘h4 f4 14 gxf4 h6 15 ♗xh6 ♗xh6 16 ♕g3 ♗g7 17 ♕xg6 ♖f8 18 ♘f5 ♗xf5 19 exf5 e4 20 f6 and Black's game is under strong attack; Holmov – Bannik, USSR 1962.

13 cxd5 fxe4
14 ♕xe4 cxd5
15 ♕c2 e4
16 ♘e5 ♘c6

According to Taimanov, Black has a promising game.

D

8 b3 *(69)*

This is a natural developing move. We should like to call the reader's attention to the fact that in the present section variations are examined in which White is not in a hurry to move his bishop to b2. Posi-

tions after the premature ♘b2 are dealt with elsewhere.

8 ...   ♕c7

Planning to meet 9 ♘b2 with 9 ... e5. Alternatively:

a) 8 ... a5 9 ♗a3! (For 9 ♗b2 see Chapter 5, variation A1113) 9 ... ♘a6 (9 ... ♕e8 10 ♕d3 ♘a6 11 ♖ad1 ♘b4 12 ♕b1 e5 13 dxe5 dxe5 14 ♘a4 e4 15 ♘d4 b5 16 ♘b6 with advantage to White; Chekhov - Vasiukov, Palma de Mallorca 1989) 10 ♖c1 ♗d7 11 d5 cxd5 12 ♘xd5 ♘e4 13 ♘d2 ♘ec5 14 ♕c2 e6 15 ♘f4 ♘b4 16 ♕b1 ♗c6 17 ♗b2 (Busch - Ditt, West Germany 1989) 17 ... e5!? 18 ♘d5 ♘xd5!? 19 cxd5 ♗e8 with equal chances.

b) 8 ... ♕a5!? 9 ♗b2 (An alternative is 9 ♗d2 ♕c7 10 d5 ♘a6 11 ♖c1 ♘c5 12 ♗e3 ♘ce4 13 ♘xe4 ♘xe4 14 ♗d4 e5 15 dxe6 ♗xe6 16 ♗xg7 ♕xg7 17 ♘d4 ♖ae8 with an equal game; Lerner - Dolmatov, USSR 1989) 9 ... e5 10 dxe5 (10 ♕d2 ♕c7 11 dxe5 dxe5 12 e4 ♘a6! 13 exf5 ♗xf5= Polugayevsky - Dolmatov, Reykjavik 1990) 10 ... dxe5 11 e4 (11 ♘a4 ♘bd7 12 ♕d2 ♕xd2

13 ♘xd2 e4 14 ♖fd1 ♖e8 15 c5 b5 16 cxb6 axb6 17 ♘c4 ♘d5 and Black has no problems; Prze- woznik - Dolmatov, Dortmund 1992) 11 ... f4! (11 ... fxe4 12 ♘d2?! e3 13 fxe3 ♗g4 14 ♕e1 ♘bd7 15 ♘de4 ♘xe4 16 ♘xe4 ♖xf1+ 17 ♗xf1 ♕c7! with a good game for Black; H. Olafsson - Dolmatov, Moscow 1989) 12 ♕d6?! (Correct was 12 a3 ♕c7 13 b4 with an un- balanced position - Dolmatov; not so good was 12 ♘a4?! ♖e8 13 ♖e1 ♗g4 14 ♕d6 ♘bd7 15 ♗c3 ♕d8 16 ♖ad1 ♗f8 17 ♕d3 ♕c7 18 gxf4 ♘h5 19 fxe5 ♘f4 and Black has good prospects against the white king; Browne - Dolmatov, Reykjavik 1990) 12 ... ♘e8 13 ♕d3 ♘a6 14 a3 ♘c5 15 ♕c2 ♕c7 16 b4 ♘e6 17 ♕b3 ♘d6 18 c5 ♘f7 and Black achieved his goals on the kingside; D. Gurevich - Dolmatov, Palma de Mallorca GMA 1989.

c) 8 ... ♘a6 9 ♗b2 transposes to Chapter 5, variation A1112.

d) 8 ... ♕e8 transposes to Chapter 1, variation B4.

9 ♗a3   a5

Alternatively:

a) 9 ... ♖d8 10 ♕c2 e5 11 dxe5 dxe5 12 ♖ad1± - Euwe.

b) 9 ... ♘g4 10 ♕d2 ♘d7 11 h3 ♘h6 12 d5 c5 13 ♘g5 ♘f6 14 ♗b2 and White has the better chan- ces; Wojtkiewicz - Donguines, Bacolod 1991.

10 ♖c1   ♘a6

In this position Karpov found an important innovation.

11 ♕d2! *(70)*

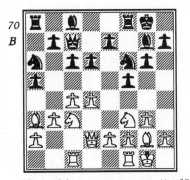

70
B

The older move was 11 d5 ♘c5 (Bad is 11 ... ♖d8 12 ♘d4 e5 13 dxe6 ♘c5 14 ♕d2 a4 15 b4 ♘xe6 16 ♘d5!± Pirc – Fuderer, Yugoslavia 1953; Taimanov recommends 11 ... ♗d7!?) 12 ♘d4 e5?! (12 ... ♗d7 – Taimanov) 13 dxe6 ♖e8 14 ♘db5 cxb5 15 ♘xb5 ♕b6 16 ♕xd6 ♕xd6 17 ♘xd6 ♘xe6 18 ♘xe8 ♘xe8 19 ♖fd1 with advantage to White; Gulko – Kaiszauri, Vilnius 1978.

11	...	♗d7
12	♖fe1	♘b4
13	♗b2	e5?!

A mistake would have been 13 ... ♘e4?! 14 ♘xe4 fxe4 15 ♘g5±. Karpov recommends 13 ... ♖ae8!?±.

14	a3	♘a6
15	dxe5	dxe5
16	♘b5!	cxb5
17	cxb5	♘c5
18	♗xe5	♕b6
19	♗xf6	

White has the advantage; Karpov – Yusupov, Linares 1989.

E

| 8 | ♗g5 | *(71)* |

In the last section of this chapter we shall examine rare possibilities for White's eighth move.

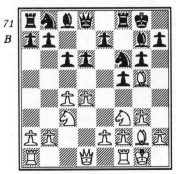

71
B

In addition to the diagram move White has chosen several other possibilities:

a) 8 ♗f4?! h6 9 ♕c2 ♕e8 10 d5 g5 11 ♗d2 ♕h5 12 e3 c5 13 a3 ♘bd7 14 ♘b5 ♘e8 15 ♗c3 ♘e5 with initiative to Black; Stahlberg – Nei, Erevan 1965.

b) 8 ♕b3?! ♔h8 (Consideration should be given to 8 ... ♕b6 9 ♕xb6 axb6= Keller – Bogoljubow, Dortmund 1951; 8 ... ♘a6 also leads to equality: 9 ♖d1 ♘c7 {*Botvinnik recommends here 9 ... ♘c7!? and 9 ... ♕e8!?*} 10 d5 ♘c5 11 ♕c2 e5 12 dxe6 ♗xe6 13 ♗f4 ♖ad8 14 ♘g5 ♕e7= Novotelnov – Hasin, USSR 1956) 9 ♖d1 (9 ♗f4?! h6 10 ♖ad1 ♕e8 11 ♗c1 ♘a6 12 a3 e5 13 d5 ♘c5 14 ♕c2 cxd5 15 cxd5 ♗d7 with advantage to Black; Wexler – Panno, Mar del Plata 1968) 9 ... ♘a6 10 d5 (10 h3?! ♕e8 11 ♕a3 ♘e4 12 ♘g5 ♘xc3 13 bxc3 h6 14 ♘f3 ♕f7 15 d5 c5∓ Naranja – Larsen, Manila 1974) 10 ... ♘c5 11 ♕c2 cxd5 12 ♗e3

♘ce4 13 ♘xd5 ♘g4 14 ♘d2 ♘xe3 15 ♘xe3 ♘f6∓ Marovic - Lombardy, Banja Luka 1976.

c) 8 ♖b1?! ♘e4 (8 ... a5 9 a3 ♘e4 *{9 ... ♘h5?! 10 b4 axb4 11 axb4 f4 12 e3 e5 13 c5!± Marschner - Gallinns, West Germany 1988}* 10 ♘xe4?! fxe4 11 ♘g5 d5 13 ♗e3 h6 13 ♘h3 g5 14 cxd5 ♕xd5 and Black seized the initiative in Hergott - Kuczynsky, St John 1988) 9 ♗f4 h6 10 ♕c2 ♘xc3 11 bxc3 *(11 ♕xc3!? - Botvinnik)* 11 ... g5 12 ♗c1 e5 13 ♗a3 ♖f7∓ Suetin - Smejkal, Ljubljana 1973.

d) 8 b4 a5 9 b5 e5= - Botvinnik.

e) 8 ♕d3 ♔h8 9 ♗g5 ♗e6 10 ♖fe1 ♘bd7 11 b3 d5 12 cxd5 ♗xd5 13 ♘xd5 cxd5 14 ♗f4 ♕b6 15 ♖ec1 ♖ac8= Bilek - Holmov, Havana 1965.

8   ...   ♘bd7

Alternatively:

a) 8 ... ♕e8!? 9 ♗xf6 ♗xf6 10 e4 ♕f7 11 e5 ♗g7 12 ♕e2 f4 13 h3 dxe5 14 dxe5 ♘a6 15 ♖ad1 h6 and Black has sufficient counterplay; Sideif-Zade - Malaniuk, Baku 1983.

b) 8 ... h6!? 9 ♗xf6 ♗xf6 (9 ... exf6?! 10 e3 ♖e8 11 ♕d2 ♘d7 12 ♖fd1 ♘f8 13 b4 a5 14 b5 h5 15 ♘e1± Lutckis - Pelikan, Argentina 1969) 10 e4 e5 11 exf5 gxf5 12 dxe5 dxe5 13 ♕c2 ♘a6 14 ♖ad1 ♕e7 15 ♗h3 (Guimard - Pelikan, Mar del Plata 1968) 15 ... ♗g7 16 ♘h4 ♕f6= - Botvinnik.

9   ♕d2

Also playable is 9 ♕b3 ♕c7?! (9 ... h6!?) 10 ♖ad1 e5 11 c5 d5 12 ♘xe5 ♘xe5 13 dxe5 ♕xe5 14 ♗e3 ♕e7 15 ♗d4 ♗e6 16 e3 ♖f7 17 ♘e2 g5∞ (17 ... ♘e4!?) Nedeljkovic - Fuderer, Yugoslavia 1951.

9   ...   e5

Alternatively, 9 ... ♕c7 10 ♖ad1?! (10 ♗h6 e5 11 ♗xg7 ♔xg7 12 dxe5 dxe5 13 e4! fxe4 14 ♘g5 with better prospects for White - Botvinnik) 10 ... e5 11 dxe5 dxe5 12 ♗h6 ♗xh6 13 ♕xh6 e4 14 ♘d4 ♘e5 15 ♕c1 ♗d7 16 b3 ♖ae8 and Black has the initiative; Usachi - Stein, USSR 1957.

10   ♗h6

Less effective is 10 dxe5 dxe5 11 ♗h6 e4 12 ♗xg7 ♔xg7 13 ♘e1 ♘e5 14 ♕c1 ♗e6 15 b3 ♕a5 and Black has more space; Szabo - Hasenfuss, Kemeri 1939.

10   ...   ♕e7
11   ♗xg7   ♔xg7
12   dxe5   dxe5
13   ♖ad1   ♘c5

An interesting possibility is 13 ... e4!?.

14   ♕d6 *(72)*

The game is equal; Abroshin - Liebert, corr. 1957.

3 Main Line with 7 ... ♞c6

	1	d4	f5
	2	g3	♞f6
	3	♗g2	g6
	4	♞f3	♗g7
	5	0-0	0-0
	6	c4	d6
	7	♞c3	♞c6 *(73)*

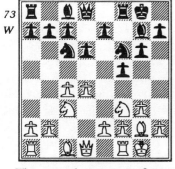

This popular system favoured White in the past and seemed to have been thoroughly analysed. However, a number of new ideas have been introduced and now the situation is less clear. Invariably White responds 8 d5 but other moves have been tried on occasion:

A 8 d5
B 8 ♕c2 and others

A

 8 d5

Black can choose between:

A1 8 ... ♞e5
A2 8 ... ♞a5

A1

 8 ... ♞e5

The sharpest continuation which White can meet by:

A11 9 ♞xe5
A12 9 ♕b3 and others

A11

 9 ♞xe5 dxe5 *(74)*

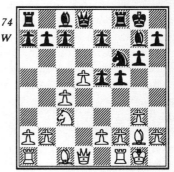

White must choose between:

A111 10 e4
A112 10 ♕b3 and others

A111

 10 e4

Here Black can choose between the sharp 10 ... f4 and the more conservative 10 ... e6.

A1111   10 ... f4
A1112   10 ... e6 and others

A1111
10   ...   f4!? (75)

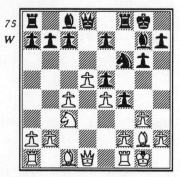

The question of whether the variation beginning with 8 ... ♘e5 is playable or not largely depends on how Black's last move is evaluated. For a long time chess books unanimously considered the position after 10 ... f4 to be favourable for White. During the preparation of this book no new information has emerged to overturn this verdict.

11   b4
White again has a choice of several alternatives:

a) An immediate breakthrough with 11 c5 has also been tried: 11 ... g5 12 ♕b3?! (12 b3 ♕e8 13 d6?! exd6 14 cxd6 c6 15 ♗a3 ♗d7 16 b4 *{Kirillov - Raud, Latvia - Estonia 1990}* 16 h5!? with chances of attack for

Black) 12 ... ♔h8 13 ♘b5 c6 14 ♘c3 ♕e8 15 ♕d1 ♗d7 16 b4 ♖d8 17 ♗b2 ♘g4 18 h3 ♕h5 19 gxf4 gxf4 20 hxg4 ♗xg4 21 f3 ♗c8 22 ♔f2 cxd5 23 ♖h1 ♕g6 24 exd5 e4 and Black gained a formidable attack in Wells - C. Hansen, Kiljava 1984.

b) 11 b3 gives chances for both sides: 11 ... g5 12 ♗a3 g4 (12 ... h5?! 13 ♖e1 h4 14 gxf4 exf4? *{14 ... gxf4}* 15 e5 ♘g4 16 e6! f3 17 ♗h3 ♘h6 18 ♘e4 g4 19 ♗f1 ♘f5 and it is not clear how Black can develop his queenside without great losses; Vukic - Knezevic, Bajmok 1975) 13 ♖e1 f3 (13 ... h5?! 14 gxf4 exf4 15 e5 ♘d7 16 e6 ♗xc3 17 exd7 ♗xd7 18 ♕d3± - Botvinnik) 14 ♗f1 h5 15 c5 (Black has satisfactory replies in other variations too, for example: 15 ♖c1 h4 16 ♖c2 ♘h7 17 c5 ♕e8 18 ♕d3 ♕h5 *{18 ... c6 - Ciric}* 19 ♗c1 *{Ciric recommends 19 d6 exd6 20 cxd6 cxd6 21 ♕xd6 with a safe position, but after 21 ... ♘g5 Black has good chances}* 19 ... ♗d7 20 ♗e3 {20 c6!} 20 ... ♗h6 and Black has a powerful attack; Sieglen - Wessein, West Germany 1989) 15 ... h4 16 d6 (Taimanov suggests 16 ♗c4 but if we continue with 16 ... hxg3 17 hxg3 ♔h7 then it seems that Black still has a very strong attack) 16 ... hxg3 17 hxg3 c6! 18 ♗xc4+ e6 19 ♕d2 ♗d7 20 ♕g5 ♔f7 (76) In the diagram position Black's attack will soon reach a critical

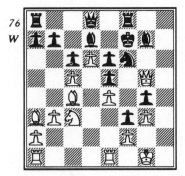

point, when the h-file can be used to great effect; Douven - Plaskett, Groningen 1980.

c) 11 gxf4 ♘h5 (11 ... exf4!? 12 e5 {12 ♗xf4 ♘xe4 13 ♗g3 ♘xg3 14 hxg3 e6= Hodakowsky - Hübner, Aibling 1965} 12 ... ♘g4 13 e6 ♘e5 14 ♖e1 {14 ♕b3 f3 15 ♗h3 b6! with the idea of ♗a6∓} 14 ... ♘xc4! {A mistake would be 14 ... f3? 15 ♗f1 ♘g4 16 ♘e4 h6 17 h3 ♘e5 18 ♘g3 b5 19 ♕c2± Zajcik - Bjelajac, USSR - Yugoslavia 1977} 15 ♖e4 ♘d6 16 ♖xf4 c6∞) 12 fxe5 {12 f5 ♘f4 with unclear complications - Avshalumov) 12 ... ♗xe5 13 ♘e2 ♕d6 14 f4! ♘xf4 15 ♘xf4 ♗xf4 16 ♗xf4 ♖xf4 17 ♖xf4 ♕xf4 18 ♕d4 e5!? (Alternatively: 18 ... ♕g5 19 ♔h1 {19 ♖f1?! ♗h3 20 ♕f2 ♗xg2 21 ♕xg2 ♕e3+ 22 ♔h1 ♖f8 23 ♖xf8+ ♔xf8∓ Taenav - Raud, Estonia 1990} 19 ... ♗g4 20 e5 {20 ♖f1? ♗e2 21 ♖e1 ♕g4 22 h3 ♕h5 23 e5 ♗f3∓} 20 ... ♖f8 21 d6∓; or 18 ... ♗g4!? 19 ♖f1 ♕g5 20 ♕f2 ♗h3= - Avshalumov) 19 ♕c5 ♕g5! 20 ♔h1 ♕d8 21 ♖f1 b6 22 ♕f2 ♕e7 23 c5! ♗a6 24 ♕f6!± Nizynsky - Jzdebski, corr 1990.

d) Not to be recommended is 11 f3?! c6 12 dxc6 ♕b6+ 13 ♔h1 bxc6 14 b3 g5 15 ♘a3 ♔f7! 16 gxf4 gxf4 17 ♘a4 ♕c7 18 ♕e1 ♖g8∓ Hjartarson - Plaskett, Hastings 1985/86.

11 ... g5

Black cannot afford to lose time with 11 ... e6?! 12 ♗b2 exd5 13 exd5 ♗f5 14 ♖e1 and due to the control over the e4-square White's position is better; Bannik - Yukhtman, Ukraine Ch 1964.

12 ♖e1

12 c5 has also been played: 12 ... h5?! (12 ... g4!?) 13 ♗b2 h4 14 gxf4 h3 15 ♗f3 exf4 16 e5 ♘d7 17 e6 and White managed to paralyse Black's queenside in D'Amore - Fernandez, Andorra zt 1987.

12 ... g4!?

After 12 ... a6 13 ♗b2 ♕e8 White can choose between:

a) 14 ♖c1 ♘g4 15 f3 (15 ♖c2?! ♕h5 16 h3 f3 and Black has the attack; Farago - Poutiainen, Budapest 1975) 15 ... ♘e3 (15 ... ♕h5! with a difficult game - Kristiansen, but after 15 ... ♘xh2 16 g4 Black does not have sufficient compensation for his knight) 16 ♖xe3 fxe3 17 g4 with excellent compensation; Reicher - Ungureanu, Rumania 1975.

b) 14 c5 ♕f7 (14 ... ♗d7?! 15 c6! bxc6 16 dxc6 ♗xc6 17 ♘d5) with an unclear game and possibilities for both sides - Kristiansen.

13 c5 f3

14 ♗f1   h5

The chances are equal; White attacks on the queenside and Black on the kingside.

A1112

10 ...   e6 *(77)*

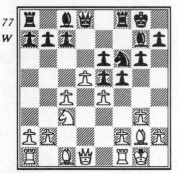

77
W

Compared to 10 ... f4, considered in the previous chapter, this move has long been considered weak, but it is not as bad as has been thought.

First of all, let us consider a misguided plan: 10 ... fxe4? 11 ♘xe4 ♘xe4 12 ♗xe4 ♘h3 (12 ... ♗f5 13 ♕e2 ♕d7 14 ♗g5 ♖f7 15 ♖ae1 with the disadvantage of double pawns; Menchik - Seitz, England 1930) 13 ♖e1 ♕d7 14 ♗e3 ♗f5 15 ♕c2 with a clear advantage for White in Radulov - Kolarov, Varna 1968.

11 ♕b3

There are many other possibilities here:

a) 11 exf5 gxf5! (After 11 ... exf5 White stands better: 12 ♗e3 *{12 ♕e2 e4 13 f3 exf3 14 ♕xf3 ♕e7 15 ♕e2 ♕xe2= Toran - Larsen, Hastings 1956/57}* 12 ... e4 *{12 ... ♘g4!? 13 ♗c1 ♖e8}* 13

♗d4 ♖e8 14 ♖e1 b6 15 f3± Collins - Sherwin, New York 1952) 12 ♖e1 (Instead of this, consideration should be paid to 12 ♗g5!? and 12 b3!?) 12 ... e4 13 f3 exf3 14 ♗xf3 e5! 15 ♖xe5?! (Taimanov suggests 15 c5!?) 15 ... ♘e4 16 ♖xe4 fxe4 17 ♘xe4 ♕e7 with possibilities for both sides.

b) 11 b3 exd5 12 ♘xd5 (12 exd5) 12 ... ♘xe4 (12 ... ♘xd5 cxd5 f4 14 ♗a3 ♖f7 15 ♖c1± Meduna - Pederzolli, Olmoutc 1977) 13 ♗a3 ♖e8 14 f3 ♘d6 (14 ... ♘f6? 15 ♗e7) 15 ♘xc7 ♕xc7 19 ♗xd6 ♕f7= - Taimanov.

c) 11 c5 exd5 12 exd5 h6 13 b4 ♔h7 14 ♕b3 e4 with possibilities for both sides; Berliner - Hearst, Omaha 1959.

d) 11 f3 exd5 12 cxd5 c6 13 dxc6 ♕b6+ 14 ♔h1 ♕xc6 15 ♗e3 ♗e6= Kramer - Hübner, Hamburg 1965.

e) 11 dxe6 c6 12 exf5 gxf5 ♕xd8 (13 ♖e1 ♕xd1 14 ♘xd1 e4= - Botvinnik) 13 ... ♖xd8 14 e7 ♖e8; Kozma - Franko, Oberhausen 1961.

f) 11 ♗g5 h6 12 ♗xf6 ♕xf6 (12 ... ♖xf6!? - Botvinnik) 13 ♕b3 f4 14 f3 ♖d8 15 c5± Ingerslev - Milner-Barry, Moscow 1956.

11 ...   exd5

This is better than:

a) 11 ... f4? (Schroeder - Joppen, West Germany 1967) 12 gxf4 exf4 13 ♗xf4 ♘xd5 14 cxd5 ♖xf4 15 dxe6 ♔h8 16 e7± - Botvinnik.

b) 11 ... ♔h8 12 ♗e3 ♕e7 13

f3± Donner - Johanessen, Beverwijk 1965.

12 cxd5 *(78)*

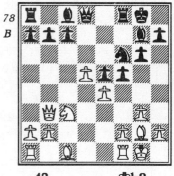

12 ... ♔h8

Without this prophylactic move White can advantageously open the centre: 12 ... ♘e8?! (Rovner - Vinogradov, Leningrad 1947) 13 exf5 gxf5 14 d6+ ♔h8 15 dxc7 ♘xc7 16 ♖d1 ♕e8 17 ♗e3 ♘e6 18 ♘b5± - Botvinnik.

13 ♗e3 ♘e8
14 exf5 gxf5
15 f4 e4

With equality; Tartakower - Alexander, Hastings 1953/54.

A112

10 ♕b3 *(79)*

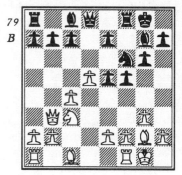

This queen move was for a long time considered to be good for White. Here, however, we will examine some new ideas that Black has found for counterplay. This section also includes unusual possibilities for White on move 10:

a) 10 b3 e4 (10 ... a6 11 ♗b2 ♕e8 12 ♕d2 h6 13 f4 e4 14 e3 e6 15 ♖fd1 ♗d7 16 ♗f1 g5 and Black has active play; Pavlovic - Nikac, Yugoslavia 1991) 11 ♕c2 (11 ♗a3!? ♘g4?! *{11 ... ♖f7 12 f3! exf3 13 exf3 f4 14 ♖c1± Dlugy - Gallego, Sharjah 1985}* 12 ♕c2 a6 13 ♖ad1 ♗d7?! *{13 ... ♕e8}* 14 c5 ♕e8 15 c6!? bxc6 16 dxc6 ♗xc6 17 ♘d5 ♗xd5 18 ♖xd5 c6 19 ♖dd1 with excellent compensation for the pawn as Black's queenside is completely destroyed; Palatnik - Avshalumov, Baku 1988) 11 ... c6 (11 ... e6 12 ♘a3 ♖f7 13 dxe6 *{13 ♖fd1 exd5 14 cxd5 ♘e8 15 ♖ac1 ♗d7 16 e3 ♗e5 17 ♘e2 ♕f6 18 ♘f4 ♘d6 and Black gained the better position in Cvitan - Raud, Bela Crkva 1990}* 13 ... ♗xe6 14 ♖ad1 ♕e8= Ivkov - Larsen, Palma de Mallorca 1968) 12 dxc6 bxc6 13 ♗f4 ♘h5 14 ♖ad1 ♕a5 15 ♗d2 ♕e5 16 ♘a4 with equal chances.

b) Here 10 f4?! is not appropriate: 10 ... e4 11 ♗e3 ♘g4 12 ♗d4 e5 13 ♗c5 b6! (13 ... exf4 14 gxf4 ♖f7 15 e3 g5 with possibilities for both sides; Krasnov - Vinogradov, USSR 1962) 14 ♗xf8 ♕xf8 and Black has excellent counterplay on the dark squares – Vinogradov.

c) 10 ♖e1 e4! with an unclear position – Botvinnik.

d) 10 b4 e4 11 ♕b3 e6 12 ♖d1 ♕e7 13 ♗f4 e5 14 ♗e3 ♕f7 15 ♗c5 ♖e8 16 b5 b6 17 ♘a3 with an unbalanced position, Cramling – Pomes, Terrassa 1990.

e) 10 ♕c2 e6=.

10 ... h6!? *(80)*

With this move, Black prevents the troublesome ♗g5 and gains good prospects for counterplay.

Other moves are sometimes seen:

a) 10 ... ♔h8 11 ♖d1 (11 c5 a6! 12 ♖d1 ♖b8 *{Intending ... b5}* 13 a4 h6 14 ♗d2 g5 was fine for Black in Hardicsay – Mi. Tseitlin, Budapest 1992) 11 ... a6 (11 ... h6!? is considered under the move order 10 ... h6 11 ♖d1 ♔h8) 12 ♗d2?! ♕e8 13 ♖ac1 h6 14 ♗e1 g5 15 c5 e4 16 d6 c6 17 ♘a4 e5 18 f3 f4 19 d7? ♘xd7 20 ♖d6 ♘f6 and White has no compensation for the pawn; Dresen – Ingenerf, Wuppertal 1986,

b) 10 ... ♘h5?! 11 ♖d1 ♔h8 12 a4 a5 13 c5 h6 14 ♗d2 g5 15 ♖ac1

f4 16 ♗e1 ♘f6 17 ♘e4 ♗g4 18 ♕b5 with the advantage; Andersson – Mascarinas, Rio de Janeiro 1985.

c) 10 ... ♘d7?! 11 ♖d1 a5 (Alternatively: 11 ... ♔h8 12 a4 a5 13 ♕a3 e4 14 ♗g5 ♖f7 15 ♘b5 ♘f6 16 ♗f4± Griego – Salman, Philadelphia 1991; or 11 ... h6 12 ♕a3 ♖f6 13 c5 ♘f8 14 b4 g5 15 ♕b3 ♔h8 16 ♗b2± Kavalek – Mack, West Germany 1986) 12 ♗e3 f4 13 ♗d2 ♘c5 14 ♕a3 b6 15 d6 ♖b8 16 dxc7 ♕xc7 17 ♘b5 ♕d7 18 ♗xf4 ♕g4 19 f3 ♕e6 20 ♘c7 ♕xc4 21 ♗e3± Saidy – Ivanov, St John 1988.

d) 10 ... e6 11 ♖d1 (11 ♗e3 exd5 *{11 ... ♕e7? does not lead to equality: 12 ♘b5 a6 13 ♘a7 ♖xa7 14 ♗xa7 b6 15 c5 ♕xc5 16 ♖ac1 ♕e7 17 ♗b8 exd5 18 ♗xc7 with a decisive material advantage in Pigusov – Meister, Voronez 1988}* 12 cxd5 ♘e8 13 ♘b5 ♘d6 14 a4 a6 15 ♘xd6 cxd6± Darga – Toran, Madrid 1957) 11 ... ♕e7 *(11 ... exd5 12 ♘xd5 {12 cxd5 ♔h8 [12 ... ♘e8 does not work because of 13 d6+ ♔h8 14 d7 ♗xd7 15 ♕xb7 – Taimanov] 13 ♗e3 ♘e8 14 ♗c5 ♘d6 [White will also gain the advantage after 14 ... ♖f6 15 ♖ac1 a6 16 d6! ♘xd6 17 ♘d5 ♗e6 18 ♗xd6 ♗xd5 19 ♖xd5 ♖xd6 20 ♕xb7 Karasev – Kondratiev, Leningrad 1959] 15 ♘b5 a6 16 ♘xd6 cxd6 17 ♗b6 ♕f6 18 ♖ac1 and due to the control of the c-file White has an advantage – Taimanov}* 12 ... c6 13 ♗g5 cxd5 14 ♗xd5+ ♔h8 15

♗xb7 ♕xd1+ 16 ♖xd1 ♖b8 17 ♕a3 ♗xb7 18 ♗xf6 ♗xf6 19 ♕xa7± Ribli – Barbero, Lugano 1985) 12 ♗g5 (12 ♗d2!? – Donaldson) 12 ... h6 13 ♗xf6 ♗xf6 14 e4 *(81)*

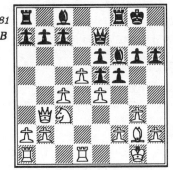

81
B

This position appeared in the game Schmid – Menvielle, Tel Aviv 1964. White has slight advantage after Botvinnik's recommendation 14 ... ♖b8, i.e. 15 ♘b5! with the idea of d6 is powerful, e.g. 15 ... c6 16 d6 ♕d8 17 ♘c7± (17 ♘xa7? ♗d7 18 c5 ♕a5 19 ♕b6 ♕xb6 20 cxb6 ♗d8 and the knight is lost).

11   ♖d1 *(82)*

Or:

a) 11 c5 ♔h8 12 ♖d1 g5 transposes to the main line.

b) 11 ♗e3 ♔h8 12 ♖ad1 g5 13 ♗c5 (13 c5 a6 14 ♕b4! ♕e8 *(14 ... f4 is suggested by Malyshev)* 15 d6 exd6 16 cxd6 cxd6 17 ♕xd6 f4 18 ♗c5 ♕h5?! 19 ♕xf8!! ♗xf8 20 ♖d8± Fominyh – Malyshev, Miskolc 1989) 13 ... a6 14 e3 ♘d7 15 ♗a3 e4 16 f3 (Bad is 16 c5 ♘e5 17 d6 c6 18 ♘a4 ♖f6! 19 ♘b6 ♗e6 20 ♕c2 ♖b8∓) 16 ... exf3 17 ♖xf3 ♘e5 18 ♖ff1 ♕e8 19 ♘e2 ♗d7! 20 ♕c2 ♕h5 21 ♘d4 ♘g4 22 ♘f3 f4!

and Black seized the initiative in Magerramov – Avshalumov, USSR 1987.

c) 11 e4 f4 12 gxf4 ♘h5 13 fxe5 e6 (13 ... ♗xe5 14 ♘e2 – Donaldson) 14 f4 ♕h4 15 ♘e2 exd5 16 cxd5 and White has imposing central pawns; Jasnikowski – Pyda, Warsaw 1990.

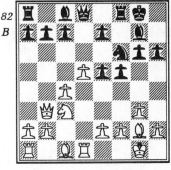

82
B

11   ...   g5

11 ... ♔h8 12 ♗d2 g5 13 c5 a6 transposes to the next note. In this line 13 ♗e1 is strongly met by 13 ... h5 14 c5 h4, as in Vukic – Illincic, Cetinje 1992.

12   c5

Alternatively, 12 ♗d2 a6 13 c5 ♔h8 14 ♗e1 ♕e8 (Black continued on similar lines in Adianto – Spraggett, Novi Sad 1990: 14 ... ♖b8 15 a4 ♕e8 16 d6 exd6 17 cxd6 c6 18 a5 ♗e6, whilst 14 ... e4 15 ♖ac1 left White slightly better in Petrosian – Yagubov, Berlin 1991) 15 d6 cxd6 16 cxd6 e4 17 ♘a4 exd6 18 ♖xd6 f4 and Black has some attacking chances, Stangl – Arkhipov, Kecskemet 1990.

12   ...   ♔h8
13   ♕c4

Probably not the most accurate choice here. Alternatives:

a) 13 ♗d2 usually transposes to the previous note after 13 ... a6 since 13 ... f4 14 ♗e1 ♗f5 15 ♕xb7 ♖b8 16 ♕xa7 ♖xb2 17 ♕a3 worked out badly for Black in Ibragimov - Glek, USSR Team Ch 1991.

b) 13 ♕a3 ♕e8 14 d6 c6 15 b4 exd6 16 cxd6 ♕h5 17 b5 f4 18 bxc6 bxc6 19 f3 e4 and Black is prising open the kingside; Wilson - Djurhuus, Gausdal 1992.

c) 13 ♘b5 a6 14 ♕a3! ♗d7 15 ♘c3 ♕e8 16 d6!± Lagunov - Malyshev, USSR 1989.

13	...	a6
14	b3	♕e8
15	♗a3	e4
16	c6	b6
17	♗b2	♘g4
18	♘a4	♘e5
19	♕c2	♕g6
20	♗d4	♖d8
21	♘c3	e6
22	♕b2	♘f7
23	♗xg7+	♕xg7
24	dxe6	♗xe6 *(83)*

The position favours Black;

Morovic - Avshalumov, Belgrade 1988.

A12
9 ♕b3

Here White rejects the opportunity to take the black knight and seeks other ways to seize the initiative. Practice to date would suggest that it is not fully effective.

To begin with let us consider other, less useful moves for White.

a) 9 b3? (This loses material) 9 ... ♘e4 10 ♘xe4 ♘xf3+ and Black wins.

b) 9 c5?! ♘xf3+ 10 ♗xf3 dxc5 11 ♗e3 ♘d7 12 ♕b3 (12 ♘a4 b6 13 d6 ♖b8 with an extra pawn for Black) 12 ... ♔h8 13 ♗g2 a6 14 ♖ad1 ♖b8 15 ♕c4 b6 16 ♗g5 ♘e5 17 ♕h4 ♗f6 18 e4 ♘f7 19 ♗xf6 exf6 20 ♖fe1 ♘d6 and White has no compensation for the pawn; Dydyshko - Zhuravlev, Tallinn 1980.

c) 9 ♘d2 leads to positions with equal chances: 9 ... c5 (Also possible are: 9 ... ♘fd7 10 f4 ♘g4 11 ♘f3 ♘c5 12 h3 ♘f6 18 gxf4 ♗d7 with counterplay on the black squares; Schuh - Borngässer, West Germany 1985; and 9 ... c6 10 b3 *{10 h3 ♕b6 [Dubious is 10 ... ♕c7 11 ♔h2 ♘ed7 12 ♘f3 ♘c5 13 ♘d4 ♗d7 14 ♗e3 e5?! 15 dxe6 ♘xe6 16 ♘xe6 ♗xe6 17 ♗f4 ♖ad8 18 c5± Tatenhorst - Borngässer, West Germany 1987]* 11 ♘a4 ♕c7 12 f4 ♘f7 13 ♘c3 e5∓ Taimanov -

Vinogradov, Leningrad 1946} 10 ... cxd5 11 cxd5 ♘e4 *{11 ... ♘h5 12 ♗b2 f4∞ Bellin}* 12 ♘dxe4 fxe4 13 ♗xe4 ♗h3 14 ♗g2 ♗xg2 15 ♔xg2 ♘g4 and in compensation for the pawn Black has good play; Horowitz – Kostic, Prague 1931) 10 h3 (10 ♕c2 ♖b8 11 a4?! ♕e8 12 f4 ♘eg4 13 ♘f3 ♘e4 14 ♘xe4 fxe4 15 ♘g5 ♗d4+ 16 e3 ♗xe3+∓ Liebert – Holm, Aarhus 1971) 10 ... ♗d7 11 ♖b1 ♘e8 12 f4 ♘f7 13 ♕c2 ♘c7 14 e4 e5 15 dxe6 ♘xe6 16 ♕d3 ♘d4= Vaganian – Borngässer, Athens 1971.

Returning to the position after 9 ♕b3 *(84)*.

84
B

9 ... ♘ed7
Also perfectly playable is 9 ... ♘xf3+ 10 exf3 (10 ♗xf3 ♘d7=) 10 ... e5 11 dxe6 ♗xe6 12 ♖e1 (12 ♕xb7 ♗xc4 13 ♖d1 ♕d7 14 f4 a5 15 b3 ♖ab8 16 ♕a7 ♘e4 17 ♘xe4 ♗xa1 18 ♘g5 with tactical possibilities for both sides; Anic – Santo Roman, Montpellier 1991) 12 ... ♕d7 13 f4 c6 14 ♗e3 ♕f7 15 ♕a3 ♗xc4 with an equal game; Pilnik – Tartakower, Paris 1954/55.

However, 9 ... ♘fd7 allowed White a slight advantage after 10 ♘xe5 ♘xe5 11 ♖d1 ♔h8 12 f4 ♘g4 13 h3 ♘f6 14 ♗e3 in Mortazavi – Flear, London 1985.

10 ♗e3
Botvinnik has suggested 10 ♘d4 ♘c5 11 ♕c2 ♘xd5 12 ♗xd5+ e6=.

10 ... ♖e8
ECO mentions 10 ... ♘c5 11 ♕c2 a5 12 ♖ad1 ♗d7 with equality; Troianescu – Ciocaltea, Romania 1952. However, White can play 11 ♗xc5 dxc5 12 ♘g5!, as in Seirawan – Pellant, 1983, which finished: 12 ... ♖b8 13 ♕a3 a6 14 ♕xc5 b6 15 ♕b4 h6 16 ♘f3 b5 17 ♘e5 1–0.

	11	♖ad1	♘f8
	12	♘d4	♔h8
	13	♗c1	e5
	14	dxe6	♘xe6
	15	♘xe6	♖xe6
	16	c5	c6
	17	cxd6	♖xd6
	18	♗f4	

18 ♕f7!? – Botvinnik.

	18	...	♖xd1
	19	♖xd1	♕e7

The game Alatortsev – Vinogradov, Odessa 1951, demonstrated that the position is equal.

A2
8 ... ♘a5
White has two main ways to meet the threat to his c-pawn:

A21 9 ♘d2
A22 9 ♕d3 and others

A21

9 ♘d2 c5

Not 9 ... c6? 10 b4 ♘xd5 11 cxd5 ♕xc3 12 ♖b1 ♗xd2 13 ♕xd2 ♘c4 14 ♕c3 when White regains the pawn, with a pair of bishops and good attacking chances – Botvinnik.

After 9 ... c5 White has:

A211 10 ♕c2
A212 10 a3 and others

A211

10 ♕c2

Here Black can choose between:

A2111 10 ... e5
A2112 10 ... a6 and others

A2111

10 ... e5 (85)

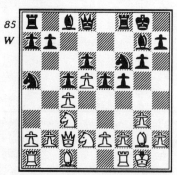

This position is similar to the Yugoslav variation of the King's Indian Defence, with Black having played ... f7 – f5. The present section is devoted to the variation in which White employs a strategy analogous to that used in the King's In-

dian Defence. At present, theory considers that this creates no serious problems for Black.

11 a3

Or:

a) A modest alternative is 11 b3 e4 12 ♗b2 ♕e7 13 ♘d1 ♗d7 14 ♗c3 b6 with a good game for Black; Palmason – Ghitescu, Havana 1966.

b) An interesting possibility is 11 dxe6!? ♗xe6 12 ♖d1 (The pseudo-active 12 ♘d5?! backfires, e.g. 12 ... ♘c6 13 e3 ♗f7 14 a3 ♖c8 15 ♖d1 ♘xd5 16 cxd5 ♘e5 17 a4 c4 with a good game for Black; Grünberg – Lutikov, Lasi 1976. After the passive 12 b3?! d5! 13 cxd5 ♘xd5 14 ♗b2 ♘b4 Black seizes the initiative; Suba – Bjelajac, Pernik 1978) 12 ... ♕e7 (12 ... ♘c6 13 ♘b3! *{Alternatively: 13 a3?! ♘d4 14 ♕b1 f4 15 gxf4 ♗f5 16 e4 ♗g4 17 f3 ♗e6 with good compensation in Ilic – Knezevic, Yugoslavia 1977; or 13 e3 ♕e7 14 ♕a4 ♘e5 [14 ... ♖fd8! 15 ♗xc6 bxc6 16 ♕xc6 d5 with an active game for the pawn – Vukic] 15 f4 ♘d3?! 16 ♘f1 ♘xc1 17 ♖axc1 and White stood better in Vukic – Bjelajac, Novi Sad 1978}* 13 ... ♕e7 *{Browne's suggestion is an improvement: 13 ... ♘b4!? 14 ♕b1 ♕b6! 15 ♗f4 ♖ad8}* 14 ♗f4 *{14 ♕d2!? – Browne}* 14 ... ♖ad8 *{14 ... ♖fd8 15 a3 [15 ♘d5!? ♗xd5 16 cxd5] 15 ... ♗xc4 16 ♗xc6 bxc6 17 ♘a5 ♕e6 and it is not clear which side has the better* *position; Jezek - Mi. Tseitlin, corr 1987-91}* 15 ♗xc6! bxc6 16 ♘a5 ♛c7 17 ♛a4 ♘h5 *{Unsuitable is 17 ... ♘e4?! 18 ♘xe4 fxe4 19 ♘xc6 ♗d7 [19 ... ♖xf4? 20 ♘xd8 ♗d7 21 ♘e6± - Browne]* 20 ♘e7+±}* 18 ♘xc6 ♘xf4 *{No better is 18 ... ♖d7 19 ♘d5! ♗xd5 20 cxd5 ♗xb2 21 ♖ab1± - Browne}* 19 ♘xd8± Browne - Cripe, USA 1987) 13 b3 ♘c6 14 ♗b2 (14 e3 ♘b4 15 ♛b1 d5 16 a3 d4 with an excellent game for Black - Zlochevski) 14 ... ♘d4 15 ♛d3 f4! and Black seized the initiative in Piket - Gurevich, Lucerne 1989.

11	...	b6
12	b4	♘b7
13	♗b2	

Nor does White gain the advantage after 13 ♘b3 ♛e7 14 bxc5 bxc5 15 a4 ♗d7 16 a5 a6 17 ♘a4 ♗xa4 18 ♖xa4 e4; Gheorghiu - Ghitescu, Romania 1961.

13	...	♛e7

Also possible is the aggressive 13 ... g5 14 e3 ♗d7 15 b5 ♛e8 16 ♖ae1 ♛h5= Kraidman - Mi. Tseitlin, Tel Aviv 1992.

14	♖ae1 *(86)*

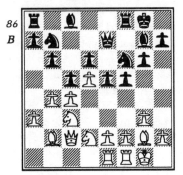

In contrast to the course of the game in the previous section, here Black does not consolidate his position in the centre but tries to organise an immediate counterplay on the queenside.

Now after the redeployment of the queen's knight into the game the chances become equal.

14	...	♘d8
15	e3	♘f7
16	f4=	

Vaganian - Tal, USSR 1970.

A2112

10	...	a6 *(87)*

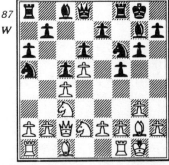

If White plays correctly, he can gain the advantage. The following are examples of incorrect play:

a) 10 ... ♖b8 11 a3 b6 12 b4 ♘b7 13 ♖b1 (13 ♗b2!? - Botvinnik) 13 ... e5 14 dxe6 ♗xe6 15 ♘d5 ♛d7 16 ♗b2± Lundquist - Blom, Marianske Lazne 1961.

b) 10 ... ♗d7 11 b3 ♛e8 12 ♗b2 g5 13 e3 ♛h5 14 ♖ae1 ♖f7 15 f4 h6 16 h3 ♗h8 17 ♘e2 b6 18 e4 with a clear advantage to

White in Neverov – Akopian, Tbilisi 1989.

11   b3

Not 11 ♖b1 ♖b8 12 a4 ♗d7 13 ♕d3 ♘g4 14 ♘f3 ♘b3 15 ♗f4 h6∓ Reilly – Pietsch, Madrid 1960.

11   ...   ♗d7

Alternatives are:

a) 11 ... e5 has been tried: 12 dxe6 ♗xe6 13 ♗b2 ♘c6 14 ♖ad1 ♘d4 15 ♕d3± Averkin – Jansen, Dresden 1969.

b) 11 ... ♖b8 12 ♖b1 (Also good is 12 ♗b2 b5 13 ♖ae1 bxc4 14 bxc4 e5 15 ♘d1! ♕c7 16 ♗c3 ♘b7 17 f4 e4 18 ♘e3 ♗d7 19 g4 and White has seized the initiative both in the centre and on the kingside) 12 ... b5 13 ♗b2 (Less promising is 13 cxb5 axb5 14 b4 cxb4 15 ♖xb4 ♕c7 with possibilities for both sides; Bolbochan – Matulovic, Siegen 1970) 13 ... e5 14 dxe6 ♗xe6 15 ♘d5 ♗xd5 16 cxd5 ♖c8 17 ♗c3 ♖e8 18 ♖fe1 b4 19 ♗b2 with a better game for White in Vukic – Matulovic, Yugoslavia 1978.

12   ♗b2   b5
13   ♖ab1 *(88)*

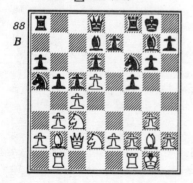

Other rook moves also give White the advantage:

a) 13 ♖fe1 bxc4 14 bxc4 ♖b8 15 ♖ab1± Kluger – Haag, Hungary 1958.

b) 13 ♖ae1 ♖b8 14 ♘d1 bxc4 15 bxc4 e5 16 dxe6 ♗xe6 (Najdorf – Pelikan, Argentina 1973) 17 ♗c3± – Botvinnik.

13   ...   ♖b8
14   e3

Also good is 14 h3!? e5 15 dxe6 ♗xe6 16 ♘d5 ♗xd5 17 cxd5 ♖c8 18 ♗c3± (18 ♖bc1!? – Botvinnik) Bozic – Friedgood, Holland 1968.

14   ...   ♕c7

Other possibilities are no better for Black:

a) 14 ... ♕e8 15 ♘e2 e5 (Lengyel – Johanessen, Beverwijk 1965) 16 dxe6± – Botvinnik.

b) 14 ... bxc4 15 bxc4 ♖b4 16 ♘e2 ♕c7 17 ♗c3 ♖xb1 18 ♖xb1 ♘h5 19 ♗xg7 ♘xg7 20 ♕b2± Gerber – Känel, Switzerland 1988.

15   ♘e2   e5

Declining to make this advance does not enable Black to equalise:

a) 15 ... ♘b7 16 ♘f4 ♘d8 17 h4 and White has a useful space advantage, as confirmed by the two games Averbakh – Spassky, USSR 1958, and Ribli – Horvath, Hungary 1976.

b) 15 ... ♖b6 16 ♗c3 ♘b7 17 ♘f4 and again the initiative is with White: Reshevsky – Grefe, USA Ch 1975.

16   dxe6   ♗xe6

17	♘f4	♗f7
18	♗xf6	♗xf6
19	♘d5	♕d8
20	b4	

White's chances are better; Züger - Lombardy, New York 1987.

A212
10 a3

Two other alternatives have been tried:

a) 10 b3?! ♘xd5 (10 ... a6!? 11 ♗b2 ♖b8 12 e3 b5 13 cxb5?! axb5 with a good position for Black; Sliwa - Ghitescu, Marianske Lazne 1962) 11 ♗xd5+ e6 12 ♗b2 (12 ♘db1 exd5 13 ♕xd5+ ♖f7 14 ♗f4 ♘c6! with powerful counterplay - Taimanov) 12 ... exd5 13 cxd5 f4 14 ♕c2 ♗h3 15 ♖fe1 fxg3 16 hxg3 ♕f6 17 ♘d1 ♕f7 18 ♗xg7 ♕xg7 19 ♕c3 b5 20 ♕xg7 ♔xg7=. White managed to parry Black's attack in the game Serper - Makarov, USSR 1989.

b) 10 ♖b1 e5 11 dxe6 ♗xe6 12 ♘d5 (Alternatively: 12 b4 cxb4 13 ♖xb4 ♖f7 14 ♘d5 ♖c8 15 ♗b2 ♘xd5 16 cxd5 with a balanced position in Rechlis - Mi. Tseitlin, Ostrava 1991; or 12 b3 leads to an unclear game: 12 ... d5 13 ♗a3 ♖c8 14 ♘a4 b6 15 b4 cxb4 16 ♗xb4 dxc4; Pinter - Bjelajac, Pernik 1978) 12 ... ♖b8 (Worse is 12 ... ♖c8 13 b3 ♗xd5 14 cxd5 b5 15 b4 cxb4 16 ♖xb4 ♕d7 17 ♘b3 ♘xb3 18 ♕xb3 ♖fe8 19 ♗f3 a6 20 a4± H. Olafsson - Tseitlin, Belgrade GMA 1988. Even after

the exchange 12 ... ♗xd5 13 cxd5 b5 or 12 ... ♘xd5 13 cxd5 ♗d7 White gains the advantage by 14 b4 - Taimanov) 13 b3 b5 14 ♘f4 ♗f7 15 cxb5 ♖xb5 16 e4 g5 17 ♘d5 ♘xd5 18 exd5 ♕a8 *(89)*

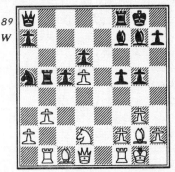

In this position the game Karlsson - Knezevic was agreed drawn, but, according to Taimanov, White could have attempted to gain the advantage by 19 ♕f3.

c) 10 dxc6 bxc6 has been seen twice recently. Kamsky - Lin Ta, Manila izt 1990, continued 11 b3 d5! 12 ♗b2 dxc4 13 b4 ♘d5! 14 ♗xd5 cxd5∞ and in Lobron - Lin Ta from the same event White played the more sedate 11 ♖b1 ♗e6 12 b3 ♕c7 13 ♗b2 ♔h8 14 ♕c1 and secured a slight advantage.

10 ... ♗d7

Others:

a) 10 ... ♘g4 11 ♕c2 ♗d7 12 e3 a6 13 b3 b5 14 ♗b2 bxc4 15 bxc4 ♖b8 16 ♘d1± Miralles - Haik, Budel zt 1987.

b) 10 ... b6 11 ♕c2 ♗d7 12 b3 a6 13 ♗b2 b5 14 ♘d1 ♖b8 15 ♗c3 e5 16 dxe6 ♗xe6 17 ♘e3 ♖e8 18

♖fd1 ♘h6 and Black went on to win in a difficult ending in Vianin - Keserovic, Geneva 1991.

11 ♕c2

The attempt to take the piece by 11 b4? is unsuccessful after 11 ... cxb4 12 axb4 ♘xc4 13 ♘xc4 ♕c7 14 ♕b3 ♖fc8.

11 ... ♕c7
12 b3 a6

After 12 ... e5 13 dxe6 ♗xe6 14 ♗b2 White has the better position.

13 ♗b2 b5
14 ♘d1!

The threat is 15 cxb5 axb5 16 b4 - Botvinnik.

14 ... bxc4
15 bxc4 ♖ab8
16 ♗c3 ♘g4

A probable improvement is 16 ... ♖b7, when after 17 ♖b1 ♖fb8 18 ♖xb7 ♖xb7 19 ♘b2 ♕b8 Black was slightly better in Magerramov - Mi. Tseitlin, Balatonbereny 1989.

17 ♗xg7 ♔xg7
18 ♕c3+ ♔g8
19 ♘b2 ♖b7
20 ♘d3

White has a slight but evident advantage; Botvinnik - Matulovic, Belgrade 1970.

A22

9 ♕d3 (90)

9 ♕d3 is the most troublesome alternative to 9 ♘d2 for Black but others have also been seen:

a) Rarely played is 9 b3!? ♘e4 10 ♘xe4 ♗xa1 11 ♘eg5 c5

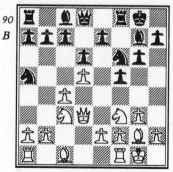

12 ♕e1 ♗g7 13 ♗d2 b6 14 e4 ♘b7 15 exf5 gxf5 16 ♕e2 with compensation; Udovcic - Gufeld, Leningrad 1967.

b) 9 ♕c2!? is an interesting idea since 9 ... ♘xc4 10 ♘b5 a6 11 ♘bd4 ♘b6 12 ♘g5 is clearly better for White. After 9 ... c5 White has 10 dxc6! (10 ♘d2 e5 11 dxe6 ♗xe6 12 ♖d1 ♕e7! 13 b3 ♘c6∞ Piket - Gurevich, Lucerne 1989) 10 ... bxc6 11 ♖d1 ♖b8 (11 ... ♘xc4 12 ♘d4+) 12 ♘d4 ♗d7 13 c5± Agadzarjan - Nadanyan, USSR 1991.

c) 9 ♕a4 c5 has been seen more often recently (Not 9 ... b6 10 ♕c2! ♗d7 {10 ... ♘xc4? 11 ♘b5 a6 12 ♘bd4 b5 13 ♘g5 and *White controls the white squares; Schmidt - Matulovic, Helsinki 1972*} 11 b3 c5 12 ♘d2 {*Not bad is 12 dxc6 ♘xc6 13 ♗b2*} 12 ... a6 13 ♗b2 b5 14 e3 ♖b8 15 ♖ab1± Averbakh - Lutikov, USSR 1959) 10 dxc6 ♘xc6?! (10 ... bxc6!? 11 ♘d4 {*Pinter recommends 11 ♖d1 ♕c7 12 c5!±, but Black can improve with 11 ... c5 12 ♘e5 ♖b8 13 ♘c6 ♘xc6 14 ♗xc6 ♗d7! with good* chances according to Mi. Tseitlin} 11 ... ♗d7 {11 ... c5 12 ♘db5 ♖b8 13 ♘xa7 ♗d7 14 ♘ab5 ♔h8 15 ♗g5 and White has made inroads into Black's position; Larsen – Tisdall, London 1990} 12 ♘xc6 ♘xc6 13 ♗xc6 ♖c8 14 ♗xd7 ♕xd7 15 ♕b3 ♔h8 with an initiative for the sacrificed pawn – Kuzmin) 11 ♖d1 ♕a5 (Alternatively: 11 ... ♘a5? 12 c5 ♗d7 13 ♕a3 ♘e8 14 ♗g5± Keres – Korchnoi, USSR Ch 1952; not much better is 11 ... ♘e4?! 12 ♘xe4 fxe4 13 ♘g5 ♘d4 14 c5 dxc5 15 ♕c4+ e6 {Liptay – Bilek, Hungary 1965} 16 ♗e3 with a white advantage – Botvinnik) 12 ♕b3 (12 ♕xa5 ♘xa5 13 ♘d5 ♘xd5 14 cxd5 ♗d7 15 ♖b1 ♖fc8 and chances are equal; Vladimirov – Gastonyi, Leningrad – Budapest 1961) 12 ... ♕b4 13 ♕xb4! ♘xb4 14 ♘d4 ♘g4 (14 ... ♖b8±) 15 ♖b1 ♘e5 16 ♗g5± Yusupov – Gurevich, Linares 1991.

9 ... c5

Parrying the threat of 10 b4.

The opening of the centre is advantageous for White: 9 ... e5 10 dxe6 ♗xe6 11 b3 ♔h8 (11 ... ♘c6 12 ♗a3, with the idea of 13 ♖ael and advantage to White – Taimanov, or 12 ♗b2 ♘e4 13 ♖ac1 ♖e8 {13 ... ♘b4 14 ♕b1 ♘xc3 15 ♗xc3 ♗xc3 16 ♖xc3 ♕f6 17 ♕a1 ♖ae8 and Black has no problems; Gomez – Zsu. Polgar, San Sebastian 1991} 14 ♖fd1 ♗f7 with a sound position for Black; van Scheeren – Chernin, Am-

sterdam 1980) 12 ♗b2 (12 ♘g5 ♗d7 13 ♗b2 h6 14 ♘f3 ♘e4 15 ♕c2 ♕f6 16 ♘d1 ♕f7 17 ♘d2 ♘c5 18 ♗xg7 ♕xg7 19 ♕c3 ♘d4 20 ♗d5+ ♔h7 21 ♔g2 ♘xe2 22 ♕xg7+ ♔xg7 and the liquidation of pieces gives an ending where Black has good chances; Dorfman – Zsu. Polgar, Debrecen 1990) 12 ... ♗d7 13 ♘d4 ♗g8 14 ♖ad1 ♘e5 15 ♕c2 ♘ac6 16 ♘xc6 bxc6 17 c5± Azmaiparashvili – Akopian, Belgrade 1988.

10 b3

This is one of the fundamental positions of the 7 ... ♘c6 8 d5 ♘a5 variation. White has to choose between immediate action in the centre and a slower build-up aimed at exploiting the misplaced black knight on a5. Black aims for counterplay with ... a6, ... ♖b8, ... ♗d7 and ... b5, similar to the King's Indian Defence.

a) Serious consideration should be given to 10 e4!? (91)

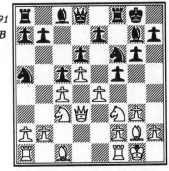

10 ... a6 (10 ... e5!?) 11 ♖e1 ♖b8 12 e5 ♘g4 13 ♗f4 b5 14 cxb5 axb5 15 h3 ♘xe5 16 ♘xe5 dxe5 17 ♗xe5 ♗xe5 18 ♖xe5 b4 19 ♘a4

♕d6 20 ♖ae1 and Black had to face some difficulties in Saeed – Bouaziz, Damascus 1989.

b) On the other hand, weaker is 10 ♘g5 a6 (10 ... h6 11 ♘e6 ♗xe6 12 dxe6 ♘c6 13 e4± Podgaets – Mozes, Ybbs 1968) 11 e4 (Alternatively, 11 ♖b1 ♖b8 12 ♗d2 ♕e8 13 b3 b5 14 a3 ♘g4 15 ♘f3 bxc4 with a black initiative in Benko – Tal, Bled 1959; or 11 ♘e6!? ♗xe6 12 dxe6 ♘c6 and in Euwe's estimation both sides have chances) 11 ... b5 12 cxb5 axb5 13 ♘xb5 fxe4 14 ♘xe4 ♘xe4 15 ♗xe4 ♗a6 16 a4 c4 and Black has counterplay for the pawn; Dely – Gufeld, Debrecen 1970.

c) A further possibility is 10 ♗d2 a6 11 ♖ac1 (11 ♖ab1 b6 *{11 ... ♘e4? 12 ♘xe4 fxe4 13 ♕xe4 ♗f5 14 ♕h4 ♗xb1 15 ♘g5 h6 16 ♘e6 g5 17 ♗xg5 ♕e8 18 ♗d2±* Andric – Ivkov, Yugoslavia 1953}* 12 b3 ♖b8 13 ♘h4?! ♘g4 14 f4 b5 15 h3 ♘h6 16 e4 bxc4 17 bxc4 ♖b4! with an unclear position in Wirtensohn – Känel, Switzerland 1976) 11 ... ♗d7 12 b3 ♖b8 13 e4 b5 14 e5± Bikov – Tolush, USSR 1957.

d) Recently 10 ♖b1 has become quite fashionable, e.g. 10 ... ♘e4 11 ♘g5! ♘xc3 12 bxc3 ♕e8! 13 ♖b5 b6 14 ♘e6! ♗xe6 15 dxe6 ♖b8 16 ♗d5± Sergeev – J. Novikov, USSR 1991.

e) Finally, White can try 10 ♘d2 a6 11 a3 ♘g4 12 e3 ♗d7 13 a4± Petursson – Tisdall, Reykjavik 1990.

10 ... a6 *(92)*

Neither can Black achieve equality after 10 ... ♘e4 11 ♘b2 a6 12 ♖ac1 (12 ♘d2 b5 13 ♘dxe4 fxe4 14 ♗xe4 bxc4 15 bxc4 ♖b8 with unpleasant threats, despite the pawn deficit in Udovcic – Matulovic, Yugoslavia 1960) 12 ... b5 13 ♗a1± – Botvinnik.

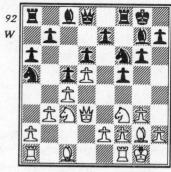

92
W

**11 ♗b2 ♖b8
12 ♘g5**

Others:

a) 12 ♖ae1 b5 13 ♗a1 (13 cxb5 axb5 14 ♘xb5 *{The gain of the pawn is temporary}* 14 ... ♗a6 15 a4 ♕b6) 13 ... bxc4 14 bxc4 ♖b4 (14 ... e5!? – Botvinnik; 14 ... ♘g4!? – Bellin) 15 ♘d2 ♘g4 16 a3 ♖b8 17 ♕c2 ♗d7 18 e3 ♘e5 19 ♘e2 ♕e8 20 ♖b1 ♗a4 21 ♕a2 and, due to the bad position of the knight at a5, White stands better; Nikolac – Bertok, Yugoslavia 1969.

b) 12 ♘d2 ♗d7 13 ♖ab1 (13 a4? ♘e4! 14 ♖a3 *{Inadequate is 14 ♗xe4 fxe4 15 ♕xe4 ♗f5}* 14 ... ♕b6 – Taimanov) 13 ... b5 14 h3 (The advantage cannot be obtained with 14 e3 ♕c7 15 ♗a1

♘g4 16 ♘e2 ♘e5 17 ♕c2 bxc4 18 bxc4 ♖xb1 19 ♖xb1 ♖b8 20 ♖xb8 ♕xb8= Valvo - Ivkov, New York 1987) 14 ... ♕e8 15 ♗a1 g5 16 cxb5 axb5 17 b4 ♘b7 18 a3 c4 19 ♕e3 ♕g6 20 f4 with a better game for White in D. Gurevich - Kontic, Belgrade 1988.

12	...	♘g4
13	♘e6	♗xe6
14	dxe6	b5
15	cxb5	axb5
16	♕c2	

Thanks to the greater activity of the his pieces, White's position is preferable; Petkevich - Arhipkin, Riga 1976.

B

8   ♕c2 *(93)*

93
B

Finally, we consider the possibilities for White if he rejects the idea of immediately advancing d4 - d5.

Before considering the diagram position, let us tackle other possibilities:

a) 8 ♖b1 ♘e4 9 e3 e5 10 ♘e2 ♔h8 11 b4 a6 12 a4 ♕e8 13 b5 ♘a5 14 ♕c2 ♗e6 (Garcia - Haag,

Havana 1962) 15 dxe5 dxe5 16 ♘d2 with chances for both sides - Botvinnik.

b) 8 ♕b3?! (The queen is misplaced here) 8 ... ♘e4 9 ♗e3 ♘xc3 10 bxc3 e5 11 c5+ ♔h8 12 cxd6 cxd6 13 dxe5 dxe5 14 ♗c5 ♖f6 15 ♖fd1 ♕e8∓ Kuzminyh - Vinogradov, Leningrad 1945.

c) 8 h3 a6 9 ♗e3 h6 10 d5 (10 ♖c1 g5 11 d5 ♘e5 12 ♘xe5 dxe5 13 c5 ♔h8 14 ♕b3 ♕e8 15 ♕b4 f4 and Black has good possibilities on the kingside; Golombek - Gufeld, Kecskemet 1968) 10 ... ♘e5 11 ♘xe5 dxe5 12 f4= - Botvinnik.

d) 8 ♗g5 ♘e4 9 ♘xe4 fxe4 10 ♘d2 ♘xd4 (10 ... ♗xd4!?) 11 ♘xe4 ♗f5= Cuellar - Alexander, Amsterdam 1954.

e) 8 b3 ♘e4 (Possible is 8 ... e5!? 9 dxe5 dxe5 10 ♗a3 ♖e8 *{Or, even 10 ... e4 11 ♗xf8 ♕xf8 12 ♘d4 ♘xd4 13 ♕xd4 ♗e6∞ Spacek - Motwani, Luxembourg 1990}* 11 ♖c1?! *{11 e4!?}* 11 ... e4 12 ♘e1 ♗e6 13 ♘c2 ♗g4 14 ♘a4 ♕g5∓ Voruna - Kontic, Vrnjacka Banja 1989) 9 ♗b2 e5 10 dxe5 ♘xc3 11 ♗xc3 dxe5 (11 ... ♕e8! 12 ♕c2 dxe5 13 ♕b2 ♕e7 14 ♖fd1 g5∓ Welsh - Alexander, Cheltenham 1954) 12 ♕d5+ ♔h8 (12 ... ♕xd5? 13 cxd5 ♘d4 14 ♗xd4 exd4 *{Thomas - Seitz, Nice 1931}* 15 ♖ac1± - Botvinnik) 13 ♕xd8 ♖xd8 14 ♘g5 ♖e8 (Worse is 14 ... ♖f8?! 15 ♗xc6 bxc6 16 ♖fd1 e4 17 ♘f7+ ♔g8 18 ♗xg7 ♖xf7 19 ♘e5 ♗e6 20 f4! ♔f8 21 ♖d2 ♔e8 22 ♖ad1 ♖c8 23 ♔f2 with advantage to White in Groszpeter – Videki, Kecskemet 1988) 15 ♖ad1 (15 ♗xc6 bxc6 16 ♖ad1 e4 *{16 ... ♗g8 17 ♕a5 h6 18 ♘h3 f4 19 ♔g2± – Botvinnik or 16 ... f4 17 f3 a5 18 ♖d2 ♔g8∞ Vladimirov – Mi. Tseitlin, Hastings 1991}* 17 ♘f7+ ♔g8 18 ♗xg7 ♔xf7 19 ♗h6 a5 20 ♗f4 ♖a7=) 15 ... ♗f6!= – Taimanov. Worse are the following: 15 ... e4 16 ♗xg7 ♔xg7 17 f3±; and 15 ... h6 16 ♘f7+ ♔g8 17 ♗xc6 bxc6 18 ♘d8± Pomar – Paredes, Barcelona 1977.

8 ... e5

Pointless is 8 ... ♔h8 9 b3 ♗d7 10 ♗b2 a6?! (10 ... e5!?) 11 d5 ♘a5 12 e4 with an obvious advantage for White; Sudoplatov – Vasiukov, USSR 1960.

9 dxe5 dxe5
10 ♖d1 *(94)*

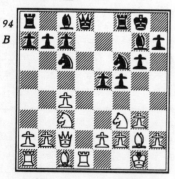

94
B

10 ... ♗d7

A risky attempt to seize the initiative is 10 ... ♕e7?! 11 ♘d5 ♘xd5 12 cxd5 ♘d8 (Considerably worse are 12 ... ♘b4? 13 ♕b3 ♕d6 14 ♘d2 b5 15 a3 ♘a6 16 ♕xb5 with a winning position

for White, as in Toran – de Greiff, Mar del Plata 1955; and 12 ... ♘d4?! 13 ♘xd4 exd4 14 ♗f4!±) 13 ♗e3 ♖e8 (A poor move is 13 ... ♘f7? 14 ♖ac1 e4 15 ♘d4 with a clear advantage; Benkner – Parliazos, Amsterdam 1954) 14 ♖ac1 e4 15 ♘d4 c6 16 dxc6 ♘xc6 17 ♘xc6 bxc6 18 ♗c5! (After 18 ♕xc6 ♗e6 19 b3 a5 and Black has a good game for the lost pawn; Koskinen – Ciocalatea, Prague 1954) 18 ... ♕f7 19 b3 ♗e6 20 e3 a5 and White stood better in Lisenko – Tseitlin, Lvov 1983.

11 ♗e3

A bad mistake is 11 ♘d5? e4 12 ♘xf6+ ♗xf6 13 ♘e1 ♘d4 14 ♕d2 ♗a4 15 b3 ♗xa3!∓ Bertok – Ghitescu, Reggio Emilia 1968/69.

11 ... ♘g4

Also to be considered is 11 ... e4 12 ♘d4 ♘g4 13 ♘xc6 (Action with 13 ♘e6?! backfires after 13 ... ♘xe3 14 fxe3 ♗xe6! 15 ♖xd8 ♖axd8 16 ♘d5 when 16 ... ♘e5 gave Black more than enough compensation for the queen in Peev – Nikolayevsky, Varna 1968) 13 ... ♘xe3 14 ♕c1 ♕e8 15 ♕xe3 ♗xc6 16 ♖d2= – Botvinnik.

12	♗g5	♕e8
13	♘d5	♖c8
14	h3	♘f6
15	♘xf6+	♗xf6
16	♗xf6	♖xf6
17	♕c3	♖f8

With equality; Sofrevsky – Matulovic, Yugoslavia 1966.

4 Avoiding the Main Lines

1	d4	f5
2	g3	♘f6
3	♗g2	g6
4	♘f3	♗g7
5	0-0	0-0
6	c4	(95)

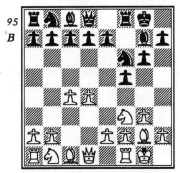

95
B

Both White and Black can avoid the main variations which arise after 6 ... d6 7 ♘c3, and we shall consider their possibilities to do so here.

A 6 ... c6
B 6 ... d6

A

6 ... c6 (96)

A shrewd move order pretending to gain a tempo by 7 ... d5, but in fact the intention after 7 ♘c3 is to equalise immediately with 7 ... ♘e4. It is a pity that this variation is so rarely employed in tournaments because it is very interesting.

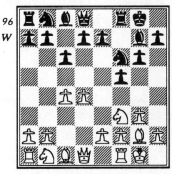

96
W

7 d5

According to Botvinnik, there is nothing to be gained by 7 ♘c3 ♘e4! (7 ... d5 {For 7 ... b6 8 d5, see 7 d5 b6 8 ♘c3} 8 cxd5 cxd5 9 ♘e5 ♗e6 10 ♗f4 ♘c6 {In Botvinnik's opinion it is better to play 10 ... ♘bd7!?} 11 ♘a4 ♘d7 12 ♘xc6 bxc6 13 ♕d2 ♗f7 14 ♖ac1 ♘b6 15 ♘c5 ♘c4 16 ♕c3 ♖e8 17 ♘d3 ♕b6 18 e3 ♖ec8 19 b3± Miles - Bronstein, Hastings 1975/76) 8 ♕c2 (More active, but not better is 8 d5 ♘xc3 9 bxc3 ♘a6 {Risky is 9 ... ♗xc3 10 ♖b1 ♘a6 11 ♗h6 ♗g7 12 ♗xg7 ♔xg7 13 ♕d4+ ♔g8 14 e4 Shamkovich - Kotkov, USSR 1958} 10 e4 d6= - Botvinnik) 8 ... d5

(Possible is 8 ... ♘xc3 9 ♕xc3 *{9 bxc3!? - Taimanov}* 9 ... d6 10 b3 ♘d7 11 ♗b2 e5 12 dxe5 ♘xe5 13 ♘xe5 *{13 ♕d2 f4!? with counterplay - Taimanov}* 13 ... ♗xe5 14 ♕d2 ♕f6 15 ♖b1 ♗e6= Whiteley - Zwaig, Hastings 1976/77) 9 cxd5 cxd5 10 ♘f4 ♘c6 11 ♖fd1 ♗e6 12 ♖ac1 ♖c8 13 ♕b3 ♘a5 14 ♕b4 ♖c4 15 ♕a3 ♘c6= Langeweg - Zwaig, Amsterdam 1977.

The possibility 7 b3 d5 8 ♗b2 is considered in the next chapter.

7 ... ♘a6

An original idea is 7 ... b6?! 8 ♘c3 ♗b7 (8 ... cxd5 9 cxd5 ♗b7 10 e4 fxe4 11 ♘g5 ♘a6 12 ♘gxe4 ♖c8?! *{12 ... ♘xe4!? - Botvinnik}* 13 ♘xf6+ exf6 14 ♗e3 ♘c5 15 b4± Korchnoi - Marszalek, Oberhausen 1961) 9 ♘d4 (9 d6!?±) 9 ... cxd5 10 cxd5 (10 ♘xd5!? ♘e4) 10 ... ♘a6 11 ♘f4 (11 d6!? ♗xg2 12 dxe7 ♕xe7 13 ♔xg2 ♘c5=; 11 ♗g5!? h6 12 ♗xf6 ♗xf6 13 e3 - Tukmakov) 11 ... ♘c5 12 ♕d2 ♘ce4 13 ♘xe4 ♘xe4 14 ♗xe4 fxe4 15 d6 exd6 16 ♗xd6 e3 17 ♕xe3 ♖e8 18 ♕b3+ ♔h8 19 ♖ad1 a5 20 f3 with an edge for White; Rashkovsky - Tukmakov, Sverdlovsk 1987.

If 7 ... ♘e4, then Botvinnik recommends 8 ♘fd2! whilst 7 ... d6 transposes to variation B1 below.

8 ♘c3 ♘c5

Or 8 ... ♕e8 9 ♖b1 e5 10 dxe6 dxe6 (10 ... ♕xe6 11 b3 d6 12

♗a3± - Botvinnik) 11 ♗f4 ♖f7 12 ♘e5 ♖e7 13 ♕d6 with advantage to White; Grigorian - Kundshin, USSR 1960.

9 ♗e3 *(97)*

97
B

9 ... ♘fe4

No better is 9 ... ♕a5 10 ♕d2 ♘a4 11 ♘xa4 ♕xa4 12 b3 ♕a6 13 ♗d4 cxd5 14 cxd5 ♕d6 15 ♖fd1 ♕xd5 16 ♕b4 ♕f7 17 ♘g5 ♕e8 18 ♗xb7± Darga - Cobo, Havana 1964.

10 ♘xe4 ♘xe4
11 ♘d2 cxd5

11 ... ♗xb2 (11 ... ♗d4!? - Botvinnik) leads to great confusion: 12 ♘xe4 fxe4?! (More exact is 12 ... ♗xa1) 13 ♗xe4? (For some reason Taimanov does not consider the possibility 13 ♖b1! with the idea of ♗xe4, ♕d3 h4, ♔g2 with an attack on the kingside as well as superiority in the centre) 13 ... ♗xa1 14 ♕xa1 ♕e8 and now possibly 15 ♗h6 ♖f6 or 15 ♕d4 d6.

12 cxd5 ♘d6
13 ♕b3

According to Botvinnik, the position favours White.

B

6   ...   d6

The standard move, after which White normally chooses between:

B1   7 d5
B2   7 b4
B3   7 ♘c3

A fourth possibility, 7 b3, is considered in the next chapter.

B1

7   d5

Now Black usually responds with:

B11   7 ... c6
B12   7 ... ♘a6
B13   7 ... c5

B11

7   ...   c6 (98)

White's aim with his seventh move is to prevent 7 ... ♘c6. After 7 ... c6 the game need not necessarily transpose into the system 7 ♘c3 c6 8 d5, White can take the game into unusual paths.

8   ♘d4   ♕b6

The main line is 8 ... c5 9 ♘c2 (Alternatively: 9 ♘f3 *{Compared to the variation 7 d5 c5, White has a tempo less}* 9 ... ♘a6 *{9 ... h6!?}* 10 ♘c3 ♘c7 *{According to Taimanov, correct was 10 ... b6}* 11 a4 ♔h8 12 ♖b1 b6 13 b3 a6 14 b4! and White seized the initiative in Kochiev - Tal, USSR 1978; or 9 ♘e6?! *{Tal}* 9 ... ♗xe6 10 dxe6 ♘c6 11 ♘c3 ♕c8 12 ♗g5 ♔h8 13 ♗xf6 ♗xf6 14 ♘d5 ♘d4 and White has insufficient compensation for the pawn - Taimanov) 9 ... b5!? (Suggested by Tal. Worse is 9 ... ♘a6 10 ♘c3 ♖b8 and White has won a tempo compared to 7 d5 c5 8 ♘c3 ♘a6 9 ♘e1 ♖b8 10 ♘c2) 10 cxb5 a6 and Black has good compensation;   the position resembling that of a Benko Gambit.

9   ♘c3

9 ♘b3 is quite playable.

9   ...   ♘e4
10   ♘xe4   ♕xd4

More accurate than 10 ... ♗xd4 11 ♘g5 ♗g7 12 ♖b1± Borisenko - Nikolaevsky, USSR 1966.

11   ♕xd4   ♗xd4 (99)
12   ♖d1

Before this game theory only considered the variation 12 ♘g5 ♗d7 with the idea of ... ♘a6 (Taimanov) or 12 ... c5 (Yudovich) and judged the position as equal. This game does not alter this general assessment.

12	...	c5
13	♘g5	a5
14	♖b1	♘a6
15	a4	♘b4
16	♗d2	♗d7
17	♗xb4	axb4
18	b3	h6

In the game Naumkin – Berkovich, Moscow 1986, Black tried to seize the initiative by 18 ... f4, but after 19 gxf4 ♗f5 20 e3 ♗xb1 21 ♖xb1 ♗c3 22 ♘e6 ♖f6 23 ♗e4 found himself in a difficult position.

In the main line chances are equal.

B12

| 7 | ... | ♘a6 (100) |

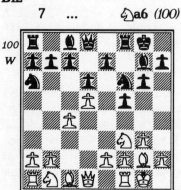

In Taimanov's opinion this plan is the simplest way to equalise, though 7 ... ♘bd7 may also lead to equality.

8 ♘d4

After 8 ♘c3 ♕e8 9 ♖b1 ♘c5 10 ♘d4 a5 11 b3 ♗d7 12 ♘a3 c6 13 ♗xc5 dxc5 14 ♘e6 ♗xe6 15 dxe6 ♕b8 16 ♘a4 ♕e5 Black has no problems; Mohr – Vasiukov, Voskresensk 1990.

8 ... ♘c5

Worthy of consideration is 8 ... ♗d7!? 9 ♘c3 ♕e8 which transposes into a well-known position of the variation 7 ♘c3 ♕e8 8 d5 ♗d7 9 ♘d4.

9 ♘c3 a5

Also possible is the immediate 9 ... e5!?, for example: 10 dxe6 c6 11 b3 ♕e7 12 ♗f4 ♘fe4?! (12 ... ♖d8) 13 ♘xe4 ♘xe4 14 ♖c1 ♖d8 15 ♕d3± Cvetkovic – Ilincic, Yugoslavia 1992.

10	b3	e5!
11	dxe6	c6
12	♗b2	

No advantage is to be had by 12 ♗a3 ♕e7 13 ♕d2 (13 ♖c1 a4 *{Necessary is 13 ... ♗xe6 as the pair of bishops is no advantage}* 14 b4 ♘xe6 15 e3 ♘g4 16 b5 with a White advantage; Eisenstadt – Novikov, Leningrad 1956) 13 ... a4!? (13 ... ♗xe6) 14 ♖fd1!? (14 b4 ♘xe6 15 e3) 14 ... axb3 15 axb3 ♗xe6 with a good position for Black, Aronson – Kuzminyh, Leningrad 1958.

12	...	♕e7
13	e3	♗xe6
14	♘xe6	♕xe6

15 ♘e2 a4

Black has equalised; Novikov – Kuzminyh, Leningrad 1974.

B13

7 ... c5 *(101)*

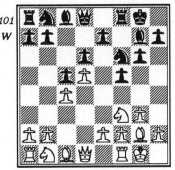

101
W

Black seizes the opportunity to switch into a position reminiscent of the King's Indian Defence, where his advanced f-pawn may prove useful.

8 ♘c3 ♘a6

Illogical is 8 ... ♘bd7?! 9 ♕c2 ♘b6 10 b3 e5 11 dxe6 d5 12 cxd5 ♘fxd5 13 ♘xd5 ♕xd5 14 ♗g5! ♕b6 (14 ... ♕d6 15 e7 ♘xe7 16 ♖ad1 ♕c7 17 ♘d4 – Taimanov) 15 e7 ♖e8 16 ♖ad1 ♗e6 (Minev – Larsen, Halle 1963) and now 17 ♗c1 with a threat of 18 ♘g5 would have given White the advantage – Taimanov.

9 ♖b1

Others:

a) White cannot hope for advantage by opening the centre, e.g. 9 e4 fxe4 10 ♘g5 ♗g4 11 ♕b3 ♕b6 12 ♘gxe4 ♘xe4 13 ♗xe4 ♕xb3 14 axb3 ♘b4= Bouwmeester – Bronstein, Amsterdam 1968,

b) More interesting, however, and worthy of consideration is 9 ♘e1 ♖b8 10 ♘c2 (10 ♕d3?! ♗d7 11 b3 ♘e4 12 ♗b2 *{12 ♗xe4? fxe4 13 ♕c2 ♗h3 14 ♘g2 ♘b4 15 ♕d2 e3 16 fxe3 ♖xf1+ 17 ♔xf1 e6!∓ Rukavina – Larsen, Leningrad izt 1973}* 12 ... ♘b4 *{12 ... b5 13 ♗xe4 with an unclear position – Botvinnik}* 13 ♕e3 ♘xc3 14 ♗xc3 f4= – Larsen) 10 ... ♘c7 11 a4 b6 (Incorrect is 11 ... a6?! 12 a5 ♘g4 13 ♖a3 b5 14 axb6 ♖xb6 15 ♘a4 ♖b8 16 b3 ♗d7 17 f3 ♗xa4 18 ♖xa4 ♘f6 19 ♕d3 ♕d7 20 ♗d2± Vaganian – Matulovic, Vrnjacka Banja 1971) 12 ♖b1 ♘g4 (Interesting is 12 ... e5 13 dxe6 ♗xe6 or 13 b4!? with possibilities for both sides – Taimanov) 13 h3 ♘e5 14 ♘a3 a6 15 ♗d2 (Botvinnik believes that White has the advantage after 15 f4 ♘d7 16 e4! fxe4 17 g4! but Taimanov adds that after 15 ... ♘f7 16 e4 e5 Black has no problems) 15 ... ♗d7 16 f4 ♘f7 17 ♔h2 e5 18 dxe6 ♗xe6= Korchnoi – Tal, Moscow 1968.

c) There is no sense in the move 9 ♘g5?! ♘c7 10 ♕c2 ♕e8 11 a4 h6 12 ♘f3 ♘a6 13 ♘e1 ♘b4 14 ♕d1 g5 with an unclear game; Pavlovic – Timoshchenko, Belgrade 1988.

d) A different strategy would be called for after 9 a4 *(102)*.

This position occurred in the game Ubilava – Oll, USSR 1986, which continued: 9 ... ♘c7?! (The knight could be useful on

102
B

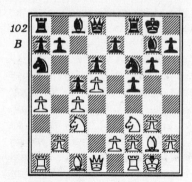

the b4-square in order to counter Ubilava's plan. Therefore the prophylactic 9 ... ♔h8! is interesting) 10 ♕d3 ♖b8 11 ♖a3 ♔h8 12 e4 fxe4 13 ♘xe4 ♘xe4 14 ♕xe4 e6? (14 ... e5!?) 15 ♘g5 ♕f6 16 dxe6 h6 17 ♘f7+ ♔h7 18 ♕f4 with an extra pawn for White.

9 ...   ♖b8

Similar play occurs after 9 ... ♗d7 10 b3 ♘c7 (More accurate is 10 ... ♖b8 11 ♗b2 ♘c7 12 a4 a6 13 a5 ♘ce8 14 ♖a1 ♘g4 15 ♖a3± H. Olafsson – Larsen, Reykjavik 1985) 11 a4 a6 (Botvinnik recommends 11 ... b6!?) 12 b4! cxb4 13 ♖xb4 ♖b8 14 ♕b3 and due to the pressure on the b-file White has a slight advantage; Petrosian – Matulovic, Sarajevo 1972.

10 b3   ♘c7
11 ♗b2   a6

Not 11 ... b5 12 cxb5 ♘xb5 13 ♘xb5 ♖xb5 14 ♘d2 ♗a6 15 ♖e1 ♖b8 with advantage to White; Novikov – Alekseev, USSR 1974.

12 e3

Or 12 ♕c2 b5 13 ♘d2 b4 14 ♘d1 e6 15 dxe6 ♘xe6= Dunkel-

blum – Szabo, Tel Aviv 1958.

12 ...   b5
13 ♘e2   a5!?

Not bad is 13 ... ♗d7 14 ♘c3 ♘a8! (14 ... ♘ce8 15 ♘g5± – Botvinnik or 15 ♘f4± – Keene) 15 ♘f4 (15 ♘g5 ♗h6 leads to an unclear position; Keene – Ree, Paignton 1970) 15 ... ♘e4 16 ♗xg7 ♔xg7 17 ♕c2 bxc4 18 bxc4 ♕a5= Keene – Matulovic, Siegen 1970.

14 ♘f4   a4
15 h4   axb3
16 axb3   bxc4
17 bxc4   ♖b4
18 ♘d2   ♗a6
19 ♕c2=

Keene – Jansa, Nice 1974.

B2

7 b4 *(103)*

103
B

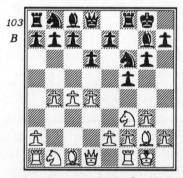

As it is not easy for White to gain the advantage in the main variations, new possibilities are being sought all the time. One of them involves an early advance of the b-pawn. Before dealing with this possibility, let us consider the move 7 ♕c2. This should present no problems for Black, e.g. 7 ... ♘c6 8 d5 ♘e5 9 ♘d4 ♗d7 10 ♖d1 c5 11 dxc6 bxc6 12 ♘c3 ♖e8 (12 ... ♘xc4 13 ♘xc6±) 13 b3 ♘f7 14 ♘f3 ♕a5 with an unclear position; Drasko – Maksimovic, Zagreb 1982.

7 ... e5

The most logical reply, although other possibilities have been tried too:

a) Vladimirov recommends 7 ... a5 8 b5 and only then 8 ... e5.

b) 7 ... ♘e4!? 8 ♗b2 c5 9 b5 ♘d7 (9 ... a6!? 10 a4 axb5 11 axb5 ♖xa1 12 ♗xa1 ♕a5 {12 ... ♘d7!?} 13 ♗b2 {13 ♘bd2 ♘c3} 13 ... ♕b4 14 ♕c2. In this complicated position White's chances are slightly preferable – Bangiev) 10 ♘c3 ♘b6 11 ♕c2!? cxd4 (A mistake would be 11 ... ♘xc4? 12 ♘xe4 ♘xb2 13 ♘ed2; White could gain a slight advantage after 11 ... ♘xc3 12 ♗xc3 ♘xc4 13 dxc5 – Bangiev) 12 ♘xe4 fxe4 13 ♘xd4 e5 14 ♘b3 ♗e6 15 ♗xe4 ♘xc4 (15 ... ♖c8 16 c5!) 16 ♗xb7 ♖b8 17 ♗c6 and White is better; Bangiev - Karpman, Lvov 1988.

8 dxe5 dxe5

Worse is 8 ... ♘fd7?! 9 ♘c3 (9 ♗g5 ♕e8 10 ♘c3 ♘xe5 11 ♘xe5 ♗xe5 12 ♘d5 ♖f7=) 9 ... ♘xe5 (9 ... dxe5 10 ♗g5 ♗f6 {10 ... ♕e8 11 ♘d5±} 11 ♗xf6 ♕xf6 12 e4 with a slight advantage to White) 10 ♘xe5 ♗xe5 (10 ... dxe5 11 ♕xd8 ♖xd8 12 ♗g5 with the idea of ♖ad1± – Vladimirov) 11 ♗b2 and White's lead in

development gives him a slight advantage; Vladimirov - Malaniuk, Tashkent 1987.

9 ♗b2

Clearly bad is 9 ♘xe5? ♘fd7 (And not 9 ... ♘g4?! 10 ♕xd8 ♖xd8 11 ♘xg4 fxg4 12 ♗g5 ♖e8 13 ♘d2 ♗xa1 14 ♖xa1 with good compensation - Vladimirov) 10 ♕d5+ ♔h8 11 ♗f4 c6 with a win of material.

9 ... e4
10 ♘d4 ♘a6

Also possible is 10 ... ♕e7 11 ♕b3 ♔h8 12 ♘a3 ♘c6 13 ♘ac2 ♘e5 14 ♖ad1 ♗d7 15 b5 with a slight advantage to White; Bangiev - Tokariev, Simferopol 1988.

11 b5

11 ♕b3 c5! - Bangiev.

11	...	♘c5
12	♘a3	♕e7
13	♘ac2	♗d7
14	♗a3	♖ad8
15	♕c1	♖fe8
16	♖d1	

This position arose in Bangiev - Legky, Simferopol 1988. In Bangiev's opinion, White's chances are somewhat better.

B3

7 ♘c3 (104)

In this final section we shall deal with variations where Black rejects the classical possibilities 7 ... ♕e8, 7 ... c6 and 7 ... ♘c6 and chooses something else.

To begin with, let us consider two very rarely played

possibilities:

a) 7 ... ♔h8 8 ♗g5!? ♕e8 9 ♕d2 e5 10 dxe5 dxe5 11 e4 fxe4 12 ♘h4 ♘a6?! (12 ... ♘c6!?) 13 ♘xe4 ♘xe4 14 ♗xe4 ♘c5 15 ♗g2 ♕f7 16 ♖ae1 ♖e8 17 b3 ♘e6 18 ♗h6 ♘d4 19 ♗xg7+ ♔xg7 20 f4 c5 21 fxe4 and Black has lost a pawn; Suba – Erenska, Palma de Mallorca 1989.

b) 7 ... ♗d7 8 ♗g5!? ♘c6 9 d5 ♘a5 10 ♕d3 c5 11 dxc6 ♘xc6 12 ♖ad1 ♕a5 13 ♗xf6 ♗xf6 14 ♘d5 ♗xb2 15 ♖b1 ♗g7 16 ♖xb7 ♖fd8 17 ♘g5 ♖ac8 18 ♘f4 ♗f6 19 ♗d5 with a winning position for White; Murshed – Hjorth, Copenhagen 1982.

Slightly less rare, although still highly unusual are:

B31 7 ... a5
B32 7 ... e6

B31

    7   ...   a5
    8   ♗g5!?

There is little sense in 8 ♕b3 ♘c6 9 d5 ♘b4 10 ♘g5 ♘a6 11 ♗e3 (11 ♕c2= – Botvinnik) 11 ... ♘g4 12 ♗d2 ♘c5 13 ♕c2 h6 with

a good game for Black; Cafure – Pelikan, Argentina 1965.

    8   ...   ♘bd7

Or 8 ... ♘c6 9 d5 ♘e5 10 ♘xe5 dxe5 11 ♕d2 e4 12 ♖ad1 (12 ♗h6 ♗xh6 13 ♕xh6 e6 14 ♖fd1 ♕e7 15 ♕e3 ♘g4= Rossetto – Pelikan, Mar del Plata 1966) 12 ... ♘g4 13 f3 ♘e5 14 b3 and, as in the main variation, White gains the advantage; Smyslov – Pelikan, Mar del Plata 1966.

9	♕d2	c6
10	♖ad1	♕c7
11	♗h6	♘b6
12	♗xg7	♔xg7
13	b3	a4
14	♖fe1	axb3
15	axb3	♘e4
16	♕c2	

White's position is more comfortable; Guimard – Pelikan, Mar del Plata 1966.

B32

    7   ...   e6 *(105)*

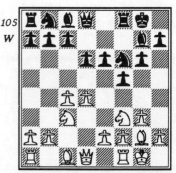

7 ... e6 was played by Botvinnik with Black against Tal in 1960. The move is directed against the advance d4 – d5, on which Black could reply ... e6 –

e5. Regrettably, this modest move is too passive and, as recent practice has shown, the advance d4 - d5 is, in fact, ineffective.

8 ♕c2

8 b3 is passive and allows Black some chances to equalise, for example:

a) 8 ... ♘c6 9 ♗b2 (9 ♘a3 ♘e4 10 ♕d3 ♘xc3 11 ♕xc3 ♗d7 12 ♖ad1 and White has a space advantage; Ionov - Zysk, Dortmund 1992) 9 ... e5 (Sharper is 9 ... ♕e7 10 d5 ♘e4! 11 ♕c1 ♘xc3 12 ♗xc3 ♘d8 13 ♗xg7 ♕xg7 14 e4 e5± Dautov - Zysk, Dortmund 1992) 10 dxe5 dxe5 11 ♕xd8 ♖xd8 12 ♖fd1 ♖xd1+ 13 ♖xd1 e4 14 ♘e1 ♗e6= Ivkov - Menvielle, Havana 1966.

b) If instead 8 ... ♕e8 9 ♘a3 h6 10 ♕c2 g5 11 ♖ad1 ♘a6 12 ♖fe1 ♕h5 13 b4 ♘c7 with chances for both sides; Summermatter - Gavrikov, Berne 1991.

8 ... ♘c6

Less good is 8 ... ♕e7 9 e4 ♘xe4 10 ♘xe4 fxe4 11 ♕xe4 ♘c6 12 ♗g5 ♕f7 13 ♖ad1 ♗d7 14 ♕h4 ♖ae8 15 ♗h6 ♗xh6 16 ♕xh6 ♕g7 17 ♕d2 with advantage to White; Gligoric - Stoltz, Helsinki 1952.

9 ♖d1

White has other possibilities:

a) 9 d5?! ♘b4 10 ♕b3 ♘a6 11 ♗e3 (11 dxe6 ♘c5 12 ♕c2 ♗xe6 13 b3 ♘fe4 14 ♗b2 ♘xc3 15 ♗xc3 ♗xc3 16 ♕xc3 ♘e4 17 ♕c2 ♕e7 18 ♘d2 d5= Cvitan - Bjelajac, Belgrade 1988) 11 ... ♘g4= -

Tal.

b) 9 b3 ♕e7 10 ♗b2 e5 11 dxe5 dxe5 12 ♘d5 ♕d6 13 ♖fd1 ♘xd5 14 cxd5 ♘b4 15 ♕c4± Johansson - Menville, Havana 1966.

9 ... ♕e7 *(106)*

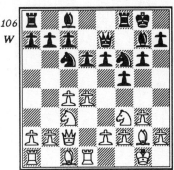

10 ♖b1

Others:

a) Not good is 10 d5? ♘e5 11 dxe6 ♘xc4 12 ♘b5 a6 13 ♕xc4 axb5 14 ♕xb5 ♘e4 15 ♘d4 c6 16 ♕b3 d5∓ Altshul - Vinogradov, Leningrad 1940.

b) Nothing more than equality is gained by 10 e4 fxe4 11 ♘xe4 e5 12 dxe5 ♘xe4 13 ♕xe4 dxe5= Podgaets - Tal, USSR 1969.

c) Botvinnik recommends 10 a3!?.

10 ... a5

Other possible moves are worse:

a) 10 ... e5? 11 dxe5 dxe5 12 ♘d5 ♘xd5 13 cxd5 ♘d8 14 b4 or 14 ♗e3. These are Euwe's and Filip's recommendations and both give White the advantage.

b) 10 ... ♗d7? 11 b4 ♖ae8 12 b5 ♘d8 13 ♗a3± - Botvinnik.

11	a3	♞d8
12	e4	fxe4

12 ... e5 13 ♗g5 c6 14 c5! is not helpful – Tal.

13	♞xe4	♞xe4
14	♛xe4	♞f7

Or 14 ... e5 15 dxe5 ♗f5 16 ♛d5+ ♛f7 17 ♖a1 dxe5 18 ♞g5± – Euwe.

15	♗h3	♛f6
16	♗d2	d5

Botvinnik suggests 16 ... e5!?.

17	♛e2	dxc4
18	♗f4	♞d6
19	♞g5	

White has a slight advantage; Tal – Botvinnik, World Ch 1960.

5 Systems with an early b3

1	d4	f5
2	g3	♘f6
3	♗g2	g6
4	♘f3	♗g7
5	0-0	0-0
6	b3 *(107)*	

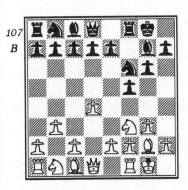

The development of the bishop to the b2-square has always been a popular counter to the Leningrad variation. In the lines considered in this section, move order is important, as identical positions frequently arise from different sequences.

The material has been arranged as follows:

A 6 ... d6
B 6 ... ♘e4
C 6 ... c6 and others

A

6	...	d6

Normally White now fianchettoes immediately but we also consider 7 c4 (which often arises via 6 c4 d6 7 b3).

A1 7 ♗b2
A2 7 c4

A1

7	♗b2	

Obviously Black has a wide choice here too:

A11 7 ... c6
A12 7 ... ♕e8 and others

A11

7	...	c6 *(108)*

Here White usually chooses between:

A111 8 c4
A112 8 ♘bd2

A111

8   **c4**

Now Black has:

A1111 8 ... ♕e8
A1112 8 ... ♘a6
A1113 8 ... a5

Simen Agdestein has successfully tried 8 ... ♕c7 here: 9 ♘bd2 ♘g4!? (Not 9 ... ♖e8? 10 d5!) 10 e4 (According to Ribli White should play 10 h3 ♘h6 11 e4±) 10 ... f4 11 ♕c2 (Again 11 h3 is recommended by Ribli) 11 ... fxg3 12 hxg3 e5 13 dxe5 dxe5 14 c5 b5 15 a4 a5∞ 16 b4 axb4 17 axb5 ♖xa1 18 ♖xa1 cxb5 19 ♕b3+ ♔h8 20 ♕xb4 ♗d7∓ 21 ♖c1 ♘c6 22 ♕b3 h6 23 ♘b1 b4 24 ♘bd2 g5 25 ♘c4 ♗e6 26 ♕d3 b3 27 ♘d6 ♘b4 28 ♕e2 ♘a2! 29 ♖c4 ♘xf2 30 ♘xe5 ♔h7! 31 ♕h5 ♗xe5 32 ♕xe5 ♘g4 33 ♗h3 ♗xc4 34 ♗xg4 ♕xc5+ 0-1 Stohl – Agdestein, Manila izt 1990.

A1111

8   **...**   **♕e8** *(109)*

Black's last move is popular in other lines as well (compare with Chapter one, for example). This variation is very common in modern practice.

9   ♘c3   ♘a6

Illogical is 9 ... h6 10 ♖e1 e5 11 e4 fxe4 12 dxe5 dxe5 13 ♘xe4 ♘xe4 14 ♖xe4 ♗f5 15 ♖e3 ♗g4, as in Damljanovic – Zsu. Polgar,

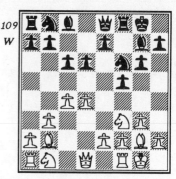

Wijk aan Zee B 1990.

10   **d5**

Alternatives are:

a) 10 ♕c2 ♘b4? (10 ... h6!?) 11 ♕d2 a5 12 a3 ♘a6 13 b4 with a great positional superiority for White; Zaitseva – Titorenko, Moscow 1984.

b) 10 a3 leads to an unclear position: 10 ... e5 11 e3 e4 12 ♘d2 ♗e6 13 b4 ♘c7 14 ♖e1 g5 15 ♘f1 ♗f7 16 a4 ♖d8 17 ♕c2 ♘h5 18 ♖ab1 ♖f7 19 a5 d5 20 b5 f4, as in Adonov – Ermenkov, St John 1988, when 21 a6 is possible.

10   **...**   **♗d7**

After 10 ... c5 11 ♕d2 h6 12 ♖ae1 ♕f7 13 e4 fxe4 14 ♘xe4 White stands better; Todorcevic – Arencibia, Leon 1991.

11   **♖c1**

White may also try:

a) 11 ♘d4 also serves well in the fight for the advantage: 11 ... ♘c5 (11 ... ♘c7 12 b4±) 12 ♖b1 ♖c8 13 b4 ♘ce4 (13 ... ♘a6?! 14 ♘c2?! {More exact was 14 dxc6!? bxc6 15 b5 cxb5 16 cxb5 ♘c5 17 ♘c6± - Titov} 14 ... ♘c7 15 ♕d2 ♕f7 16 f4?! {16 a4} 16 ... cxd5 17 cxd5 ♘a8 18 e4 fxe4 19

♘xe4 ♘xe4 20 ♗xe4 ♘b6 21 ♘e3 ♘a4!∓ Titov – Basin, Belgorod 1989) 14 ♘xe4 ♘xe4 (14 ... fxe4 15 ♘e6 ♗xe6 16 dxe6 with the idea of ♕d4± – Titov) 15 ♘e6! ♗xe6 16 ♗xg7 ♔xg7 17 dxe6 ♘f6 18 ♕d4 b6 19 c5 ♕d8 20 ♖fd1 bxc5 21 bxc5 d5 22 ♖b7 with advantage to White; Reshevsky – Vasiukov, Palma de Mallorca 1989.

b) 11 ♕c2 h6 12 ♖ad1 ♖ac8 13 ♕b1 g5 14 ♘d4 ♘g4 15 h3 ♘e5 16 f4 gxf4 17 gxf4 ♘g6 with an unclear position; Sandic – Savchenko, Belgrade 1988.

c) 11 ♕d2 ♖c8 12 ♖ad1 cxd5 13 ♘xd5 ♘xd5 14 ♗xg7 ♘e3 15 fxe3 ♔xg7 16 e4 ♘c5 and Black has a good game; Danielian – Rublevsky, Jurmala 1991.

d) 11 ♖b1 ♖c8 12 ♘d4 ♘c7 13 e3 c5 14 ♘c2 b5∞ Wl. Schmidt – Vyzmanavin, Copenhagen 1991.

11 ... h6

Also perfectly playable are 11 ... ♖d8 12 ♗a3 ♘c5 13 ♘d2 a5 14 b4 axb4 15 ♗xb4 e5∞, as in Lobron – Yusupov, Hamburg SKA 1991; 11 ... ♘c7 12 ♕d2 h6 13 ♘e1 ♕f7 14 ♘d3 ♖fd8 15 ♖fd1± Portisch – Malaniuk, Moscow GMA 1990; and 11 ... ♖c8!? 12 ♘d4 ♕f7 13 ♗a3 g5 14 e3 f4 15 exf4 gxf4 16 ♘ce2 ♘h5 17 ♗f3 ♗e5 18 ♗xh5 ♕xh5 19 ♘xf4 ♕xd1 20 ♖fxd1 ♗xf4 21 gxf4 ♖xf4 22 ♖d3 ♔f7 23 ♖e1 ♖g8± Moldobaiev – Kramnik, Belgorod 1989.

12 e3

More active is 12 ♘d4!? ♖c8

13 ♕d2 ♘c5 (13 ... ♕f7 14 e4±) 14 b4 ♘ce4 15 ♘xe4 ♘xe4 16 ♗xe4 fxe4 17 ♘e6 ♗xb2 18 ♕xb2 ♗xe6 19 dxe6 ♖f6 20 ♕d4 ♖xe6 21 ♕xa7± – Malaniuk.

12	**...**	**♖c8**
13	**♘d4**	**♕f7**
14	**♗a3**	**cxd5**
15	**♘xd5**	**♘e4**
16	**f3**	**♘ec5** (110)

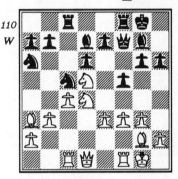

17 ♘b5

A suitable move for seizing the initiative is 17 e4!? – Malaniuk.

17	**...**	**♗xb5**
18	**cxb5**	**♘c7**
19	**♘xc7**	**♖xc7**
20	**♗xc5**	**dxc5**
21	**f4**	

A draw was agreed here in Kasparov – Malaniuk, Moscow 1988.

A1112

8	**... ♘a6**
9	**♘c3** (111)

This variation is somewhat similar to the system 7 ... c6 considered in Chapter 2. There is limited material on this variation from recent practice.

The alternative knight development 9 ♘bd2, is considered in variation A11211, whilst 9 d5 c5 10 ♘c3 h6 11 ♖b1 g5 12 e3 ♗d7 was unclear in Wl. Schmidt - Malaniuk, Copenhagen 1991.

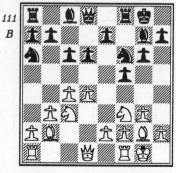

111
B

| 9 | ... | ♘c7 |

Many other moves are possible here:

a) Worse is 9 ... ♗d7 10 ♖e1 b5 (10 ... ♕a5 11 e4 fxe4 12 ♘xe4 ♖ae8 13 ♘eg5 ♘c7 14 ♕d2 ♕xd2 15 ♘xd2 h6 16 ♘gf3 g5 *(Panno - Bronstein, Amsterdam 1956)* 17 ♖e2± - Botvinnik) 11 cxb5 cxb5 12 ♘d2 ♖b8 13 e4±.

b) 9 ... ♔h8 10 ♕d2 ♘c7 11 d5 cxd5 (11 ... e5!? - Botvinnik) 12 ♘xd5 ♘cxd5 13 cxd5 ♗d7 14 ♖ac1 ♕b6 15 ♗d4 ♕a6 16 ♖c7± Csom - Ciocaltea, Ljubljana 1973.

c) 9 ... ♖b8 10 d5 (10 a4 ♘b4 11 e3 a5 12 ♕e2 h6 13 ♖ad1 g5 14 d5 c5 15 ♘e1 f4 16 exf4 gxf4 17 ♘d3 ♗g4 with some complications; van Doeland - Bhend, Lenk 1991) 10 ... e5 (10 ... ♗d7 11 ♖b1 c5 12 ♕d2 ♘c7 13 a4 b6 14 e4 fxe4 15 ♘g5 a6 16 ♘cxe4 b5 17 axb5 axb5 18 ♗c3 h6 19 ♘xf6+

exf6 20 ♘f3 with a more advantageous position for White; Schmidt - Espig, Dresden 1985) 11 dxe6 ♗xe6 12 ♘g5 ♗c8 13 ♕d2 h6 14 ♘f3 ♘c5 15 ♖ad1± Birbrager - Lutikov, USSR 1966.

d) The transferrence of the knight to the wing is interesting: 9 ... ♘h5!? 10 d5 e5 11 dxe6 ♗xe6 12 ♕d2 ♕e7 13 ♖ad1 ♖ad8 14 ♘d4 ♗c8 15 a3 ♘c5 16 b4 ♘e4 17 ♘xe4 fxe4 18 f4 exf3 19 exf3 ♕f7= Razuvaev - Lutikov, USSR 1976.

e) 9 ... ♘e4 10 ♕c1 e5 11 dxe5 dxe5 12 ♘xe4 fxe4 13 ♘g5 ♘h6 14 h4 ♗f5 15 ♗xe5 ♕e7 16 ♗b2 ♖fe8 17 ♕e3 and White is much better; Csom - Maenner, Lenk 1991.

f) 9 ... ♘c7 10 ♖c1 (10 ♖e1 e5 11 e4 and the slight lack of harmony between the ♘a6 and ♕c7 gives White the better game - Taimanov) 10 ... e5 11 ♘b5?! (With this move White obtains no more than equality) 11 ... ♕d8 12 dxe5 dxe5 13 ♘d6 e4 14 ♘g5 ♕e7 15 h4 h6 16 ♘xc8 ♖axc8 17 ♘h3 ♘h5 with an equal game; van Schlechtinga - van der Weide, Wijk aan Zee 1973.

g) 9 ... ♕e8 transposes to variation A1111.

| 10 | ♕c2 |

Here 10 ♖e1, with the intention of opening the centre by e2 - e4, as Botvinnik recommends, does not seem bad.

| 10 | ... | ♖b8 |

Black has no problems either

after:

a) 10 ... ♘h5 11 d5 e5 12 dxe6 ♗xe6 13 e3 ♕e7 14 ♘a3 ♖ad8 15 ♖ad1 a6 16 ♖d2 c5 17 ♖fd1 b5 with equal chances; Pelc – Lutikov, USSR 1961.

b) 10 ... ♔h8 11 ♖ad1 ♗d7 12 e3 ♕e8 13 ♖fe1 ♖d8 14 ♖d2 ♘h5 15 d5 ♕f7 and again Black has equal chances; Brzozka – Bronstein, Miskolc 1963.

	11	a4	a5
11	a4	a5
12	♖ad1	♘a6
13	d5	♕b6
14	♘d4	♗d7
15	e3	♘c5
16	♖b1	♖be8

Black has a sound game; Smyslov – Lutikov, Tbilisi 1976.

A1113

	8	...	a5
	9	♘c3	*(112)*

112
B

This rather solid system has not been examined recently, either in theory or in practice. The alternative, 9 ♘d2, is considered in variation A1122.

	9	...	♘a6

Alternatively:

a) 9 ... ♘e4 has a worse reputation than the text move: 10 ♖c1 d5 11 cxd5 cxd5 12 ♘e5 ♗e6 13 ♘a4 ♘d7 14 f3 ♘ef6 15 ♕d2± Portisch – Zwaig, Raach 1969.

b) 9 ... ♕c7 10 d5 ♘a6 11 ♘d4 ♗d7 (11 ... e5 12 dxe6 ♘c5 13 ♖c1 ♘xe6?! *{13 ... ♗xe6}* 14 ♘xe6 ♗xe6 15 ♕d2 ♖fd8 16 ♖fd1 ♕f7 17 ♘a4± Csom – Casper, Berlin 1979) 12 ♖b1 (Approximately equivalent to the text is 12 e4 fxe4 13 ♘xe4 ♘xe4 14 ♗xe4 ♘c5 15 ♗g2 a4 with an unclear position; Baumbach – Ghitescu, Zinnowitz 1964) 12 ... ♘c5 13 ♕c2 f4 14 ♖bd1 fxg3 15 hxg3 ♕b6 16 ♗a1 ♖ac8 17 e3 a4= Averkin – Knezevic, Dubna 1976.

10 ♕c2

This is probably a better choice than:

a) Unfavourable is 10 a3?! ♗d7 (10 ... ♕c7 11 ♖c1 e5 12 ♘b5 ♕e7 13 dxe5 dxe5 14 ♗xe5 ♖d8 15 ♕c2 f4 16 ♘bd4 fxg3 17 hxg3 ♘c5 18 ♖cd1 ♗g4 with active play for Black; Tosic – Berkovich, Pula 1990) 11 d5 ♘e4 12 ♘d4 ♘xc3 13 ♗xc3 ♕b6 and the initiative is with Black, Zivkovic – Sahovic, Yugoslavia 1974.

b) 10 ♖c1 ♗d7 11 ♕c2 (11 d5?! ♘c5 12 ♕c2 ♕b6 13 ♘d2 a4 14 bxa4 ♕a6 15 ♕b1 ♘xa4 with a slight advantage to Black; Jakobsen – Zwaig, Raach 1969 or 11 ♕d2 ♖e8 12 ♖fd1 ♕c7 13 e4 ♖ad8= Mednis – Ftacnik, Amsterdam 1988) 11 ... ♕c7 12 ♖fd1 e5 13 c5 e4 14 cxd6 ♕xd6 15 ♘e5 ♘b4 16 ♕d2 ♗e6 with a good game for Black; Kozlov - Berkovich, Moscow 1986.

c) 10 ♕d2?! ♗d7 11 ♖fe1 b5 12 cxb5 cxb5 13 ♖ac1 (Fauland - Buecker, Budapest 1988) 13 ... ♖b8 and Black has a good position.

10 ... ♕c7 *(113)*

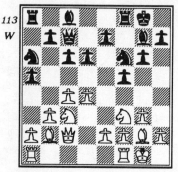

Black paves the way for equalising the chances in the centre. This is more logical than 10 ... ♘b4?! 11 ♕b1 with the idea of a2 - a3± - Botvinnik.

11 ♖ad1 e5

There are some other possible moves:

a) 11 ... ♗d7 12 a3 ♖ae8 13 d5 e5 14 dxe6 ♗xe6 15 ♘d4 ♗c8= Stoltz - Kostic, Bled 1950.

b) 11 ... ♔h8 12 d5 ♘c5 13 ♘d4 ♗d7 14 e3 ♖ac8 15 ♕b1 ♕b6= Kovacs - Knaak, Polanica Zdroj 1975.

12 c5 e4

Clearly this is better than:

a) 12 ... exd4 13 cxd6 ♕xd6 14 ♘xd4± - Botvinnik.

b) 12 ... dxc5 13 dxe5 ♘g4 14 ♘a4 with a better position for White; Pachman - Gerusel, Mannheim 1975.

13	cxd6	♕xd6
14	♘e5	♘b4
15	♕b1	♗e6

According to Botvinnik, the game is equal.

A112

8 ♘bd2 *(114)*

After this move, as after 8 c4, Black has a choice:

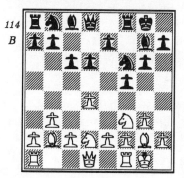

A11211 8 ... ♘a6
A11222 8 ... a5
A11223 8 ... ♔h8 and others

Now White has:

A11211 9 c4
A11212 9 ♘e1 and others

A11211

9 c4 *(115)*

White plays c4 having already stationed the knight on the d2-square. In spite of the somewhat passive position of the pieces White has surprisingly good prospects of emerging from the opening with an advantage.

9 ... ♕e8

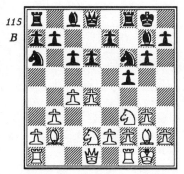

This is the most common reply, although not necessarily the best. Instead:

a) 9 ... e5?! has been tried: 10 dxe5 ♘d7 11 ♗a3 ♘xe5 12 ♘xe5!? (12 ♖b1 ♘xf3+?! *{It would have been better to avoid the exchange by 12 ... ♘f7!?}* 13 ♗xf3 ♘c5 14 b4±) 12 ... ♕xe5 13 ♘f3 ♕xa1 14 ♕xa1 ♘c5 15 ♖d1 ♕f6 16 ♕c1 ♕e7 17 ♗b2 ♘e4 18 ♕e3 and Black has difficulties in defending his king; Shirov - Bareev, Lvov zt 1990.

b) 9 ... ♗d7 10 ♖e1 ♔h8 11 a3 d5 12 ♕c2 ♗e6 13 ♘e5 ♖c8 14 b4 (14 c5!?) 14 ... ♘d7 15 ♘d3 ♕b6± Mikhalchishin - Vasiukov, USSR 1982.

c) 9 ... ♔h8 with the idea of ... ♗e6 - g8 - Mikhalchishin.

d) 9 ... ♕c7!? 10 a3 ♗d7 11 b4 (11 ♖c1 ♖ae8 12 b4 ♕b8 13 ♕b3 ♔h8 14 a4± Csom - Espig, Kecskemet 1972) 11 ... ♖ae8 12 c5 ♕b8 13 ♘c4 ♗e6 14 ♖c1 ♔h8 15 e3 ♖d8 16 ♕e2 ♗d5 17 ♘g5 ♗xg2 18 ♔xg2 ♘c7 19 f3 ♕c8 20 ♘h3= Balashov - Bareev, Moscow 1989.

10 ♕c2

Here attention should also be paid to other possibilities:

a) 10 ♖e1 ♘c7 (10 ... d5?! 11 ♘e5 ♗e6 12 f3 with a positional advantage to White; Stohl - Kontic, Vrjncka Banja 1989) 11 e3 b5!? 12 ♕e2 bxc4 13 bxc4 ♖b8 14 ♘c3 ♗a6 with possibilities for both sides; Ilic - Georgiev, Wijk aan Zee 1984.

b) 10 e3!? ♘c7 11 ♕e2 h6 12 e4 fxe4 13 ♘xe4 ♘xe4 14 ♕xe4 ♗f5 15 ♕e3 and White has occupied the e-file; Akhmilovskaya - Stepanovaya, Sochi 1987.

c) 10 ♖c1 h6 11 ♕c2 g5 12 ♖fe1 ♕h5 13 a3 ♘c7 14 d5? cxd5 15 c5 ♘ce8 and White did not obtain adequate compensation for the sacrificed pawn; Okkanen - J. Polgar, Columbia 1989.

10 ...   ♘c7 *(116)*

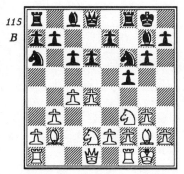

Instead of this, 10 ... h6!? can be recommended, when Smejkal - Topalov, Altensteig 1990, continued 11 a3 g5 12 e3 ♕h5 13 ♖fe1 ♖f7 14 ♘f1 ♗d7 15 ♖e2 ♖af8 with good attacking chances for Black. White does better to prepare the e4-break with 11 ♖ae1 g5 12 e4 fxe4 13 ♘xe4± Dreev – Motwani, Berlin 1991.

11	♖ae1	♗d7
12	e4	fxe4
13	♘xe4	♗f5
14	♘xf6+	♗xf6
15	♕d2	♕d7
16	♖e3	♖ae8
17	♖fe1	♖f7
18	d5	c5
19	♘h4	

White's pressure on the e-file is obvious; Pigusov – Odeev, Minsk 1986.

A11212

| 9 | ♘e1 *(117)* |

117
B

White again plays ♘b1 – d2 temporarily rejecting c2 – c4. The lines presented below are very complicated. Before the manoeuvre with the knight it is also possible to play 9 e3 ♕e8 and only now 10 ♘e1. For example: 10 ... g5 (Possible is 10 ... e5!? 11 ♘c4 exd4 12 exd4 *{12 ♘xd6? ♕e6 13 ♘xc8 dxe3! with the idea of 14 ... e2. Or 13 ♕xd4 ♘e8 and Black wins – Ftacnik}* 12 ... ♕d8 13 ♘d3 with equal

chances) 11 ♘d3 ♕g6 (11 ... ♕h5 12 ♕xh5 ♘xh5 13 f4!? or 12 f3 and in both cases White has a slight advantage – Ftacnik) 12 ♕e2 ♔h8?! (Ftacnik suggests 12 ... ♗d7!? with the idea of ... ♖d8) 13 ♖ae1?! (White does better to play 13 c4!? with the idea of b4 – b5) 13 ... ♗d7 with an unclear position.

| 9 | ... | ♗e6 |

Black has two good alternatives:

a) Consideration should be given to the possibility of 9 ... c5!? 10 d5 ♘c7 11 c4 a6 12 ♘d3 b5 13 e4 bxc4 14 bxc4 fxe4 15 ♘xe4 ♖b8 16 ♘xf6+ ♗xf6 17 ♗xf6 *(118)*

118
B

17 ... ♖xf6?! (Preferable was the elimination of the weakness on the e-file with 17 ... exf6!?=) 18 ♖e1 with a positional advantage to White; Torre – Meulders, Brussels 1987.

b) Also possible is 9 ... ♘c7 10 ♘d3 ♕e8 11 e4?! (Slightly too early; 11 c4!?) 11 ... fxe4 12 ♘xe4 ♘xe4 13 ♗xe4 ♘e6= Espig – Chekhov, Berlin 1988.

| 10 | ♘d3 | ♕b6!? |

11	c4	♖ad8
12	♕c2	♗f7
13	♖ad1	♖fe8
14	♕c1	♖d7
15	♕a1	♕d8
16	♘f3	♘e4

With an unclear position and possibilities for both sides; Vegh - Vasiukov, Budapest 1986.

A1122

8 ... a5 (119)

119
W

Similar to 8 ... ♘a6, this is another solid reply to the plan chosen by White. This variation makes frequent appearances in practical play.

9 c4

White has four other possibilities here:

a) Seldom seen is 9 e3 ♘a6 10 ♘e1 ♗d7 11 ♕e2 ♔h8 12 c4 ♘c7 13 ♘d3 a4 14 ♖fe1 ♕e8 15 f3 b5 16 f4 bxc4 17 bxc4 ♕f7± Bogdanovski - Kontic, Belgrade 1988.

b) 9 ♘e1 ♕c7 (Taimanov recommends 9 ... a4!?) 10 ♘d3 ♘bd7 11 ♘f4! ♘b6 12 e4 fxe4 13 ♘xe4 ♘xe4 14 ♗xe4 d5 15

♗g2± Udovcic - Dimc, Yugoslavia 1953.

c) 9 a4 ♘a6 10 ♘e1 (10 e3 ♔h8 11 ♘e1 ♘b4 12 c3 ♘bd5 13 ♘d3 ♕b6 14 ♖e1 ♘c7 15 c4 ♗e6 with an unclear position; Milic - Bronstein, Beverwijk 1963) 10 ... ♘b4 (Serious consideration should be given to 10 ... e5!? 11 dxe5 ♘g4 12 ♘d3 ♘xe5 13 ♘xe5 dxe5 14 e4 ♕c7 15 ♕e2 f4 16 ♗a3 ♖e8 17 ♖ad1 ♗f8= Romanishin - Kovacevic, Sarajevo 1988) 11 c3 ♘bd5 12 ♘d3 ♕b6 13 e3 ♗d7 14 ♖c1 ♖ad8 15 ♗a3 ♕a6 16 c4± Panno - Gheorghiu, Varna 1962.

d) 9 a3 ♘a6 (Alternatively: 9 ... a4 *{This aims to blockade the queenside and the centre}* 10 b4 b5 11 c4 d5 12 c5 ♕c7 13 ♘e5 ♘bd7 14 ♘d3 ♘e4 15 f3 ♘xd2 16 ♕xd2 ♘f6 17 ♕f4 ♕xf4 18 gxf4 and neither side was able to break the pawn chain in Panno - Dolmatov, Moscow 1989; or 9 ... ♘e4 10 c4 ♕b6 11 e3 ♘xd2 12 ♘xd2 ♘a6 *{12 ... ♘d7!?}* 13 ♘c3 ♗e6 14 ♕c2 ♗f7 15 ♖fb1 e5 16 c5 dxc5 *{16 ... ♕a7 17 b4±}* 17 dxe5± Ree - Bohm, Amsterdam 1980) 10 e3 (Also: 10 ♖e1 *{This attempt to open the centre is unsuccessful}* 10 ... ♘e4 11 ♘xe4 *{11 e3 ♘c7 12 c4 ♘e8 13 ♕c2 ♘8f6 14 ♖ac1 ♘g4 15 ♖e2 ♗d7 with a balanced position; Kallai - Sax, Hungary 1991}* 11 ... fxe4 12 ♘d2 d5 13 f3 exf3 14 ♗xf3 *{14 exf3 c5 - Taimanov}* 14 ... ♘c5 with an unclear position; Bielicki - Pelikan, Mar del Plata 1960; or 10 ♘e1 ♕c7 11 ♘d3 ♗d7

12 e4 fxe4 13 ♘xe4 ♘xe4 14 ♗xe4 ♘h3 15 ♖e1 ♕d7 and White has a very slight advantage; Gerusel – Gallinnis, West Germany 1988) 10 ... ♘c7 (Or 10 ... ♗d7 11 ♕e2 ♕c7 12 e4 fxe4 13 ♘xe4 ♖ae8 14 ♖ae1; Bolbochan – R. Garcia, Mar del Plata 1966) 11 ♕e2 ♔h8 12 ♘e1 ♗e6 13 c4 ♗g8 14 ♘d3 ♘d7 and White, with the plan of f2 – f4, is slightly better; Sanguinetti – Pelikan, Argentina 1968.

9 ... ♘a6
10 a3 *(120)*

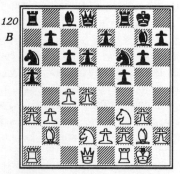

120
B

Instead of the text move, one could also try 10 ♕c2!?.

10 ... e5

The most logical continuation. Also possible are:

a) 10 ... ♘c7 11 ♖c1 (11 ♕c2) 11 ... ♗d7 12 ♕c2 ♖b8? (Black cannot find a plan) 13 ♗c3 ♘a6 14 ♗a1 ♔h8± Hofmann – Gallinns, West Germany 1988.

b) 10 ... ♕c7 11 ♕c2 (11 ♖e1 ♗d7 12 e4 ♘xe4 13 ♘xe4 fxe4 14 ♖xe4 ♗f5 15 ♖e1 ♖ae8= Bouwmeester – Stahlberg, Zevenaar 1961) 11 ... ♗d7 (11 ... ♔h8) 12 c5 ♔h8 13 ♖ac1 ♖ae8 14 ♘c4

♗e6 (Weaker is the following continuation: 14 ... dxc5 15 dxc5 ♘xc5 16 ♘xa5 ♕xa5 17 b4± – Botvinnik) 15 ♖fd1 ♘e4 16 ♘fd2= Portisch – Uhlmann, Stockholm izt 1962.

11 dxe5 ♘d7?!

Black would be better advised to play 11 ... ♘g4!? 12 h3 ♘xe5= 13 ♕c2 ♘xf3+ 14 ♘xf3 ♗xb2 15 ♕xb2 ♕f6!.

12	♘d4	♘xe5
13	♕c2	♗d7
14	♗c3	♘c7
15	e3	♕e7
16	♖fe1?!	

It would be preferable to occupy space in the centre with the plan 16 h3!? intending f4, ♖ae1, e4±.

16	...	♘g4
17	h3	♘f6
18	b4	axb4
19	axb4	d5

Andersson – Dolmatov, Clermont-Ferrand 1989. The game soon ended in a draw.

A1123

8 ... ♔h8 *(121)*

121
W

Here we will continue to

consider the positions arising after 8 ♘bd2, concentrating on those variations where Black plays neither 8 ... ♘a6 nor 8 ... a5.

The text is a popular king move, but two other examples should also be considered:

a) 8 ... ♘bd7 (The start of an original manoeuvre) 9 e3 ♕c7 10 ♘g5 ♘b6 11 c4 h6 12 ♘f3 ♗e6 13 ♖c1 ♗f7 14 ♖c2 ♘bd7 15 ♖e1 e5 16 dxe5 dxe5 17 e4 f4 18 gxf4 ♘h5 19 f5 ♘f4 20 ♗f1 ♖ae8 21 ♖e3 with a complicated position in Orlov - Shabalov, Leningrad 1989.

b) 8 ... ♕c7 9 c4 ♘h5 (With this move Black achieves ... e7 - e5, but he does not reach equality) 10 ♕c2 e5 11 dxe5 dxe5 12 c5 e4 13 ♘d4 ♕e7 14 b4 ♘d7 15 ♘c4 ♘e5 16 ♘d6 b6 17 f4 exf3 18 exf3 bxc5 19 bxc5 ♗a6 20 ♖fe1 ♕d7 21 ♖ad1 and Black lacks an adequate defence; Dreev - Dolmatov, USSR Ch 1989.

9   c4

The most logical move in every respect.

9 ♖e1 has also been played (As ... d6 - d5 coincides with Black's plans anyway, the move with the rook seems unnecessary) 9 ... d5 (9 ... a5 10 a3± Najdorf - Schweber, Mar del Plata 1968) 10 ♘e5 ♗e6 11 ♘d3 ♘bd7 12 f3 ♕b6 13 ♔h1 ♖ae8 14 c4 ♕c7 15 ♕c2 ♕d6 16 ♖ac1 ♘h5 17 cxd5 ♕xd5 18 e3 ♕d6 19 ♘c4 ♗xc4 20 bxc4 g5 21 e4?! (The

initiative could have been gained by 21 c5!?, followed by e3 - e4 - e5 when Black's pieces would have been out of the game) 21 ... ♗xd4 with an unclear position; Ribli - Yusupov, Belfort 1988.

9   ...   d5

Black switches to a Stonewall formation, even at the cost of a tempo.

Not good is 9 ... e5?! 10 dxe5 ♘fd7 11 ♗a3 ♘xe5 12 ♘xe5 ♗xe5 13 ♖c1 with the idea of ♘f3± - Malaniuk; or even 13 ♘f3!?.

10   ♘e5   ♗e6
11   ♘d3   ♘bd7
12   ♖c1

Or 12 f3 ♕b6 13 e3 c5!? with an unclear position - Malaniuk.

12   ...   ♘e4
13   ♘f4   ♗f7
14   cxd5   cxd5
15   f3   ♘d6

Chances are equal; Yusupov - Malaniuk, USSR Ch 1987.

A12

7   ...   ♕e8 *(122)*

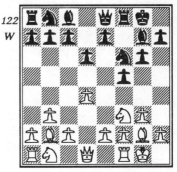

In this section we shall consider the variation where

Black rejects the traditional advance ... c7 - c6. In addition to the text move, Black has no less than nine other possible continuations.

First of all we deal with the more unusual possibilities. It should be added here that Black can play 7 ... ♘a6 in conjunction with the advance ... c7 - c6, transposing to material we have already covered, and can transpose to variation B1 by playing 7 ... ♘e4.

a) 7 ... e6!? (This move is not in accord with modern plans but it cannot be considered bad for this reason alone) 8 ♘bd2 a5 9 a3 ♘c6 10 ♖e1 ♘e4 with chances for both sides; Torre - Ilmaz, Dubai ol 1986.

b) 7 ... ♘c6 (Provoking the advance d4 - d5 and aiming for counterplay on the queenside - Taimanov) 8 d5 ♘a5 9 ♘fd2 c5 10 a4 ♗d7 11 c3 (This square for the pawn is better than the square c4 - Taimanov) 11 ... ♖c8?! (Instead of this move Taimanov recommends 11 ... ♘e8!, e.g. 12 ♖a2 ♖c8 13 b4 cxb4 14 cxb4 ♗xb2 15 ♖xb2 ♘c4 16 ♘xc4 ♖xc4 17 ♕b3 ♕c7 with good prospects for Black) 12 b4 cxb4 13 cxb4 ♘c4 14 ♘xc4 ♖xc4 15 ♕b3 ♖c8 16 ♘d2 ♕e8 17 e3 h6 18 ♗d4 b5 19 axb5 ♗xb5 20 ♖fc1 and Black's position is difficult; Larsen - Reyes, Lugano 1968.

c) 7 ... h6 (This move is evidently a loss of time here) 8 ♘bd2 g5 9 e3 c6 10 ♘e1 ♕e8 11 ♘d3 ♕g6 12 ♕e2 ♘e4 13 ♘c4 ♘d7 14 f3 ♘ef6 15 e4 fxe4 16 fxe4 ♘b6 17 e5 ♘e8 and Black remained under relentless pressure; Nogueiras - Afifi, Lucerne 1989.

d) 7 ... e5? (Too early) 8 dxe5 ♘g4 9 h3 ♘xe5 10 ♕d5+ ♘f7 (After 10 ... ♔h8 11 ♘xe5 dxe5 12 ♗xe5 Black loses a pawn - Taimanov) 11 ♗xg7 ♔xg7 12 ♘c3 ♕f6 13 ♕d2 ♘e5 14 ♘d5 and White has a superiority in the centre; van Geet - van Baarle, Holland 1971.

e) 7 ... ♘bd7?! 8 ♘bd2 ♖e8 (Also 8 ... ♕e8 9 e4 ♘xe4 10 ♘xe4 fxe4 11 ♘g5 ♘f6 12 ♘xe4 gives White a good game; Sokolov - Simic, Yugoslavia 1971) 9 ♘c4 ♘b6 10 ♕d3 c6 11 a4 ♗e6 12 ♘xb6 ♕xb6 13 ♘g5 ♗d7 14 ♕c4+ and the initiative is with White; Najdorf - Quinteros, Buenos Aires 1968.

f) 7 ... a5 8 c4 (Black is fine after 8 a4 ♘c6 9 ♘bd2 ♕e8 10 ♖e1 ♘e4∞ Tukmakov - D. Gurevich, Reykjavik 1990, and 8 ♘bd2 a4 9 c4 c6 10 ♕c2 ♕e8 11 b4 a3∞ Dreev - D. Gurevich, New York 1990) 8 ... ♘a6 9 a3 c5 10 ♘c3 ♘e4 11 e3 ♘xc3 12 ♗xc3 ♖b8 13 ♕d2 b6 14 ♖fe1 ♗b7 15 d5 ♗xc3 16 ♕xc3 ♘c7 17 b4 and White enjoys a great positional advantage; Gofstein - Nevednichi, Tbilisi 1983.

g) 7 ... ♔h8?! 8 ♘bd2 ♘c6 9 c4 e5 10 dxe5 ♘g4 11 ♕c2 ♘gxe5 (11 ... dxe5±) 12 ♖ad1 a5 13 c5±

Najdorf - Canobra, Mar del Plata 1969.

h) 7 ... ♘h5!? 8 e3 (Ivkov suggests 8 c4) 8 ... ♘c6 9 ♘a3 (9 c4 e5∓ - Ivkov; 9 ♘c3 e5 10 dxe5 dxe5 11 ♕d5+ ♕xd5 12 ♘xd5 e4 13 ♘d4 ♘xd4 14 ♗xd4 c6 15 ♘c7!? ♖b8!= Cebalo - Ivkov, Cetinje 1977) 9 ... e6 10 c4 ♕e7 11 ♘c2 a5 (*123*)

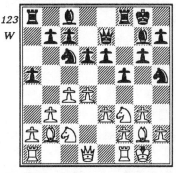

12 ♕d2 (Ivkov and Sokolov recommend 12 a3!? with the idea of b4) 12 ... ♗d7 13 ♖ab1 ♘d8 14 ♖fd1 ♘f6 with an un-clear position; Franco - Haag, Oberhausen 1961.

8 ♘bd2

Also worth consideration are:

a) 8 d5 (Preventing 8 ... ♘c6) 8 ... ♘a6 (8 ... c6 9 c4 ♘a6 10 ♘c3 ♗d7 11 ♖c1 ♖d8 12 ♗a3 ♘c5 13 ♘d2 a5 14 b4 axb4 15 ♗xb4 e5 16 ♘b3 ♗xb3 17 axb3 c5 18 ♗a3 e4 19 ♗b2 ♘g4 and Black begins his kingside attack; Lob-ron - Yusupov, Hamburg 1991) 9 c4 c5!? 10 ♘c3 ♗d7 11 ♖b1 (Also possible is 11 ♕d2 ♘c7 12 e4 b5?! 13 e5 ♘g4 14 exd6 exd6 15 ♘xb5 ♘xb5 16 ♗xg7 ♔xg7 17

♖fe1 ♕d8 18 cxb5 and Black has lost a pawn; Krasenkov - Zaru-bin, Moscow 1984) 11 ... h6 (According to Matsukevich, equality can be achieved by 11 ... b5 12 ♘xb5 ♗xb5 13 cxb5 ♕xb5 14 ♘d2) 12 ♘e1 g5 13 e4?! (13 ♘d3) 13 ... ♕g6 14 ♕e2 fxe4 15 ♘xe4 ♗g4! 16 ♕e3 (16 f3 ♘xe4; 16 ♘xf6+ exf6 17 ♕xg4 ♕xb1 18 ♕e6+ ♖f7 19 ♘c3 ♘c7! 20 ♕xd6 ♗f8 - Matsukevich) 16 ... ♘f5 17 f3 b5 and Black seized the initiative in Konopka - Malan-iuk, Frunze 1987.

b) 8 ♕d3 ♘c6 9 ♕c4+ e6 10 b4 a6 11 ♕b3 ♔h8 12 a4 e5 13 dxe5 dxe5 14 b5 ♗e6 15 ♕e3 and White has wasted valuable tempi with his queen; Muse - Videki, Kecskemet 1990.

c) 8 c4!? (In practice this move is the best for White) 8 ... e5?! (Better is 8 ... ♘a6 {8 ... h6 9 ♘c3 g5 10 e3 ♔h8 [10 ... a5∞] 11 d5! a5 12 ♘d4 led to a crush-ing win for White in Shirov - Piskov, Moscow 1991} 9 ♘c3 {Alternatively: 9 d5 c5 10 ♘c3 h6 11 ♘e1 g5 12 ♘d3 ♕g6 13 ♕d2 ♗d7 14 f4 ♘g4 and Black had sufficient counterplay in Tuk-makov - Malaniuk, Lvov zt 1990; or 9 ♘bd2 e5 10 dxe5 ♘g4 11 ♖b1 dxe5 12 h3 ♘h6∞ Velikov - Bareev, Marseille 1990} 9 ... c6 with transposition into varia-tions already considered above; but 8 ... ♘h5?! cannot be re-commended: 9 ♘c3 f4 10 ♕d2 c6 11 d5 {With simple moves White gains a great advantage}

11 ... ♘a6 12 ♘a4 c5 13 ♗xg7 ♔xg7 14 e4 h6 15 e5. Black's knights are badly positioned on the wings and there is a threat of 16 e6 which may spoil the co-operation of his pieces. Black is thus strategically lost; Romanishin – Gurevich Tallinn 1987) 9 dxe5 ♘g4 10 ♘c3 ♘xe5 11 ♕d2 (White will gain a slight advantage after 11 ♕c2 ♘a6 12 ♖ad1 f4 13 ♘d5 ♗f5 14 ♕d2 fxg3 15 hxg3 ♖d8 16 ♘xe5 ♗xe5 17 ♘e3 c6 18 ♘xf5 ♖xf5 19 ♗d4 b6 20 ♕b2± Loginov – Malaniuk, Tashkent 1987) 11 ... ♘a6 12 ♖ad1 ♘xf3+ 13 exf3!? ♘c5 14 ♖fe1 ♕d8 15 b4 ♘d7 16 ♘d5 ♗xb2 17 ♕xb2 ♖f7 18 f4 c6 19 ♘e3 ♘f6 20 b5± Lputian – Malaniuk, Sverdlovsk 1987.

8 ... ♘c6 *(124)*

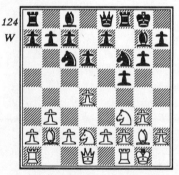

124
W

9 ♘c4

Alternatively, 9 ♖e1 h6! (9 ... e5?! 10 e4) 10 e4 fxe4 11 ♘xe4 ♘xe4 12 ♖xe4 g5! (And Black stands better already – Malaniuk) 13 ♕e2 (13 ♖e3!?) 13 ... ♕h5 14 ♖f1 ♗g4 15 ♖e3 e6! (15 ... ♖f7 and 15 ... ♔h8 are unpleasantly met with 16 d5) 16 c3 ♘e7 17 h3

(17 c4 ♘c6∓ – Malaniuk) 17 ... ♗xh3 18 ♗xh3 ♕xh3 19 ♖xe6 ♘d5 (Consideration should be given to 19 ... ♖xf3 20 ♖xe7 ♖af8 21 ♖e8∓, and not 21 ♖xc7 h5 22 ♖xb7 h4 23 ♖b8 hxg3 24 ♖xf8+ ♗xf8 and Black wins) 20 ♘h2! ♕f7 (20 ... ♘f6 21 ♖e7± – Malaniuk) 21 ♕g4 ½–½ Yusupov – Malaniuk, Moscow 1988; if 21 ... ♕xg4 22 ♘xg4 ♘f6 23 ♘xf6+ ♖xf6 24 ♖e7 ♖f7, then the game is equal.

9 ... ♔h8

Other moves have also been tried:

a) 9 ... h6 10 ♘e1 (Critical is 10 d5 ♘b4 11 ♘e3 c5 12 dxc6 bxc6 13 a3 ♘a6 14 b4 ♖b8 15 c4 c5∞ Efimov – Malaniuk, Kiev 1989) 10 ... g5 11 ♘d3 ♔h8 12 e3 ♗e6 and Black has completed his development; Tal – Sakaev, Moscow 1991.

b) 9 ... e6 10 a4 ♗d7 11 e3 h6 12 ♘e1 g5 13 ♘d3 a6 14 a5 ♖b8 15 ♕e2 ♘e7 16 ♖ae1 ♘g6 17 f3?! (Enklaar – Chernin, Amsterdam 1980); instead of this, Masukevich recommends 17 f4!? with an unclear game.

c) 9 ... ♗e6 10 ♘g5 ♗xc4 11 bxc4 ♘d8 12 ♕d3 h6 13 ♘f3 e6 14 c5 dxc5 15 dxc5 ♘c6 16 ♖ab1 ♖d8 17 ♕b3 b6 18 ♖fd1 ♖xd1+ 19 ♖xd1 ♘e4 20 ♗xg7 ♔xg7 21 cxb6 axb6 22 ♕b2+ e5 (Sosonko – Beliavsky, Tilburg 1984) 23 ♘d2± ♘xd2 24 ♗xc6 ♘c4 (24 ... ♕xc6 25 ♕xe5+) 25 ♕b5 ♕e6 26 ♖d5 with advantage to White (worse would be 26 ♗d5 ♘d6).

10	d5	♘b4
11	♘e1	c6
12	dxc6	♘xc6
13	♘d3	♗e6
14	♘f4	♗g8
15	♘d5	♖d8
16	♘xf6	♗xf6
17	♗xf6+	♖xf6 (125)

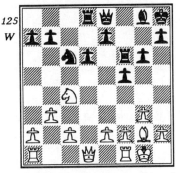

The game is equal; Sosonko - Korchnoi, Brussels 1987.

A2

| 7 | c4 (126) |

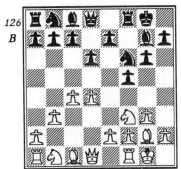

After b2 - b3 White does not need to transfer the bishop immediately to b2. This can be delayed or sidestepped altogether in favour of ♗a3!? - a possibility which we will examine here.

| 7 | ... | e5 |

Black tries to exploit the absence of the bishop at once.

Also worth considering is 7 ... c6 8 ♘bd2 (8 ♗b2 transposes to A111) 8 ... e5 9 e3 e4 10 ♘e1 d5 (White has let Black gain the upper hand in the centre) 11 a4 a5 12 ♘c2 ♗e6 13 ♗a3 ♖f7 14 ♕e2 ♘bd7 15 ♖fb1 g5 16 f4 exf4 17 ♗xf3 g4 18 ♗g2 ♘e4 19 ♘xe4 fxe4∓ Donchenko - Orlov, Belgorod 1989.

| 8 | dxe5 |

8 ♘c3 is not advisable, e.g. 8 ... ♘c6 9 ♖b1 e4 10 ♘e1 d5 11 ♘c2 ♗e6 12 ♖e1 dxc4 13 bxc4 ♘a5 14 ♘a3 ♘g4 15 e3 c5 with advantage to Black; Csom - Planinc, Amsterdam 1974.

| 8 | ... | dxe5 (127) |

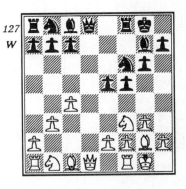

Instead of the text, attention should perhaps be paid to 8 ... ♘g4 9 ♘c3 dxe5 10 ♗a3 e4 (According to Taimanov, worse for Black is 10 ... ♖e8?! 11♕xd8 ♖xd8 12♘d5♘a6 13 ♖ad1 ♗e6 14 ♘g5) 11 ♗xf8 ♕xf8 12 ♘d4± e3 13 f4 ♘f2 14 ♖xf2 exf2+ 15 ♔xf2 ♘a6 with counterplay; Wexler -

Uhlmann, Buenos Aires 1960.

9 ♗a3

Also fine for Black is 9 ♕c2 (9 ♕xd8 ♖xd8 10 ♘xe5 ♖e8 is bad for White) 9 ... ♘c6 10 ♗a3 ♖f7 11 ♘g5 ♖d7 12 ♘e6 ♘d4!= Savon – Lutikov, USSR 1969.

	9	...	♕xd1
	10	♖xd1	♖e8
	11	♘c3	e4
	12	♘e1	c6
	13	f3	♘g4
	14	fxg4	♗xc3
	15	♖ac1	♗xe1
	16	♖xe1	fxg4
	17	♖ed1	♗f5
	18	♖d4	♘d7

White has sufficent counterplay for the pawn; Anastasian – Malaniuk, Moscow GMA 1989.

B

6 ... ♘e4

Here we consider variations in which Black tries to interfere in White's plans by activating his king's knight.

7 ♗b2

Here Black can hold back his d-pawn or support the knight in the centre:

B1 7 ... d6
B2 7 ... d5 and others

B1

7 ... d6

Now White has:

B11 8 c4
B12 8 ♘bd2

B11

8 c4 (128)

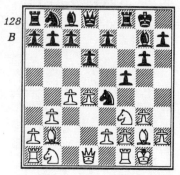

In this section, White counters Black's plan of occupying e4 by delaying the development of the queenside knight.

8 ... ♘c6

Other possibilities offer White more chances for an advantage:

a) 8 ... c5?! (There is no sense in opening the centre) 9 ♕c1 cxd4 10 ♘xd4 ♕b6 (Botvinnik suggests 10 ... ♘c6!? as a better possibility) 11 ♘b5 a6 12 ♘5c3 ♘c6 13 ♘xe4 fxe4 14 ♗xg7 ♔xg7 15 ♗xe4 and White has an extra pawn; Portisch – Gastonyi, Hungary 1957.

b) 8 ... ♘d7 9 ♕c2 ♘df6 (9 ... e6 10 ♘bd2 ♘xd2 11 ♕xd2 ♕e7= – Bellin) 10 ♘bd2 e6 11 ♘e1 ♘xd2 12 ♕xd2 ♕e7 13 ♘d3± Petrosian – Kaiszauri, Vilnius 1978.

c) 8 ... e6 9 ♘c3 ♘xc3 10 ♗xc3 ♘d7 11 ♖c1 ♕e7 12 ♗b4 ♖b8 13 ♖e1 b6 14 e4 fxe4 15 ♖xe4 ♗b7 16 d5 e5 17 ♖e1 ♗h6 18 ♗d2± Gligoric – Benko, Buenos Aires 1955.

9   ⟡e1

9 ⟡bd2 is considered later under B121, whilst 9 ⟡c3 is considered under variation B in Chapter 3 (8 b3 ⟡e4 9 ♗b2).

9   ...   ⟡g5

Or 9 ... e5 10 d5 ⟡e7 11 e3 with the idea of f3 or f4± – Botvinnik.

10   e3   e5
11   d5   ⟡e7
12   f4   ⟡f7

Conceding the centre is worse: 12 ... exf4 13 ♗xg7 ♔xg7 14 exf4± – Botvinnik.

13   ⟡c3   g5
14   ⟡d3   ⟡g6
15   ♕d2   ♗d7
16   ♖ae1

White has a slight advantage; Csom – Holm, Skopje 1972.

B12

8   ⟡bd2   ⟡c6

Now White can choose between:

B121   9 c4
B122   9 ⟡c4 and others

B121

9   c4   e5 *(129)*

This is an interesting line. The viability of the whole system starting with 6 ... ⟡e4 may depend on it. However, Black can also consider 9 ... ⟡xd2 (Or 9 ... e6 10 e3 ♕e7 11 ⟡e1 ⟡xd2 12 ♕xd2 e5 13 f4 e4 when Black has few problems; Umanskaya – Gusev, Moscow 1991) 10 ⟡xd2 e5 when Black

stood well in Illescas – de la Villa, Panplona 1990, and A. Sokolov – Avshalumov, Nimes 1991.

10   dxe5

10 d5 is also interesting: 10 ... ⟡xd2 11 ♕xd2 (11 dxc6!?) 11 ... ⟡e7 (Also fine is 10 ... ⟡b8 12 ♖ac1 {12 ⟡g5 ♕e7 13 ♖ad1 ⟡a6 [Not 13 ... h6 14 ⟡e6 ♗xe6 15 dxe6 ⟡c6 16 c5 and the white pawns are penetrating Black's position; Skembris – Santo Roman, Athens 1992] 14 b4? ⟡xb4! 15 ⟡xh7 ♔xh7 16 ♕xb4 f4∓ Moutousis – Santo Roman, Athens 1992} 12 ... ♕e7 13 b4 ⟡d7 14 c5 ⟡f6 15 ♖fd1 f4 16 gxf4 ⟡e4 17 cxd6 cxd6 18 ♕c2 ♖xf4 and Black's activity on the queenside and White's activity on the kingside counterbalance one another; Romanishin – Casper, Jurmala 1987) 12 ♖ac1 h6 13 ♖fd1 g5 14 c5 ⟡g6 15 e3 ♖f7 16 cxd6 cxd6 17 ♖c2 f4 18 exf4 gxf4 19 ⟡e1 ♗f5 and White has to organise a defence; Akhmilovskaya – Litinskaya, Tbilisi 1987.

10   ...   ⟡xd2

11 ♕xd2   dxe5
12 ♕d5+   ♚h8
13 ♕xd8   ♖xd8

It is interesting to note that this position is analogous to the variation 6 c4 d6 7 ♘c3 ♘c6 8 b3 – the only difference being that the white bishop is placed on b2 instead of c3.

14 ♘g5

14 ♖ad1 leads to an equal endgame: 14 ... ♖xd1 15 ♖xd1 e4 16 ♗xg7+ ♚xg7 17 ♘d4 ♘xd4 18 ♖xd4 ♗e6 19 f3 exf3 20 ♗xf3 (20 exf3 ♖b8 21 f4 b5 22 cxb5 ♖xb5 23 ♚f2 ♖a5 14 ♖d2 ♖a3 25 ♗c6 ♖a5 26 ♖c2 ♚f6 27 ♚e3 ♚e7 28 ♚d4 ♚d6 ½–½ Schoen – Mi. Tseitlin, Budapest 1989) 20 ... c6 21 ♚f2 ♚f6 22 e4 ♖f8 23 ♚e3 c5 24 ♖d2 b6 25 h4 fxe4 with a quick draw; Polugayevsky – Bareev, Moscow 1987.

14 ...   ♖d2 *(130)*

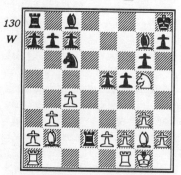

Instead of Black's last move, more exact would be 14 ... ♖e8 (see the analogous line 7 ... ♘c6 8 b3, considered under variation B in Chapter 3).

15 ♗c3   ♖c2

Dangerous is 15 ... ♖xe2?! 16 ♗xc6 bxc6 17 ♖fd1 ♘f6 18 ♚f1 ♖c2 19 ♗xe5 ♗xe5 20 ♘f7+ ♚g7 21 ♘xe5 and White has a significant advantage in the endgame; Smejkal – Fleck, Munich 1987.

16 ♖ac1   ♖xc1
17 ♖xc1   e4
18 f3   ♘d4

18 ... h6 19 ♘h3 ♘d4 20 ♚f2 exf3 21 exf3 ♗e6 22 f4 c6 23 ♖d1± – Ftacnik.

19 ♚f2   h6
20 ♖d1   c5
21 e3   hxg5
22 exd4   exf3
23 ♗xf3   ♖b8
24 ♖d3   g4
25 ♗g2   cxd4
26 ♗xd4   ♗e6
27 ♗e3   b6
28 ♖d6

The endgame favours White; Ftacnik – Henley, Hastings 1982/83.

B122

9 ♘c4 *(131)*

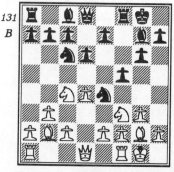

There are some interesting possibilities here. White rejects c2 – c4 and instead uses the c4-square as a basis for knight manoeuvres, ignoring the knight at e4 and at the same time preventing the liberating advance ... e7 - e5.

Also playable are:

a) 9 e3 ♘xd2 10 ♘xd2 e5 11 d5 ♘b8 (11 ... ♘e7 is strongly met by 12 f4, as in Ftacnik - Banas, Trnava 1984) 12 f4 ♘d7 13 ♘c4 b6?! (13 ... exf4!?) 14 ♖e1± Pigusov - Vyzmanavin, Togliatti 1985.

b) 9 ♘e1 d5 (9 ... ♘xd2 10 ♕xd2 e5 11 ♗xc6±) 10 ♘df3 f4?! 11 ♘d3 g5 12 c4 e6 13 ♖c1 ♘e7 14 ♘d2 and Black is forced to concede his position in the centre; Lputian - Gurevich, USSR 1983.

9   ...   e6
10 ♘fd2

Also roughly equal are:

a) 10 e3 ♕e7 11 ♘e1 ♖d8 12 ♘d3 e5 13 f3 ♘g5= Gerusel - Clemens, Solingen 1974.

b) 10 a4 a5 11 e3 b6 12 ♕c1 ♗d7 13 ♖d1 ♕e7 14 ♘fd2 ♘b4?! (According to Haritonov, equality results from 14 ... d5) 15 ♘f1 ♘d5 16 c3± Haritonov - Legky, USSR 1987.

10 ...   d5

White threatened 11 ♘xe4 fxe4 12 d5. Not 10 ... ♘xd2 11 ♕xd2 ♘e7 12 f3.

11 ♘xe4 *(132)*
11 ...   dxc4!?

Preferable to 11 ... fxe4 12 ♘e3 with a slight advantage to White.

12 ♘c5   ♗xd4!?

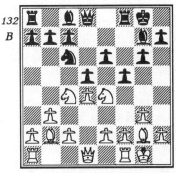

12 ... ♘xd4 leaves White slightly better: 13 e3 ♘f3+ 14 ♕xf3 ♗xb2 15 ♖ad1 ♕e7 16 ♘xb7.

13 ♘xb7   ♗xb7
14 ♗xd4   ♕xd4
15 ♕xd4   ♘xd4
16 ♗xb7   ♖ad8
17 ♗a6   c3

The game is equal; Hausner - Tseitlin, Kecskemet 1985.

B2

7   ...   d5 *(133)*

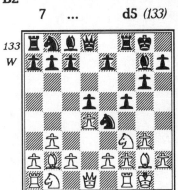

This is the last section on the move 6 ... ♘e4. Black declines to play ... d7 - d6 and instead a Stonewall-type pawn chain appears on the board. Rarely seen are:

a) 7 ... ♘c6 8 ♘bd2 d5 (8 ... d6 turns into variations already considered above) 9 e3 e6 10 ♘e1 b6 11 ♘d3 ♗a6 12 ♘f3 ♖c8 13 ♖e1= Donner - Alexander, Hastings 1954/55.

b) 7 ... c5 8 e3 (Other moves have been tried: 8 c4 ♘c6 9 e3 d6 10 ♘c3 e6 11 ♕d3 ♘xc3 12 ♗xc3 ♕e7 13 dxc5 dxc5 14 ♗xg7 ♔xg7 and Black's chances were not worse in Pfleger - Santo Roman, Royan 1988; and 8 ♕c1 cxd4 9 ♘xd4 d5?! *{9 ... ♕b6!?}* 10 ♘f3 ♘d7 11 ♗xg7 ♔xg7 12 ♕b2+ ♘df6 13 ♘bd2 ♕b6 14 c4 ♗e6 15 cxd5 ♗xd5 16 ♘xe4 ♗xe4 17 ♕e5± Csom - Kuczynsky, Warsaw 1987) 8 ... ♘c6 9 ♕e2 d5?! 10 c4 dxc4 11 ♕xc4+ ♔h8 12 ♘c3 cxd4 13 ♘xe4 fxe4 14 ♘xd4 ♘e5 15 ♕c2 ♘f3+ 16 ♘xf3 exf3 17 ♗xg7+ ♔xg7 18 ♕c3+± Najdorf - Alexander, Amsterdam 1954.

8 c4 *(134)*

Consideration should be given to the immediate attempt to exploit the weakness of the square e5 and play f2 - f3 later to remove Black's active knight: 8 ♘e5 ♘d7 (Overly sharp is 8 ... f4 9 ♘d2 ♘g5 10 ♘df3 ♘xf3+ *{10 ... ♘e6!? - Ivkov, Sokolov; but not 10 ... ♘h3+?! 11 ♔h1 fxg3 12 hxg3 ♘c6 13 ♔h2 with a winning position in Najdorf - Rodriguez, Mar del Plata 1969}* 11 ♘xf3 with a solid advantage to White - Ivkov, Sokolov) 9 f3 ♘xe5 10 dxe5 ♘c5 11 f4 c6 12 ♘d2 h6?! (12 ... ♗e6!?) 13 e3 g5

14 c4 ♗e6 15 ♕c2 ♘e4 16 cxd5 cxd5?! (16 ... ♘xd2=) 17 ♘f3± Ionescu - Zsu. Polgar, Bulgaria 1990.

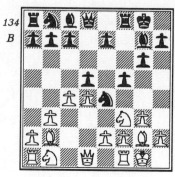

134
B

8 ... c6
9 ♘bd2

Alternatively:

a) 9 ♘c3 leads to an equal position: 9 ... ♗e6! 10 cxd5 ♘xc3 11 ♗xc3 ♗xd5, as in O'Kelly - Zwaig, Sandelfjord 1975.

b) 9 cxd5 cxd5 10 ♘a3 ♘c6 11 ♘c2 ♗e6 12 ♘ce1 with the idea of ♘d3± - Botvinnik.

9 ... ♗e6

Worse is 9 ... ♘d7 10 ♖c1 ♘df6 11 ♕c2 ♘g4 12 cxd5 cxd5 13 h3 ♘gf6 14 ♘e5 ♗e6 15 ♘xe4 ♘xe4 (Gligoric - Joppen, Belgrade 1954) 16 ♕c7± - Botvinnik.

10 e3

In the recent game Ruban - Malaniuk, USSR Ch 1991, White tried 10 ♕c2 ♘d7 11 ♖fd1 ♖c8 12 e3 ♘df6 13 ♘e5 g5 14 ♖ac1 ♘d6 15 ♘d3 h6 16 ♗a3 with a slight advantage.

10 ♖c1 does not lead to any advantage: 10 ... ♘d7 11 ♕c2 ♔h8 12 ♖fd1 ♖c8 13 e3 ♗g8 14

♘e5 ♕e8 15 ♘xd7 ♕xd7 16 ♘f3
½-½ Marin - Kuczynsky, Dresden 1989.

10 ... ♘d7!?

An interesting posibility here
is 10 ... ♔h8!? 11 ♘xe4 fxe4 12
♘g5 ♗g8 13 h4 ♘a6 14 cxd5
cxd5 15 ♕d2 ♘c7 16 ♖ac1 h6 17
♘h3 ♗e6 18 ♘f4 ♘xf4 19 exf4
♗e6 with an equal game; Wirthenson - Hölzl, Biel 1980.

11 ♖c1

A complicated position is
reached after 11 ♘xe4 dxe4
(Bad is 11 ... fxe4 12 ♘g5 ♗f5 {12
... ♗f7 13 ♗h3} 13 cxd5 cxd5 14
g4 h6 {A piece is lost after 14 ...
e6 15 ♘h3; 14 ... e5 15 gxf5 ♕xg5
16 dxe5 and Black's position
breaks up} 15 gxf5 hxg5 16
fxg6± Haritonov) 12 ♘g5 ♗f7 13
♘xf7 ♖xf7 14 f3 exf3 15 ♕xf3
e5 - Haritonov.

11 ... ♔h8

12 ♕c2

Worse is 12 ♘e1?! ♕a5.

12 ... a5!

13 a4

Also possible are:
a) 13 a3 a4 14 b4 b5!=.
b) 13 ♘e1 a4 14 ♘d3 axb3 15
axb3 ♕b6= (15 ... ♕a5?! 16 ♘f3±).

13 ... ♕e8

14 ♖fd1 ♖c8

15 ♘e1 ♕f7

16 ♘d3

Black has nothing to fear
after 16 cxd5 ♗xd5.

16 ... ♘xd2?!

Instead, Black should have
played 16 ... g5! 17 cxd5 (17
♘f3!?) 17 ... ♗xd5.

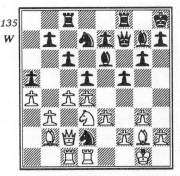

17 ♖xd2 dxc4?

According to Antoshin,
equality could still be achieved
by 17 ... g5.

18 bxc4 ♘b6

19 ♘e5!

White has a clear advantage;
Haritonov - Bareev, Sochi 1987.

C

6 ... c6 (136)

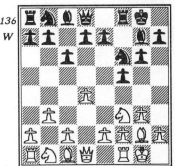

It is unusual for Black to
avoid both 6 ... ♘e4 and 6 ... d6,
but in the diagram position
Black is attempting to play his
d-pawn to d5 in one go. It is
also possible to play 6 ... d5
immediately of course.

Bent Larsen has experimented with the extravagant 6 ... b5

7 ♗b2 (In F. Olafsson – Larsen, Wijk aan Zee 1961, the game went 7 c4 bxc4 8 bxc4 c5 9 ♗b2 ♛b6 10 ♛c1 ♘c6 11 dxc5 ♛xc5 12 ♘bd2 ♜b8 13 ♘b3 ♛b6 14 ♘e5 ♗b7 with an obscure position) 7 ... ♗b7 8 ♘d2 with the idea of c2 – c4 and White has prospects to achieve an advantage – Ivkov, Sokolov.

7 ♗b2   d5

More consistent than 7 ... ♛e8 8 ♘bd2 h6?! 9 ♘e5 d6 10 ♘d3 ♛f7 11 e4 fxe4 12 ♘xe4 and Black has difficulties in choosing good plan; Tal – Meulders, Brussels 1987.

8 c4   ♗e6

After 8 ... ♔h8!? 9 ♘c3 ♗e6 10 ♛d3 ♘bd7 11 ♜ac1 the position was finely balanced in Vladimirov – Spraggett, Moscow GMA 1990.

9   ♘g5   ♗f7
10 ♘c3   ♛e8
11 ♛d3   h6
12 ♘xf7   ♛xf7
13 f3

White does not gain anything after the exchange 13 cxd5 cxd5 14 ♛b5 e6 15 ♘a4 ♘c6 16 ♘c5 ♘e4!∓ – Portisch.

13 ...   ♘bd7
14 cxd5

In the game Portisch – Smyslov, Portoroz match 1971, play continued 14 e4? dxc4 15 bxc4 ♘b6! and Black seized the initiative.

14 ...   ♘xd5

Bad is 14 ... cxd5? 15 e4.

15 ♘xd5   ♛xd5 (137)

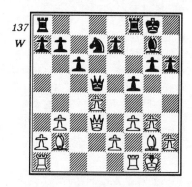

With equal chances according to Portisch.

6 Systems with ♘h3

1	d4	f5
2	g3	♘f6
3	♗g2	g6
4	♘h3	♗g7 *(138)*

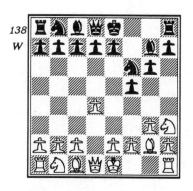

The development of the knight to h3 (known as the Karlsbad system) is a very popular way to fight against the Leningrad Variation. Both White and Black have a number of different possibilities to develop their pieces. The following sequence may be considered to be the main variation: 5 c4 0–0 6 ♘c3, after which play usually continues 6 ... d6 7 d5. However, it is possible for Black to delay or avoid 6 ... d6 and for White to delay c4.

A 5 c4
B 5 ♘f4

A

5 c4 0–0

Black can also try the immediate 5 ... c6. Seirawan – Gurevich, Belgrade 1991, continued 6 ♘f4 d6 7 d5 e5! 8 dxe6 ♕e7 9 ♘d2 0–0 10 0–0 ♗xe6 with equal chances.

6 ♘c3

Now Black has:

A1 6 ... d6
A2 6 ... ♘c6
A3 6 ... e6

A1

6 ... d6
7 d5

White has little chance of an advantage if this is delayed.

a) 7 0–0 (Enables Black to carry out the equalising advance) 7 ... e5 (7 ... ♘c6, 7 ... c6 and 7 ... e6 are also playable) 8 dxe5 dxe5 9 ♕xd8 ♖xd8 10 ♘d5 ♖d7! 11 ♗g5 ♔f7 12 f4 (In Botvinnik's opinion 12 ♗xf6 is worth trying: 12 ... ♗xf6 13 e4!?) 12 ... ♘g4 13 fxe5 ♘xe5 14 ♗f4 ♗xf4 15 ♖xf4 c6= Byrne –

Pelikan, Mar del Plata 1961.

b) 7 ♘f4 ♘c6 8 h4 e5 9 dxe5 dxe5 10 ♘fd5 ♘d4 11 ♗g5 c6 12 ♘xf6+ ♗xf6 13 e3 ♗xg5 14 hxg5 ♘e6 15 ♕xd8 ♖xd8= Bannik - Savon, USSR 1962.

After 7 d5 Black can choose between:

A11 7 ... ♘a6
A12 7 ... c6
A13 7 ... c5

Dolmatov has suggested 7 ... ♘g4!?.

A11

7   ...   ♘a6 *(139)*

This is quite a well-trodden path. Black tries to manage without ... c7 - c6 in this variation, but White has several plans to develop the initiative.

8 0-0

Let us consider other possibilities:

a) 8 ♖b1?! ♘c5 9 ♘f4 e5 10 dxe6 c6 11 0-0 ♕e7 12 ♕c2 g5 13 ♘h3 h6 14 f4 g4 15 ♘f2 ♗xe6 with an unclear position; Taborov - Gurevich, USSR 1982.

b) 8 ♘f4 ♕e8 (Interesting are both 8 ... ♘c5!? 9 ♗e3 e5 10 dxe6 ♘xe6 11 ♘xe6 ♗xe6 12 ♗xb7 ♖b8 13 ♗d5 ♗xd5 14 cxd5 ♖xb2 15 0-0 ♕e7 16 ♗d4 ♖b4 17 e3 ♘e4 18 ♗xg7 ♕xg7 19 ♘xe4= Uhlmann - Espig, Berlin 1988, and 8 ... e5!? 9 dxe6 c6 transposing to the variation 7 ... c6 8 ♘f4 e5 9 dxe6 ♘a6 considered below) 9 h4!? (Trying to exploit the weakness of 7 ... ♘a6. Less active is 9 0-0 c5 *{9 ... g5 10 ♘d3 ♕h5 11 e4± - Chernin}* 10 dxc6?! bxc6 11 ♕a4 ♘b8 12 c5! e5 13 ♘fd5 cxd5 14 ♕xe8 ♖xe8 15 ♘xd5 e4 16 ♘c7 ♘a6 17 ♘xa8 dxc5 and the white knight is lost; Espig - Malaniuk, Budapest 1989) 9 ... c6 10 0-0 ♗d7 (10 ... e5 11 dxc6 *{An unclear position is reached after 11 dxe6 ♗xe6 12 ♕xd6 ♗xc4}* 11 ... bxc6 12 ♕xd6 exf4 13 ♗xc6 ♗e6 *{13 ... ♗d7 14 ♗xa8 ♕xa8 15 ♗xf4!±}* 14 ♗xf4 ♖b8 15 ♕xe6+ ♗xe6 16 ♗xb8 ♘xb8 17 ♗d5 ♘xd5 18 cxd5 ♗f7 19 ♖fd1± - Chernin) 11 e4 fxe4 12 ♘xe4 ♘xe4 13 ♗xe4 ♘c5 (13 ... e5 14 dxe6 ♗xe6 15 ♖e1± - Chernin) 14 ♗g2 (14 ♗c2!?) 14 ... ♕f7 15 ♗e3 with a slight advantage for White; Chernin - Bareev, USSR 1987.

8   ...   ♘c5 *(140)*

The most accurate choice at this point. Less effective are:

a) It is not enough to play 8 ... e5?! 9 dxe6 ♘c5 10 ♘g5 ♖b8 11 ♗e3 ♕e7 12 ♘d5 ♘xd5 13 cxd5 ♗xb2 14 ♖b1 ♗f6 15 h4 with a positional advantage; Kotov -

Tolush, USSR 1958.

b) Too slow is 8 ... ♗d7?! 9 ♖e1 c6 10 ♖b1 ♘c5 11 ♗e3 ♘ce4 12 ♘xe4 ♘xe4 13 ♘g5 ♘f6 14 c5 ♘g4 15 ♕b3 (15 ♗d4!?) 15 ... ♔h8 16 ♗d2 dxc5 17 ♕xb7 ♖b8 18 ♕xa7 cxd5 19 ♗a5± Lutz - Zysk, West Germany 1988.

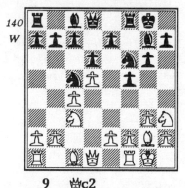

9 ♕c2

Also possible are:

a) 9 ♘f4 e5 10 dxe6 c6 11 ♗e3 (Incorrect is 11 ♕d2 g5 12 ♘h3 h6 13 ♖d1 ♗xe6 14 ♕xd6 ♕xd6 15 ♖xd6 ♗xc4 16 ♗e3 ♘ce4 17 ♘xe4 ♘xe4 18 ♖d7 ♖f7 19 ♖ad1 ♗xa2 winning a pawn in Siegel - Fleck, West Germany 1988; and 11 ♕c2?! is not good either: 11 ... ♘xe6 12 ♖d1 ♘g4 13 ♘xe6 ♗xe6 14 c5? d5 15 e3 ♕e7 16 ♘e2 ♖ae8 17 ♗d2 f4 18 ♘xf4 ♘xf2! with advantage to Black; Taimanov - Lutikov, USSR 1955) 11 ... ♘xe6 (11 ... ♕e7 12 h3 g5 13 ♘d3 ♘xe6 14 ♕d2 h6 15 f4 ♘h5 with chances for both sides; van der Sterren - van Mil, Dutch Ch 1991) 12 ♕d2 ♘g4 13 ♘xe6 ♘xe6 14 ♗g5= - Botvinnik.

b) 9 ♗e3 e5 (9 ... a5 10 ♘f4 ♖b8 11 ♖c1 ♗d7 12 b3 ♘g4 13 ♗xc5 dxc5 14 e4 ♘h6 15 ♘d3 fxe4 16 ♘xe4 ♗xc1 17 ♕xc1 b6 18 ♗h3 c6 19 ♗xg4 ♗xg4 20 ♕h6 with excellent compensation for the exchange in Santos - Lin Ta, Dubai 1986) 10 dxe6 ♘xe6 11 ♗g5 ♘g4 12 ♘xe6 ♘xe3 13 ♘xd8 ♘xd1 14 ♖axd1± - Botvinnik.

c) 9 ♖b1 a5 10 ♗e3 e5 11 dxe6 ♘xe6 (The recapture with the bishop is worse: 11 ... ♗xe6 12 b3 ♘fd7 13 ♗d4± - Botvinnik) 12 ♘d5 ♘g4 13 ♗d2 c6 14 ♘fd4= Ragozin - Lutikov, USSR 1955.

9 ... a5

Full equality is not achieved by 9 ... e5 10 dxe6 ♗xe6 (10 ... ♘xe6 11 b3 ♘g4 12 ♗b2 f4 13 ♘d5± - Botvinnik) 11 ♘f4 ♗xc4 12 ♘a4 ♗f7 13 ♘xc5 dxc5 14 ♗xb7 (After 14 ♗e3 b6 15 ♖ad1 ♕e7 16 ♗xa8 ♖xa8 Black has good counterplay for the exchange; Toth - Dely, Kecskemet 1972) 14 ... ♖b8 15 ♗g2± - Botvinnik.

10 ♘f4

Also good is 10 b3!? e5 11 dxe6 ♘xe6 12 ♗b2 ♕e7 13 ♖ad1 ♖e8 14 e3 ♘c5 15 ♘f4 with advantage to White in Szabo - Blom, Marianske Lazne 1961.

10	...	e5
11	dxe6	c6
12	b3	♕e7
13	♗a3	*(141)*
13	...	g5?!

After 13 ... ♘xe6 14 ♘xe6 ♗xe6 15 ♖ad1 ♖ad8 16 ♕d2 ♘e8 17 c5 d5 18 ♘a4 ♕c7 19 ♗b2 White would have a slight

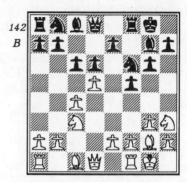

advantage. More serious consideration should be paid to 13 ... a4!?.

	14	♘d3	♘ce4
	15	♖ad1	♗xe6
	16	♘xe4	♘xe4
	17	♗xe4	fxe4
	18	♘e1	♕f7
	19	♗xd6	♖fe8
	20	♗c5	b5
	21	♗d4!	bxc4
	22	bxc4	♗xc4
	23	♗xg7	♔xg7
	24	♘g2	

White has an overwhelming advantage; Timoshchenko - Chernin, USSR 1981.

A12

	7	...	c6

Now White can opt for either 8 0–0 or the immediate 8 ♘f4.

A121 8 0–0
A122 8 ♘f4

A121

	8	0–0 *(142)*

Black's play is analogous to the variation 7 ... c6 (Chapter

two). The position of the knight at h3 instead of f3 promises White certain advantages.

	8	...	e5

Most common but evidently not the best possibility. Also played is 8 ... ♔h8 (8 ... ♗d7 9 ♖e1 ♘a6 10 e4 fxe4 11 ♘xe4 ♘xe4 12 ♖xe4 ♘c5 13 ♖e1±) 9 e4 (9 ♘f4!?) 9 ... e5 10 f4 cxd5 11 cxd5 ♘a6 12 fxe5 dxe5 13 ♔h1 ♕b6 14 ♕e2 fxe4 15 ♘f2 ♗f5 with equality; Thorbergsson - Vasiukov, Reykjavik 1968.

	9	dxe6

Nothing is gained by 9 dxc6 bxc6 10 b4 ♗e6 11 b5 e4 12 ♕a4 ♘fd7 13 ♗g5 ♘b6 14 ♕c2 ♕e8 15 ♖ad1 ♘xc4 with a slight advantage to Black; Doda - Dobosz, Sandomierz 1976.

	9	...	♗xe6
	10	♕b3	

White has two complex alternatives:

a) An unclear position is reached after 10 ♕d3 ♘bd7!? 11 ♕xd6 ♗xc4 12 ♕b4 ♗a6 13 ♘g5 c5 14 ♕b3+ c4 15 ♕d1 ♕e8 16 ♘d5 ♖c8 Magerramov - Palatnik, Baku 1988.

b) Another possibility here is 10 b3 ♘a6 (10 ... ♘e4?! 11 ♘xe4 ♗xa1 12 ♕xd6) 11 ♗f4 (11 ♘g5 ♕e7 *{11 ... ♗c8 12 ♗b2 ♕e7 13 ♘a4 ♗d7 14 e3 ♖ad8 15 ♘h3 ♘c7 16 ♕e1 ♘e6 17 ♖d1 ♗e8 18 f4± Taimanov - Knezevic, Slanchev Brjag 1974}* 12 ♘xe6 ♕xe6 13 ♗b2 ♘e4 *{13 ... ♖ad8 14 e3 ♘c7 15 ♕c2 d5 16 cxd5 ♘cxd5 17 ♘xd5 ♘xd5 18 ♗xg7 ♔xg7 19 ♖ad1 with equal chances; C. Hansen - Lobron, Hamburg 1991}* 14 ♕c1 d5 15 cxd5 cxd5 16 ♘xe4 dxe4 17 ♗xg7 ♔xg7= Taimanov - Holmov, USSR 1975)* 11 ... ♘h5 12 ♕d2 ♘xf4! 13 ♘xf4 ♗f7 14 ♖ac1 ♖e8 15 ♖fd1 ♕a5 16 ♘h3 ♘c5 17 ♘g5 ♖ad8 18 e3 ♕b4 19 ♘e2 ♕xd2 20 ♖xd2 and the position favours White; Karpov - Holmov, Rostov 1980.

10 ... ♕e7 *(143)*

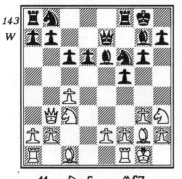

11 ♘g5 ♗f7

On 11 ... ♗c8 it is fine to play 12 e4! threatening c4 - c5 - Taimanov.

12	♘xf7	♖xf7
13	♗f4	♘a6
14	♖ad1	♘e8
15	♕a3	♕e6

15 ... ♘c5 does not save Black either: 16 b4! ♘e6 17 ♗c1 - Taimanov, and 15 ... g5 was met by 16 ♗c1± in Suba - Ivkov, New York 1987.

16	♗xc6	bxc6
17	♕xa6	♗xc3
18	bxc3	c5
19	♖fe1	♖b8
20	f3	♖b6
21	♕a4	♘f6
22	♖d3	

Black does not have sufficient compensation for the pawn; Ree - Rakic, Maribor 1980.

A122

8 ♘f4 *(144)*

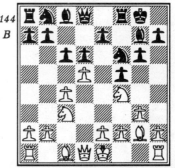

White rejects castling, aiming to prevent the advance ... e7 - e5. But as we have stated above more than once, Black does not need to hurry with this move. Consequently, it is questionable whether White should try to prevent it at all.

8 ... ♕e8

Or:

a) Another possibility to strengthen the square c6 is 8 ...

♗d7 9 0-0 (9 h4 is critical, as in Kasparov - Speelman, London 1989, which continued 9 ... ♗h8 10 e4 *{10 ♕d2! - Kasparov}* 10 ... ♘a6 11 h5 g5 12 ♘e6 ♗xe6 13 dxe6 ♘xe4 14 ♗xe4 ♗xc3+ 15 bxc3 fxe4 16 ♗xg5 ♘c5 and Black stood well) 9 ... ♘a6 (9 ... ♔h8?! 10 e4 cxd5 11 exd5 ♘a6 12 ♗e3 ♖c8 13 b3 ♘c5 14 ♗d4 g5 15 ♘d3 b6 16 ♘e2 e5 17 dxe6 ♘xe6 18 ♗b2 ♘g4 19 ♗xg7+ ♔xg7 20 ♕d2 and there is no counterplay for Black's positional weakness; Schlosser - Weidemann, West Germany 1989) 10 ♖e1 (10 ♖b1 ♔h8 11 b3 ♕e8 12 ♗b2 g5 13 ♘d3 ♕h5 14 e3 ♕h6 15 ♘e2 ♖ac8 16 ♗xf6 ♗xf6 17 f4 with an unclear game in Benjamin - Fishbein, New York 1989. The immediate opening of the centre does not promise any advantage either: 10 e4 fxe4 11 ♘xe4 ♘xe4 12 ♗xe4 ♕e8 13 ♗f3 ♕f7 14 ♗g4 ♗xg4 15 ♕xg4 ♘c7 16 ♕d7 ♖ac8 17 ♘e6 ♘xe6 18 dxe6 ♕f6 19 ♕xb7 ♕xe6 and White has made no real gains; Beutigam - Zysk, West Germany 1988) 10 ... ♘c7 11 ♕b3 c5 12 ♗d2 ♖b8 13 a4 a6?! 14 a5 ♕e8 15 e4 ♘g4 16 ♘d3± Gunawan - Kovacevic, Sarajevo 1988.

b) The third possibility is the immediate 8 ... e5 9 dxe6 ♕e7 (9 ... ♘a6 *{Now Black has to reckon with the advance of the h-pawn}* 10 h4!? ♘c5 11 h5 gxh5 *{11 ... g5 12 h6 ♗h8 13 ♘h3 g4 14 ♘f4 and Black's king is very exposed; Kaidanov - Dunworth*

Andorra 1991} 12 ♘xh5 ♘xh5 13 ♖xh5 ♗xe6 14 ♗h6 ♗xh6 15 ♖xh6 ♕g5 16 ♖h4 f4 17 ♕d2 ♗xc4 18 b3 ♗xe2 19 ♘xe2 ♕e5 with an unclear game; Eingorn - Vasiukov, Belgrade 1988. In the game Spassky - Santo Roman, French Ch 1991, White varied with 18 0-0-0 and lost quickly after 18 ... ♗xa2 19 ♕xd6 fxg3+ 20 f4 ♕xh4 21 ♕xc5 ♗b3 22 ♖f1 ♖xf4 23 ♖h1 ♕f6 24 ♘e4 ♖xe4 25 ♗xe4 ♕f4+ 0-1) 10 0-0 (10 h4!? ♗xe6 11 h5 - Botvinnik) 10 ... ♘a6 (Black does not gain equality by 10 ... ♗xe6 11 ♘xe6 ♕xe6 12 ♘f4 ♕xc4 13 ♕xd6 ♘a6 14 ♖fd1 ♘h5 15 ♗g5± Popov - Sahovic, Plovdiv 1975 and Kasparov - Gurevich, Amsterdam 1991; or by 10 ... g5 11 ♘fd5! cxd5 12 cxd5 ♘e8 13 f4 gxf4 14 ♗xf4 with excellent compensation; Seirawan - Tisdall, Reykjavik 1990) 11 ♖e1 (Worse is the opening of the centre by 11 e4?! fxe4 12 ♘xe4 ♘xe4 13 ♗xe4 ♘c5 14 ♗g2 ♘xe6 15 ♖e1 ♕f7 16 ♖b1 ♘xf4 17 ♗xf4 ♘f5 and White has certain difficulties; Kovacevic - Suba, Haifa 1989. Tempting is 11 b3!? ♘e4 12 ♘xe4 ♗xa1 13 ♕xd6 ♕xd6 14 ♘xd6 ♗f6 15 e4 and Black has no reason to be pleased about his material advantage; Hartoch - van Baarle, Holland 1971) 11 ... ♗xe6 (Black had to face even greater difficulties after 11 ... g5?! 12 ♘d3 ♘e4 13 ♘xe4 fxe4 14 ♗xe4 ♗xe6 15 ♕c2± Portisch - Naranja, Palma de Mallorca 1970) 12 e4 and, according to Botvinnik, White's position is better.

Returning to the position after 8 ... ♕e8 *(145)*

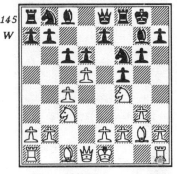

145
W

9   ♕b3

Other continuations are also promising:

a) 9 0-0 ♘a6 10 dxc6 (Consideration should also be paid to 10 ♖b1 ♗d7 11 h3 ♘c7 12 ♕b3 ♖b8 13 c5 ♔h8 14 cxd6 exd6 15 dxc6 bxc6 16 ♕a3 and Black loses material; Donchenko - Panchenko, USSR 1985) 10 ... bxc6 11 ♕a4 ♘b8 and the position is difficult to evaluate; Nowak - Sydor, Sandomierz 1976.

b) 9 h4 e5 10 dxe6 ♗xe6 11 ♕b3 (Alternatively: 11 ♘xe6 ♕xe6 12 ♗f4 ♘a6 13 ♕xd6 ♕xc4 14 ♕d2 ♖ad8 15 ♕c1 ♘g4 and Black was better in Korchnoi - Aronson, USSR 1957; or 11 b3 ♘a6 *{11 ... ♘e4 12 ♘xe4 ♗xa1 13 ♗a3 and White has a good game - Botvinnik; or even 11 ... ♕e7!? - Botvinnik}* 12 ♕xd6 ♗f7 with compensation for a pawn) 11 ... ♖f7 12 h5 ♖d7=.

c) 9 ♖b1 (the latest try) 9 ...

♗d7? (9 ... ♘a6∞) 10 c5! ♘a6 11 cxd6 exd6 12 dxc6 ♗xc6 13 ♕xd6!± Co. Ionescu - S. Grünberg, Eforie Nord 1989.

9   ...   e5
10   ♘e6

10 dxe6 ♘a6= - Botvinnik.

10   ...   ♗xe6
11   ♕xb7   ♘bd7
12   dxe6   ♕xe6
13   ♗xc6   ♘b6
14   ♗d5

14 b3? e4!?.

14   ...   ♘fxd5
15   cxd5   ♕c8

Botvinnik recommends 15 ... ♕f6!?.

16   ♕xc8   ♖fxc8

Black has compensation for his material deficit - Kovacevic.

A13
7   ...   c5 *(146)*

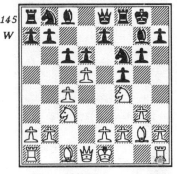

146
W

The move 7 ... ♘bd7 has no individual importance, because after 8 0-0 ♘e5 a position from the variation 6 ... ♘c6 7 0-0 d6 8 d5 ♘e5 occurs.

8   ♘f4

As usual, White can simply castle: 8 0-0 ♘a6 9 ♗d2 (9 ♘f4

♘c7 10 ♖e1 ♘g4 11 ♕c2 ♖b8 12 a4 ♘e5 13 ♘b5 a6 14 ♘xc7 ♕xc7 15 ♗d2 b5 and Black has quite active play; Scherbakov – Korzubov, Moscow 1991) 9 ... ♘c7 10 ♕c2 ♖b8 11 a4 ♗d7 12 ♘f4 a6 13 a5 with better chances for White in Taimanov – Tal, USSR 1969.

	8	...	♘a6
	9	0-0	♘c7

Or 9 ... ♖b8 10 ♖b1 ♘g4?! 11 ♘b5 ♕b6 12 ♗d2 ♘e5 13 b3 ♗d7 14 ♕e1 with the advantage to White in Farago – Hölzl, Hungary – Austria 1975.

10 ♖b1

Equality was the outcome of 10 ♕c2 ♖b8 11 a4 b6 12 ♖b1 ♗d7 13 ♗d2 a6 14 b4 cxb4 15 ♖xb4 a5 16 ♖bb1 ♘a6 17 ♘b5 ♕e8 18 ♘d3 ♘e4; Hasin – Naivelt, Leningrad 1984.

10	...	♖b8
11	a4	a6
12	b4!	cxb4
13	♖xb4	♘d7
14	♗d2	a5
15	♖b1	♘e5
16	♕b3	♘a6
17	♘d3	♗d7
18	♘b5	

White has a slight advantage; Uhlmann – Paehtz, Halle 1974.

A2

	6	...	♘c6 *(147)*

Black intends to play ... d7 – d6 and ... e7 – e5. In anticipation of these moves White has to play d4 – d5. This variation has

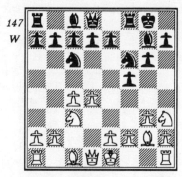

been popular in recent practice.

7 0-0

Castling can be postponed:

a) 7 ♘f4 d6 8 d5 ♘e5 9 b3 (9 ♕b3 c5 10 0-0 ♖b8 11 a4 ♕a5 12 ♘d3 ♗d7 13 ♗d2 ♕d8 14 ♘xe5 dxe5 15 ♕a3 b6 16 a5 ♘e8 with equal chances; Uhlmann – Yrjola, Tallinn 1987) 9 ... ♘e4 10 ♘xe4 fxe4 11 ♗e3 g5 12 ♘h5 ♗h8 13 h3 ♕e8 14 g4 ♕g6 15 ♘g3 ♘f3+ 16 ♗xf3 exf3 17 ♖c1 fxe2 18 ♕c2 ♕f7 19 ♕xe2= Legky – Kontic, Vrjancka Banja 1989.

b) 7 d5 ♘e5 8 ♕b3 (8 b3 ♘f7 9 ♗b2 e5 10 dxe6 dxe6 11 ♕xd8 ♖xd8= Osnos – Legky, Lvov 1984) 8 ... c5 (8 ... ♘f7 9 0-0 ♘h5 10 ♖d1 d6 11 ♗e3 ♗d7 12 c5 dxc5 13 ♗xc5 b6 14 ♗d4 with a favourable position for White; Korchnoi – Kuzminyh, USSR 1951) 9 0-0 ♘e8 10 ♗e3 d6 11 ♖ad1 ♖b8 12 ♘g5 ♘c7 13 ♘f3 ♗d7 14 ♘xe5 ♗xe5 15 ♗h6 ♖e8 16 ♕c2 b5 with an unclear position; Kloss – Haag, corr. 1959.

c) 7 ♖b1!? d6 8 d5 ♘e5 9 b3 c5 (9 ... a6 10 a4 c5 11 0-0 ♖b8 12

♗d2! ♗d7 13 ♕c2± Scherbakov –
Kramnik, USSR 1990) 10 0-0
♗d7?! (More exact is the immediate 10 ... a6 with the idea
of ... ♖b8, ... b6 and ... ♘f6 – e8
– c7) 11 ♕c2 a6 12 a4 ♖b8 13 ♗d2
♘e8 14 ♘f4 (14 ♔h1?! b6 *{14 ...*
♘c7 enables White to fix the
queen's wing: 15 a5!± Kozlov
– Legky, Tallinn 1987} 15 f4 ♘f7
{15 ... ♘g4?! 16 ♘f2 ♘xf2 17
♖xf2± Nenashev – Malaniuk,
Tashkent 1987} 16 ♘f2 ♘h6!?
and Black's position is not
worse; Haritonov – Malaniuk,
Moscow 1988) 14 ... ♘c7 (14 ...
b6!?) 15 a5 and White has a
spatial advantage; Suba – Ermenkov, Tunis izt 1985.

7   ...   d6

An unusual idea is 7 ... e6!? 8
d5 ♘e5 9 b3 (9 ♕b3 – Speelman)
9 ... ♘f7! 10 ♘a3 ♖e8 11 ♖c1 (11
dxe6±) 11 ... e5 12 d6 c6 13 b4 b6
14 e4?! (14 c5 with a complicated game) Timman – Speelman, London match 1989.

8   d5

Less effective is 8 ♘f4 (This
enables Black to free himself in
the centre) 8 ... e5 (It is not
good to capture 8 ... ♘xd4?! 9
♕xd4 e5 10 ♕d3 exf4 11 ♗xf4
♕e7 12 ♖ad1 ♖e8 13 c5! dxc5 14
♘b5 c6 15 ♘c7 ♗e6 16 ♘xa8
♖xa8 17 ♗d6 and Black loses
material; Hort–Sikora, Trecian-
ske Teplice 1979) 9 dxe5 dxe5 10
♘fd5 (Nothing is gained by 10
♗xc6 bxc6 11 ♕xd8 ♖xd8 12
♘d3 ♘d7; Dizdar – Malaniuk,
Baku 1988. An equal position is

reached by 10 ♕xd8 ♖xd8 11
♘fd5 ♖d7 – Tukmakov) 10 ...
♘e8 (10 ... ♘d4 11 f4!? *{11 ♗g5*
c6 12 ♘xf6+ ♗xf6= – Tukmak-
ov} 11 ... ♘h5 12 fxe5 ♗xe5 13
♗h6 ♖e8 14 e3 ♘e6 15 ♖xf5
gxf5 16 ♕xh5 c6 17 ♖d1 ♗d7 18
♘f4 ♕e7 19 ♕xf5 ♘f8 20 ♕h5
♗g7 21 ♘e4 with a slight advantage to White; Yuferov –
Piskov, Moscow 1989) 11 b4!? c4
12 b5 ♘d4 13 ♗e3 with an obscure position in Tukmakov –
Malaniuk, Sverdlovsk 1987.

8   ...   ♘e5
9   b3

Probably the most logical
course of action. Also:

a) In one of the original
games with this variation White
opted to defend the pawn with
his queen. However, after 9
♕b3 ♘fd7 Black has chances of
an active game: 10 ♗e3 (10
♘a4 loses time, e.g. 10 ... ♕e8 11
♘g5 ♘b6 12 ♘xb6 axb6 13 ♕c2
h6 14 ♘h3 c4 15 ♗d2 *{15 a4?*
♗d7∓} 15 ... b5 and Black seized
the initiative in Yurenok –
Golubenko, Erevan 1983) 10 ...
♘g4 11 ♗d2 ♘c5 (11 ... e5! 12
♘g5?! ♘c5 13 ♕a3 e4! 14 b4
♘e5!!∓ Poldauf – Glek, Erfort
1989) 12 ♕c2 a5 13 ♖ad1 ♗d7 14
♘f4 ♖e8 with an equal game;
Bogolyubow – Tartakower,
Karlsbad 1923.

b) The pawn may also be
defended indirectly: 9 ♕c2 ♗d7
(Possible is also 9 ... c5 10 b3 a6
11 ♗b2 ♖b8 12 a4 b6 13 ♘f4 ♘e8
14 h4 ♘c7 15 ♖fb1 h6 16 ♘d1

♕e8 with an unclear game; Dzhandzhava - Kramnik, Belgorod 1989) 10 b3 c5 11 ♘f4 ♘e8 12 ♗b2 ♘c7 13 a4 ♘a6 14 h4 ♘b4 15 ♕d2 a6 16 h5 g5 17 ♘e6 ♗xe6 18 dxe6 f4 19 ♗xb7 ♖b8 20 ♗e4 and Black has counterplay for the pawn; Georgadze - Savchenko, Simferopol 1988.

9 ... c5 (148)

It is inappropriate to play actively: 9 ... ♘e4?! 10 ♘xe4 fxe4 (Even worse is 10 ... ♘f3+? 11 exf3 fxe4 12 ♗g5! ♗xa1 13 ♕xa1 exf3 14 ♖e1 ♖f7 15 ♗f1 and White wins; Portisch - Menvielle, Las Palmas 1972) 11 ♖b1 ♗f5 12 ♘g5 ♕d7 13 ♘xe4 ♖ae8 14 ♗b2 e6 15 dxe6 and Black's counterplay for the missing pawn is insufficient; Taimanov - Hort, Wijk aan Zee 1970.

The immediate 9 ... c5 seems more accurate than 9 ... ♗d7, e.g. 10 ♗b2 (10 ♗d2 c5 11 a4 ♖b8 12 a5 ♘e8 13 f3 ♘c7 with typical play; Gavrikov - Spraggett, Moscow GMA 1990) 10 ... c5 11 dxc6 bxc6 12 c5!± Glek.

148
W

10 ♗b2
Another possibility is 10 dxc6

bxc6 11 ♗b2 ♖b8 12 ♕c2 ♕c7 13 ♖ad1 ♘f7! 14 ♗c1 e5∞ I. Hausner - Glek, W. Germany 1991.

10 ... a6
11 ♘f4 ♖b8!?

Not 11 ... g5?! 12 ♘d3 ♘g6 13 ♕d2 h6 14 f4 g4 15 e4 ♘xe4 16 ♘xe4 fxe4 17 ♗xg7 ♔xg7 18 ♗xe4 ♘f5 19 ♕c3+ ♔h7 20 ♗xf5 ♖xf5 21 ♘f2 h5 22 h3! gxh3 23 ♘xh3 with an overwhelming advantage for White; Radulescu - Fasil, corr. 1987.

12 a4 b6
With a complicated game.

A3

6 ... e6 (149)

149
W

On d4 - d5 Black intends to play ... e6 - e5, but there are additional possibilities for White to gain a lead in development. Recently some unsuccessful attempts have been made to resurrect this line.

7 d5

In several games 7 0-0 d6 has been played (Unsuccessful is 7 ... ♕e7 8 d5 e5 9 d6 ♕xd6 10 ♕xd6 cxd6 11 ♘b5 ♘c6 12 ♖d1 ♘e8 13 ♗e3 e4 14 ♖ab1 ♘e5 15 b3 a6 16 ♘xd6 ♘xd6 17 ♖xd6 b5 18 c5 with a positional advantage for White; Taimanov - Liebert, Rostov 1961) 8 b3 (8 ♘f4 c6 9 ♕b3 ♘a6 10 ♖d1 ♕e7 11 e4 (11 ♘d3!?) 11 ... fxe4 12 ♘xe4 ♘xe4 13 ♗xe4 e5 14 dxe5 ♘c5 15 ♕e3 ♘xe4 16 ♕xe4 ♗xe5∓ Nikolic - Bjelajac, Novi Sad 1982) 8 ... c6 9 ♗a3 (Less efficient is 9 ♕c2 a5 10 ♗a3 ♘a6 11 ♖ad1 ♕c7 12 ♘f4 ♘b4 13 ♕b1 e5 with an equal game; Averbakh - Gulko, USSR 1976) 9 ... ♕a5 (Better is 9 ... a5) 10 ♕c1 ♖d8 11 b4 ♕c7 12 ♖d1 ♘bd7 13 c5 d5 14 ♘g5 ♖e8 15 f4 with a better position for White; Ree - Hübner, Wijk aan Zee 1975.

7   ...   ♕e7

In Gleizerov's and Samarin's opinion 7 ... e5 is slightly better. After 8 d6! White's advantage is not as great as in the main line.

8   0-0   e5
9   d6

This is more effective than 9 e4!?.

9   ...   ♕xd6

On 9 ... cxd6 Gleizerov and Samarin suggest 10 ♗g5! with the idea of ♕d2 and ♖ad1.

10   ♕xd6   cxd6
11   ♘b5   ♘c6
12   ♖d1!

White has a great advantage; Gleizerov - Legky, USSR 1987.

B

5   ♘f4 *(150)*

Here White tries to get by without c2 - c4. This presents

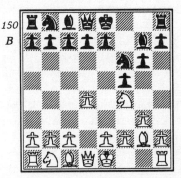

no problems for Black.

Another possibility is the immediate 5 d5 d6 (5 ... 0-0!? with the idea of ... e7 - e5) 6 ♘f4 c6! (6 ... c5 7 h4 0-0 8 h5 ♕e8 9 hxg6 hxg6 10 ♘d2 ♘a6 11 ♘f3 ♘e4 with an obscure position; Solmundarsson - Padevsky, Siegen 1970) 7 ♘c3 0-0 8 0-0 cxd5 9 ♘fxd5 ♘xd5 10 ♕xd5+ ♔h8 11 e4 ♘c6 12 ♗e3 ♗d7 13 ♕d2 fxe4 14 ♘xe4 ♕a5 15 c3 ♘e5 with the black pieces co-operate effectively - Taimanov.

White can also try 5 c3 with similar play to chapter 7, e.g. 5 ... ♘c6 6 ♘d2 d6 7 d5 ♘e5 8 ♘b3 c5! 9 dxc6 ♘xc6 10 ♘d4 ♘xd4 11 cxd4 ♕a5+= Douven - Vanheste, Holland 1986/87.

5   ...   ♘c6

Three other moves have also been seen:

a) Interesting is 5 ... e6 6 c3 c6 7 ♘d2 d6 8 ♘d3 ♕c7 9 e4 e5 10 dxe5 dxe5 11 exf5 ♗xf5 12 ♘c5 ♘bd7 13 ♘ce4 0-0-0 14 0-0 h5 15 h4 ♗h6. Unusual and imaginative play has led to an interesting position; Levin -

Shabalov, Leningrad 1989.

b) Satisfactory is 5 ... d6 6
♘c3 0-0 (6 ... c6 7 d5!? e5! {7 ...
cxd5 8 ♘fxd5!} 8 dxe6 d5 9 h4
♕e7 10 h5 g5 11 h6 ♗f8 12
♘h5!?∞ Korchnoi - Gurevich,
Rotterdam 1990) 7 e4 c6 8 0-0
♘a6 9 d5 e5 10 dxe6 fxe4 11
♘xe4 ♘xe4 12 ♗xe4 ♖e8 13 c4
♘c5 14 ♗g2 ♘xe6 15 ♕b3 ♕b6
16 ♖e1 ♗d7 17 ♗e3 ♕xb3 18 axb3
♘xf4 19 ♗xf4= Eingorn -
Malaniuk, Odessa 1989,

c) It is risky to play 5 ... 0-0
6 h4 ♘c6 (The two remaining
possibilities are weaker: 6 ... d6
7 c3 c6 8 ♕b3+ d5 9 h5 g5 10 h6
♗h8 11 ♘d3 g4 12 ♗f4 ♘bd7 13
♘d2± Savchenko - Malaniuk,
Herson 1989; and 6 ... ♗h8?! 7
♘d2 e6 {Even worse is 7 ... ♘c6
8 c3 e6 9 d5 exd5 10 ♘xd5 ♘e7
11 ♘xf6+ ♗xf6 12 ♘f3 d5 13 h5
c6 14 hxg6 ♘xg6 15 ♗e3 ♕e7 16
♕d2 ♗e6 17 ♘g5± Fokin -
Vyzmanavin, Smolensk 1989}
8 c3 c6 9 e4 d6 10 exf5 exf5 11
0-0 ♗g7 12 d5 ♖e8 13 ♘c4 ♗f8
14 a4 ♘e4 15 ♗e3 ♘a6 16 ♖e1
♘c7± Bagaturov - Galdunts,
Belgorod 1989) 7 h5 ♕e8 (7 ...
g5 8 h6! - Taimanov) 8 hxg6
hxg6 9 ♘c3 ♔f7 10 d5 ♘e5 11

♕d4 d6 (151)

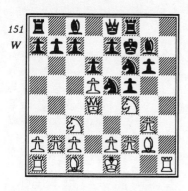

151
W

and the position is not at all
clear; Alekhine - Tartakower,
Karlsbad 1923.

| 6 | d5 | ♘e5 |
| 7 | ♘c3 | |

A sharper alternative is 7 h4
c6 8 ♘c3 0-0 9 h5 cxd5 10 hxg6
hxg6 11 ♘cxd5 ♘xd5 12 ♗xd5
e6∞ Pugachev - Rublevsky,
USSR 1991.

7	...	c6
8	♘d3	♘f7
9	0-0	0-0
10	f4	cxd5
11	♘xd5	♘xd5
12	♗xd5	e6
13	♗g2	d5

The position is equal; Rubin-
stein - Bogolyubov, Karlsbad
1923.

7 Systems with c3

1	d4	f5
2	g3	♘f6
3	♗g2	g6
4	c3	♗g7 *(152)*

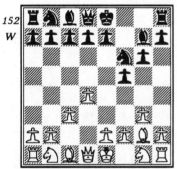

The modest advance of the c-pawn introduces a popular variation in which White's play is to a large extent based on the weakness of the diagonal g8 - a2. The chapter is divided into three sections. The first two are quite significant but the third is rarely seen:

A 5 ♘f3
B 5 ♕b3
C 5 ♗g5 and others

A

5   ♘f3

Now Black usually chooses to castle at once, although this move may be delayed:

A1 5 ... 0-0
A2 5 ... d6

A1

5   ...   0-0
6   0-0

Instead of castling Beliavsky has tried 6 ♗g5 c6 (One can also play more actively: 6 ... ♘e4!? 7 ♗f4 d6 with the idea of ... ♕e8 and ... e7 - e5 - Gurevich) 7 ♘bd2 (White intends to play 8 ♗xf6 ♗xf6 9 e4) 7 ... d5 8 ♘e5 ♘bd7 9 ♗f4 ♘xe5 10 ♗xe5 ♗h6 11 ♘f3 ♕b6 12 ♕c2 ♗e6 13 0-0 ♘d7 14 ♗f4 ♗g7 (14 ... ♗xf4 15 gxf4±) 15 ♕d2 ♗f7 16 b3 ♖fe8 17 ♖ac1 e5 and there is no longer any sign of White's initiative, Beliavsky - Gurevich, Moscow 1988.

After 6 0-0 Black may consider:

A11 6 ... d6
A12 6 ... c6 and others

A11

6   ...   d6

Now White has:

A111 7 ♕b3+
A112 7 ♘bd2

A111

7 ♕b3+ *(153)*

Although 7 ♘bd2 is more common in practice, this queen move poses very serious problems. White's idea is simple: Black is soon forced to play ... d6 - d5 and the White game will be based around the weak squares.

First, let us consider a rare continuation: 7 a4 (White usually plays this in answer to ... a7 – a5) 7 ... h6 (7 ... a5) 8 a5 a6 9 ♕b3+ ♚h7 10 ♘bd2 ♘c6 11 d5 ♘e5 12 ♘d4 ♕e8 13 ♘2f3 c5 14 ♘e6 ♗xe6 15 dxe6 ♘xf3+ 16 exf3 ♕c6 17 c4 ♖ab8 18 ♖e1 b5!? with an unclear position; Cebalo – Avshalumov, Belgrade 1988.

7 ... ♚h8
8 ♘g5

Both 9 ♘f7+ and 9 ♘e6 are threats to Black.

8 ... d5
9 c4

Also possible is more peaceful plan by 9 ♘d2 ♘c6 10 ♘df3

h6 11 ♘h3 g5 12 ♘e5 ♘xe5 13 dxe5 ♘e4 14 f3 ♘c5 15 ♕d1 ♗e6 16 ♕d4 b6 17 b4 ♘d7 18 ♗xg5! and White has gained a winning attack; Gutman – Knezevic, Wuppertal 1986.

9 ... e6
10 ♘f3

10 ♘c3 also has good prospects: 10 ... ♘c6 11 cxd6 ♘xd4 12 ♕c4 ♘xd5 13 ♘xd5 exd5 14 ♗xd5 f4?! (Better was 14 ... ♘xe2+ 15 ♕xe2 ♕xd5 16 ♖d1 ♕g8 with an unclear position) 15 ♗xf4! (15 ♘f7+ ♖xf7 16 ♗xf7 ♗d7!) 15 ... ♘xe2+ 16 ♕xe2 ♕xd5 17 ♖fd1 ♕f5 18 ♖ac1 h6 19 ♘e4 ♗d7? (19 ... c6 20 ♘d6 ♕g4!?) 20 ♖xc7 ♗b5 21 ♕e3 and White has an extra pawn; Miralles – Santo Roman, Royan 1988.

10 ... c5?! *(154)*

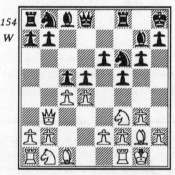

This is too impatient. Evidently 10 ... c6 or 10 ... ♘e4 should have been played, intending to fight for the e5-square.

11 dxc5 ♘a6
12 ♗e3 ♘g4
13 ♗g5 ♕e8
14 cxd5 ♘xc5

15 ♕a3

The opening up of the position has favoured White; Dokhoian - Akopian, Vilnius 1988.

A112

7 ♘bd2

Here Black has:

A1121 7 ... ♘c6
A1122 7 ... ♔h8 and others

A1121

7 ...   ♘c6 *(155)*

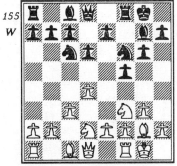

Black chooses the most active plan. 7 ... ♘c6 is played with the intention of advancing ... e7 - e5. If Black plays correctly here, he can expect to equalise.

8 ♖e1

Also possible is 8 ♕b3+!? ♔h8 9 d5 ♘e5 (9 ... ♘a5! 10 ♕a3 c5 - Bellin) 10 ♘d4 ♘fd7?! (Bad is 10 ... ♖b8?! 11 h3; but 10 ... ♕e8, with the idea of ... c7 - c5, is worth trying) and in the game Neckar - Pribyl, White could have continued by 11 ♘e6!? ♘c5 12 ♘xc5 dxc5 13 ♕a3±.

8 ...   e5

The slow 8 ... ♔h8 is hardly essential, but is interesting nevertheless: 9 e4 e5 (9 ... f4!? - Matsukevich; or 9 ... fxe4 *{The exchange in the centre is not recommended here}* 10 ♘xe4 ♘xe4 11 ♖xe4 e5 12 ♗g5 ♕d7 13 dxe5 dxe5 14 ♕e2 ♕f7 15 ♖h4 ♗e6 16 ♗e3! ♕f6 17 ♘g5 with a solid advantage for White; Gligoric - Rajkovic, Yugoslavia 1975) 10 dxe5 dxe5 11 exf5 (11 ♕b3 *{This enables Black to carry out a typical attack}* 11 ... f4 12 gxf4 ♘h5 13 f5 ♘f4 14 ♘f1 ♘xg2 15 ♔xg2 gxf5 16 exf5 ♗xf5 17 ♗g5 ♕d7 18 ♘g1 ♗e6 19 ♕b5 ♗d5+ 20 f3 ♖xf3 21 ♘xf3 ♕g4+ and White resigned in Tataev - Kramnik, Belgorod 1989) 11 ... e4 12 ♘g5 gxf5 13 ♘b3 ♕e8 14 f3 h6 15 ♘h3 ♘e5 16 ♘f4 ♕f7 17 ♗e3 ♗d7 18 ♗d4 ♖ae8 19 ♘c5± Schussler - Silva, Thessaloniki ol 1984.

9 dxe5   ♘xe5

Capturing with the pawn is a mistake: 9 ... dxe5? 10 e4 f4 11 gxf4 exf4 12 e5± - Gurevich.

10 ♘xe5   dxe5
11 e4   f4
12 ♘c4

Or 12 gxf4 ♘h5 13 fxe5 ♕h4 14 ♘f3 ♖xf3!! 15 ♕xf3 ♗xf5 16 h3 ♗e6 with the idea of ... ♖f8 and ... ♘f4 with serious threats - Gurevich.

12 ...   fxg3
13 hxg3   ♕e7
14 b3   ♖e8
15 ♗a3   ♕f7

16 ♕c2   a5! *(156)*

156
W

Black has overcome his opening difficulties; Kaplun – Gurevich, USSR 1983.

A1122

7   ...   ♔h8 *(157)*

157
W

Here we consider this prophylactic king move and other possibilities for Black, with the exception of 7 ... ♘c6. First of all some deviations:

a) 7 ... c6?! (This proves to be a loss of tempo) 8 ♖e1 (8 a4!? ♔h8 *{8 ... a5}* 9 a5 ♕c7 10 ♘c4 ♗e6?? 11 ♘b6 and White wins material; Yailjan – Orlov, Belgorod 1989) 8 ... d5? (8 ... ♘h5!? with the idea of 9 e4 f4) 9 ♘e5 ♔h8 10 ♘df3 ♗e6 11 ♗f4 ♘bd7

12 ♕c2 ♘xe5 13 ♘xe5 ♖g8 (13 ... ♘d7!?) 14 ♘d3± Tempone – Rubinetti, Buenos Aires 1979.

b) 7 ... ♕e8 (This falls in with White's plans) 8 ♕b3+ e6 9 ♖e1 d5 10 ♘e5 g5 11 c4 c6 12 cxd5 exd5 13 e4! fxe4 14 ♘xe4 ♘xe4 15 ♖xe4 ♔h8 16 ♖e1 ♕d8 17 ♗d2 and due to the active knight at e5 White has the advantage; Schussler – Ochoa, Palma de Mallorca 1989.

8   ♖e1

After 8 ♕b3 ♘c6 9 ♘g5 d5 10 f4 b6 11 ♘df3 e6 12 ♕b5 ♕e8 13 b3 h6 14 ♘h3 ♘e4 15 ♕d3 a5 Black has a good game; Sprotte – Tukmakov, Biel 1991.

8	...	d5
9	♘e5	c6
10	♘df3	♘e4
11	♗f4	♗e6
12	♘g5	♘xg5
13	♗xg5	♘d7
14	♘xd7	♕xd7
15	♕d2	♗g8
16	♗h3	♕c7
17	♗f4	*(158)*

158
B

17   ...   ♕b6?!

Equality would have been achieved by 17 ... e5.

18	♕e3	♖ae8
19	♗e5	♗xe5
20	♕xe5+	♖f6
21	b4	

With an overwhelming advantage to White in Spasov – Glek, Moscow 1989.

A12

6	...	c6 *(159)*

For the time being Black leaves it open whether to play ... d7 - d6 or ... d7 - d5.

Artificial is 6 ... a5 7 ♘bd2 ♘a6 (7 ... d6!?) 8 ♘c4 c6 9 a4 (9 ♕b3 a4!) 9 ... d6 10 ♕b3 ♗e6 11 ♘g5 ♗xc4 12 ♕xc4+ d5 13 ♕d3 ♕d7 14 ♗f4 ♖ae8 15 ♗e5± Gligoric – Kovacevic, Bugojno 1984.

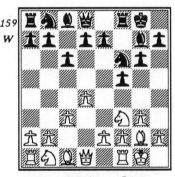

7	♘bd2	♔h8

Alternatively:

a) The transfer of the knight 7 ... ♘e4 is unsuccessful, e.g. 8 ♘xe4 fxe4 9 ♘e1 d5 10 f3 exf3 11 exf3 ♗f5 12 ♕e2 ♕d7 13 g3 ♗e6 14 ♘d3 and Black's centre is blocked; Djuric – Todorovic, Pula 1988.

b) Consideration should be given to 7 ... a5 8 a4 ♔h8 9 ♕b3

d5 10 ♘e5 ♘bd7 11 ♘df3 ♘xe5 12 ♘xe5 ♘d7 13 ♘xd7 ♕xd7 14 ♖d1 ♕d7 15 c4 ♗e6 16 cxd5 ♗xd5 17 ♗xd5 cxd5 18 ♕xd5 ♖fd8 19 ♕b5 ♖xd4 20 ♖xd4 ♗xd4 with an equal game; Kozul – Kovacevic, Sarajevo 1988.

c) A less flexible, but quite possible alternative is 7 ... d5 8 ♘e5 ♘bd7 (A modern, though not fully appropriate plan is 8 ... ♗e6 9 ♘df3 ♘e4 10 ♗f4 ♘d7 11 ♘xd7 ♕xd7 12 ♖c1 ♖fd8?! *{Better was to aim for equality: 12 ... ♘d6 with the idea of 13 ... ♘f7}* 13 ♘e5 ♕e8 14 ♘d3 ♗f7 15 ♗e5 ♗f6 16 f3 ♘d6 17 b3 ♕f8 18 g4 h6 19 ♔h1 ♔h7 20 ♘h3 fxg4 21 ♗xg4 ♕g8 22 ♖g1 and Black remained under pressure in Kovacevic – Fishbein, New York 1989) 9 ♘d3 ♘e4 10 ♘f3 e6 11 ♘fe5 ♘xe5 12 ♘xe5 ♘d6 13 a4 a5 14 b3 ♘f7 15 ♘d3 e5 16 dxe5 ♘xe5= Nemet – Bhend, Switzerland 1988.

8	♘e5	

Too slow is 8 ♖e1?! d5 9 ♘e5 ♘bd7 10 ♘d3 e5 (Black has alleviated his difficulties) 11 dxe5 ♘g4 12 ♘f3 ♘gxe5 13 ♘fxe5 ♘xe5 14 ♘xe5 ♗xe5 15 ♗e3 and here the players agreed a draw in Gligoric – Gurevich, Belgrade 1989.

8	...	d6

Instead of Black's last move, consideration should have been given to 8 ... d5, for example 9 ♘df3 ♘bd7 10 ♘d3 ♘e4!? with the idea of ... ♘d6 - f7.

9	♘d3	♘bd7 *(160)*

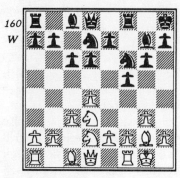

10 e4

Less active is 10 a4 e5 11 dxe5 ♘xe5 12 ♘xe5 dxe5 13 ♘c4 (13 e4!?) 13 ... e4 with equality; Szilagyi - Gurevich, Budapest 1987.

	10 ...	♘xe4
	11 ♘xe4	fxe4
	12 ♗xe4	e5
	13 dxe5	d5
	14 ♗g2	♘xe5
	15 ♘xe5	♗xe5
	16 ♖e1	♗g7
	17 ♗e3	♗f5
	18 ♗d4	♕d7
	19 ♕d2	a6
	20 ♖e3	♖ae8
	21 ♖ae1	♔g8
	22 ♗c5	♖xe3
	23 ♕xe3	♖d8
	24 h4	

White has a minimal advantage, the realisation of which is rather doubtful; Gavrikov - Malaniuk, Tallinn 1987.

A2

	5 ...	d6 *(161)*

Black does not hurry to castle at once.

	6 ♕b3

More peaceful moves are also possible:

a) 6 ♘bd2 c6 7 ♕b3 ♕b6 8 ♘c4 ♕c7 9 ♘g5! h6? (9 ... d5) 10 ♘b6! hxg5 11 ♘xa8 ♕d7 12 ♗xg5 b6 13 ♘xb6 axb6 14 ♕xb6 and White's rook and three pawns have more value than Black's two knights; Szabolcsi - Gastonyi, Hungary 1988,

b) 6 0–0 a5 (An original idea) 7 a4 e6 8 ♕b3 c6 9 ♘g5 ♕e7 10 ♘xe6 ♕xe6 11 d5 ♕d7 12 dxc6 bxc6 13 ♘d2 d5 14 ♘f3 ♘e4 and the black knight in the centre compensates for the pawn weakness; Kachur - Gofstein, Belgorod 1989.

	6 ...	c6

Attention should also be paid to 6 ... e6 7 ♘g5 d5 8 ♕a4+?! ♘c6 9 b4 0–0 10 b5 ♘e7 11 0–0 a6 12 bxa6 ♖xa6 13 ♕b3 ♘c6 14 ♖d1 ♗d7 15 ♕c2 ♘e4 and White has wasted time on the queenside; Black already has a slight advantage, Ristic - Buecker, Dortmund 1989.

	7 ♘g5

7 ♘d2 is more solid. The game Dlugy - Lean, New York

1992, continued 7 ... ♛b6 8 ♕c2 (8 ♘c4 ♕c7!) 8 ... 0-0 9 0-0 d5! 10 c4±.

7	...	d5
8	h4	0-0
9	♗f4	♛b6
10	♘d2	♛xb3
11	axb3	h6
12	♗xb8	♖xb8
13	♘gf3	♖a8
14	♘e5	♔h7
15	f4	♘e4
16	♗xe4	fxe4
17	b4	

White's early activity has not proven successful. The game Gross - Psakhis, Minsk 1986, was equal.

B

5   ♛b3 *(162)*

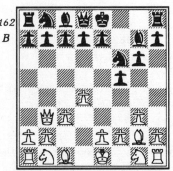

162 B

White makes a queen move before developing the knight, which may emerge on the f4-square. Practice suggests that Black is the main beneficiary of this sequence.

Black has three main alternatives:

B1 5 ... ♘c6

B2 5 ... c6
B3 5 ... d5

An interesting recent idea is 5 ... c5 6 ♗xb7 (6 dxc5 ♘a6) 6 ... c4 7 ♛b4 ♘a6 8 ♗xa6 ♗xa6 9 ♘d2 ♖b8 10 ♛a4 ♗b5 11 ♛c2 0-0 with compensation for the pawn; Henkin - Glek, USSR 1990.

B1

5	...	♘c6
6	♘h3	e6
7	♘f4	

White could also try 7 ♘d2 (White aims to prepare the attack more carefully) 7 ... d6 (Alternatively: 7 ... 0-0 8 ♘f4 ♔h8? 9 h4 e5 10 dxe5 ♘xe5 11 ♘f3 ♘eg4 12 h5 gxh5 13 ♘d4 d5 14 ♘de6 with a winning position for White in Flear - Minic, Belgrade 1988; or 7 ... d5 8 ♘f3 ♘e4 9 ♘f4 ♛e7 10 ♘d3 0-0 11 h4 b6 12 ♗f4 ♗b7 13 ♛c2 ♘d8 14 ♗e5 ♘f7 15 ♗xg7 ♔xg7 and the control of the e5-square is promising for White; Gavrikov - Vyzmanavin, Irkutsk 1986) 8 ♘f4 (Opening the centre gives no advantage: 8 e4 e5 9 exf5 gxf5 10 dxe5 dxe5 - Vanheste) 8 ... ♛e7 9 ♘xe6! ♛xe6 10 d5 ♘xd5 11 ♗xd5 ♛e7 (With the idea of ... ♘d8, ... c6, ... ♗e6) 12 ♛b5 ♛d7 13 e4 ♘e5! 14 ♛e2 (And not 14 ♛xd7 ♗xd7 15 ♗xb7 ♘d3+ 16 ♔e2 ♘xc1+ 17 ♖hxc1 ♖b8 with an overwhelming advantage to Black) 14 ... c6 15 ♗b3 fxe4 16 ♘xe4 d5 17 f4 with a very obscure position; Sosonko - Vanheste, Holland 1986/87.

Returning to the position after 7 ♘f4 *(163)*.

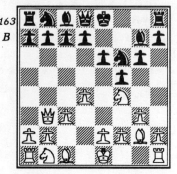

163
B

7   ...   0-0

In Malaniuk's opinion attention should be paid to 7 ... d5!? 8 h4 ♘e4 9 h5 g5 (9 ... ♛f6!?) 10 h6 ♗xd4 11 cxd4 gxf4 12 ♗xf4 ♘xd4 with unclear position.

7   h4   ♛e8
8   h5   g5

Fixing the centre by 9 ... d5 10 hxg6 hxg6 11 ♘d2 gives White a slight advantage - Malaniuk.

10   h6   ♗h8
11   ♘d3

After the retreat 11 ♘h3?! g4 12 ♘f4 ♘e7 and 13 ... ♘g6 Black's problems are solved - Malaniuk.

11   ...   ♘e4

11 ... g4?! gives White chances for attack: 12 ♗f4 d6 13 ♘d2 with the idea of opening the centre with e2 - e4.

12   g4!   d5
13   gxf5   ♘a5
14   ♛b4   ♘c6
15   ♛b3   ♘a5

16   ♛c2

After 16 ♛b4 it is more appropriate to play 16 ... ♘c6 than 16 ... b6?! 17 ♖g1! ♖xf5 18 f3! ♘d6 19 ♗h3.

16   ...   exf5
17   ♖g1 *(164)*

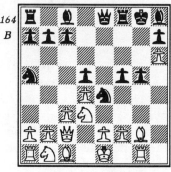

164
B

17   ...   ♗f6!

This leaves the king a secure place on the h8-square - Malaniuk.

18   f3

Malaniuk considers the variation 18 ♗xe4 fxe4 (18 ... dxe4 19 ♗xg5 exd3 20 ♗xf6+ ♔f7 21 ♛xd3 ♔xf6 22 ♛g3 with possibilities for both sides) 19 ♗xg5 ♗h8! 20 ♗xf6+ ♖xf6 21 ♘e5 ♘c6! 22 ♘xc6 bxc6 23 ♛d2 ♛h5 with compensation for the pawn.

18   ...   ♘d6
19   f4   g4
20   ♗xd5+   ♗e6
21   ♗g2   c6

Black has suffcent counterplay for the pawn; Varga - Malaniuk, Budapest 1989. In this particular game there followed 22 ♘e3? ♗xa2 23 ♘e5 ♗b3 and Black won.

B2

    5   ...   c6 *(165)*

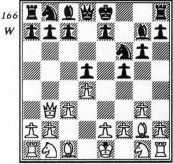

A flexible and interesting possibility on Black's part, but analysis of this variation is thin on the ground.

    6   ♘h3

6 ♘f3 and 6 ♘d2 d6 7 ♘gf3 lead to variations already considered earlier.

    6   ...   ♕b6

Ionescu recommends 6 ... e6!?.

    7   ♘d2   d6
    8   ♘c4   ♕c7
    9   ♘f4

9 ♘g5!? also leads to an advantage, e.g. 9 ... ♘d5 (9 ... d5 10 ♘e5 ♘e4 {10 ... ♘g4!? – *Malaniuk*} 11 ♘gf3 with advantage to White; Groszpeter - Yrjola, Keckemet 1987) 10 h4 h6 11 ♘h3 ♗e6 12 ♕c2 ♘f6 13 ♘d2 d5 14 ♘f3 ♘bd7 15 ♘f4 ♗f7 16 ♘d3 ♘h5 17 ♗f4 ♘xf4 18 gxf4 and White stands better; Kapstan - Hartman, Canada 1986.

    9   ...   ♘a6

Bad is 9 ... e5? 10 dxe5 dxe5 11 ♘d3 ♘bd7 (11 ... ♗e6 12 ♕xb7) 12 a4 with a positional advantage for White.

    10   ♘d2

Maybe this move is too modest?

    10   ...   ♕d7
    11   ♘d3   ♕e6

Black has successfully negotiated the opening; Ionescu - Malaniuk.

B3

    5   ...   d5 *(166)*

With this move Black fixes his pawn structure in the centre. However, White will have chances to exploit the weakness of the e5-square.

    6   ♘h3

6 ♘f3 leads to variations already considered above, but an interesting possibility is 6 h4!?, for example 6 ... c6 7 ♘h3 ♕b6 8 ♘d2 ♘g4 9 ♘f3 e5 10 ♘xe5 ♘xe5 11 dxe5 ♕xb3 12 axb3 ♗xe5 13 ♗e3 a6 14 ♘f4 ♔f7 15 b4 ♘d7 16 b5± Bischoff - Yrjola, Kecskemet 1988.

    6   ...   c6
    7   ♘d2   ♕b6

Castling brings no relief either: 7 ... 0-0 8 ♘f3 ♘g4 9 ♘f4 ♕b6 10 ♘d3 ♖e8 11 h3 ♘h6

12 h4 ♘f7 13 h5 ♘d7 14 hxg6
hxg6 15 ♗f4 ♕xb3 16 axb3 e5 17
♗xe5 ♘dxe5 18 ♘dxe5 ♘xe5 19
♘xe5 ♗xe5 20 dxe5 ♖xe5 21
♖a4! ♗d7 22 ♖ah4 and the
endgame is very difficult for
Black; Baikov - Piskov, Moscow
1989.

8 ♘f3

White may also try:

a) 8 ♘f4 ♘e4!? 9 ♘f3 ♗f6 10
h4 ♘a6 11 0-0 ♔f7 12 c4 ♕xb3
13 axb3 ♗e6 14 ♗e3 h6 15 ♖fc1
g5 16 ♘h5 ♘c7 17 ♘xf6 exf6 18
♘d2 ♘xd2 19 ♗xd2 ♖hc8 and it
is not clear whether the pair of
bishops grants White any advantage; Bönsch - Kuczynsky,
Dresden 1988.

b) 8 0-0?! (There is no rush
for this) 8 ... 0-0 9 ♘f3 ♘e4 10
♘f4 ♗d7 11 h4 ♘a6 12 ♘d3 ♘c7
13 ♘fe5 ♗c8 14 ♔h2 ♘e6 15 f3
♘d6 16 e3 ♘d8 17 ♕c2 ♘gf7 18
f4 with an equal game; Skembris - Kontic; Vrnjacka Banja
1989.

8 ... ♘g4

In Groszpeter's opinion Black
had to exchange the queens
and be satisfied with a somewhat worse endgame.

9 ♘f4 e5
10 ♘xe5 ♘xe5

10 ... ♗xe5 11 ♕xb6 axb6 12
dxe5 ♘xe5 13 ♗e3 - Knezevic.

11 dxe5 ♗xe5 *(167)*

This was the game Grosz-
peter - Knezevic, Maribor 1987.
White would have had good
chances for attack after 12 ♕c2,
intending to follow up with an

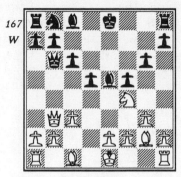

advance of the h-pawn.

C

5 ♗g5 *(168)*

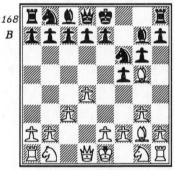

In this final section we shall
consider some rare alternatives
on White's fifth move. Naturally, these create few problems
for Black.

One possibility here is 5 ♘d2
0-0 6 ♕b3+ d5?! (Correct was
6 ... ♔h8; the text move gives
White an opportunity to attack
in the centre) 7 e4! fxe4 8
♘xe4 ♘xe4 9 ♗xe4 c6 10 f4
♕d6 (Even the weakness in the
centre is not always dangerous
for Black. We now follow the
game Skembris - Murey, Bel-
garaok 1988, where, after some

complications, White finds himself in a hopeless position)
11 ♗g2 b6 12 ♘f3 ♗a6 13 ♘e5 ♘d7 14 ♘xc6 ♕c7 15 ♘e5 ♗c4 16 ♕c2 ♗xe5 17 fxe5 ♘xe5! 18 dxe5 ♕xe5+ 19 ♔d1 ♕h5+ 20 ♔e1 ♖f6 21 ♗e3 ♖af8 22 ♕d2 ♖e6 23 b3 ♖f3 24 ♗xf3 ♕xf3 25 bxc4 ♖xe3+ 26 ♕xe3 ♕xe3-+.

5	...	♘e4!?
6	♗f4	d6
7	♘d2	♘xd2
8	♕xd2	h6
9	e4	e5
10	dxe5	dxe5

11	♕xd8+	♔xd8
12	♗e3	c6
13	♘f3	fxe4

And Black gradually frees himself from the pressure.

14	♘d2	♗e6
15	♘xe4	♘d7
16	0-0-0	♔c7
17	b3	♘f6
18	♗c5	♘xe4
19	♗xe4	♗f8
20	♗xf8	♖hxf8

Here the players agreed a draw; Nikolic - Beliavsky, Reggio Emilia 1987.

Index of Variations

8 ... ♘e5

9 ♘xe5

9 ... dxe5

10 e4

10 ... f4

11 b4 *62*